Thank you for your interest

Marvin Perry

THE THEORY AND PRACTICE
OF ISLAMIC TERRORISM

THE THEORY AND PRACTICE OF ISLAMIC TERRORISM

AN ANTHOLOGY

Edited by

Marvin Perry
and
Howard E. Negrin

palgrave
macmillan

First published in 2008 by
PALGRAVE MACMILLAN®
in the United States—a division of St. Martin's Press LLC,
175 Fifth Avenue, New York, NY 10010.

Where this book is distributed in the UK, Europe and the rest of the world,
this is by Palgrave Macmillan, a division of Macmillan Publishers Limited,
registered in England, company number 785998, of Houndmills,
Basingstoke, Hampshire RG21 6XS.

Palgrave Macmillan is the global academic imprint of the above companies
and has companies and representatives throughout the world.

Palgrave® and Macmillan® are registered trademarks in the United States,
the United Kingdom, Europe and other countries.

ISBN-13: 978–0–230–60864–1 (paperback)
ISBN-10: 0–230–60864–7 (paperback)
ISBN-13: 978–0–230–60662–3 (hardcover)
ISBN-10: 0–230–60662–8 (hardcover)

Library of Congress Cataloging-in-Publication Data

The theory and practice of Islamic terrorism : an anthology / edited
by Marvin Perry, Howard E. Negrin.
p. cm.
ISBN 0–230–60662–8 (alk. paper)   ISBN 0–230–60864–7 (alk. paper)
1. Jihad. 2. Terrorism—Religious aspects—Islam. 3. War—Religious
aspects—Islam. 4. Just war doctrine. 5. Islam and politics. 6. Qaida
(Organization) I. Perry, Marvin. II. Negrin, Howard E.

BP182.T54 2008
363.325—dc22   2008000349

A catalogue record of the book is available from the British Library.

Design by Newgen Imaging Systems (P) Ltd., Chennai, India.

First edition: November 2008

10 9 8 7 6 5 4 3 2 1

Printed in the United States of America.

CONTENTS

PART 3   THE WAR ON TERROR: SEIZING THE INITIATIVE

PART 4   SUICIDE BOMBERS: MOTIVATION, RECRUITMENT, INDOCTRINATION, AND EFFECTIVENESS

PART 5   THE THREAT TO THE WEST: TERRORISTS IN OUR MIDST

Part 6   Jews as Targets: The Islamization of European Anti-Semitic Myths

PREFACE

Since 9/11, few subjects have generated more interest or greater public concern than terrorism, specifically, Islamic terrorism. One indication that Islamic extremism has become an overriding concern of our times is the massive outpouring of books and articles on the topic. The editors of this anthology have assembled a sampling of recent literature that provides the general reader and college students with a frame of reference for understanding the theory and practice of Islamic terrorism. Included in the anthology are edited selections from books, academic journals, general interest magazines, congressional testimony, special reports, and such primary documents as published statements by terrorists.

The selections we have chosen are representative of expert opinion but should require no specialized knowledge on the part of the reader. Each of the six parts contains a comprehensive overview, and a pointed introduction precedes each selection. In editing a selection, we were careful to preserve the author's intent. We have, however, eliminated in most cases the author's endnotes, retaining only those that clarify certain references. In some cases we have inserted our own endnotes, corrected typographical errors, or added a punctuation mark for the benefit of the reader.

We wish to thank the various publishers and authors for granting us permission to reproduce material from previously published works. We would also like to express our appreciation to our wives, Phyllis Perry and Barbara Taub, for their support and encouragement. A special thanks goes to Phyllis Perry, whose finely honed computer skills enabled us to produce a professional manuscript from a hodgepodge of variously formatted documents.

MARVIN PERRY
HOWARD E. NEGRIN

INTRODUCTION

Marvin Perry and Howard E. Negrin

For some analysts, September 11 demonstrated that after the defeat of the Nazis in World War II and the collapse of the Soviet Union, the West is now confronted with another ominous threat: Islamic terrorism. Radical Islamists, or jihadists, best represented by Osama bin Laden and al Qaeda, regard terrorism—the organized, deliberate, and indiscriminate killing of civilians, including women and children, for a political purpose—as morally justifiable. For jihadists there are no innocents: they regard the bankers, bond traders, office workers, fire fighters, and other Americans who perished in the Twin Towers and Pentagon as backers and agents of a government that oppresses Muslims. Therefore their death was deserved. Jihadists regard terrorist attacks, which kill, destroy, and create an aura of fear in their wake, as legitimate means of fulfilling their sacred mission: regaining dignity for Muslims, carriers of Allah's message, by ending the humiliation and oppression imposed on them by Western infidels; overturning existing corrupt and "apostate" Muslim governments and replacing them with regimes committed to Islamic teachings; restoring the caliphate and Muslim religious and political hegemony over all lands where Islam once prevailed and ultimately over the entire planet; and imposing, by force if necessary, a stringent interpretation of Islamic law throughout the Muslim world.

Osama bin Laden and his followers describe themselves as Islamists. However, not all Islamists share bin Laden's views regarding jihadism and terrorism. Although all Islamists want to make Islam the guiding social and political force in the Muslim world and see modern, or Western ways, as a threat to traditional Islam, less radical Islamists reject both the global jihadism and terrorism advocated and practiced by al Qaeda, preferring instead the gradual Islamization of Muslim society by winning the hearts of the Muslim masses through nonviolent means.

Jihadists, a number of whom have lived in Europe, loath Western civilization which they view as materialistic, hedonistic, and godless. Islamists, who will only accept the rule of God and his Prophet, Muhammad, are repelled by secular democracies because their legal systems do not impose God's laws. For one prominent jihadist, "democracy is obvious polytheism and thus just the kind of infidelity that Allah warns against."[1] Jihadists regard democratic governments as blasphemous human contrivances that legalize equality of women, endorse freedom of expression and religion, promote interfaith dialogue, and tolerate atheism and sexual license, including homosexuality, beliefs and practices which they consider un-Islamic and even worthy of death. Even Islamists who do not support bin Laden see Western movies, literature, and dress as profane challenges to the beliefs and traditions of Islamic society. Aspiring to return to an era when the sacred predominated, Islamists are in revolt against the forces of modernity initiated and propagated by the West that, they feel, desecrate Islamic values, destabilize time-honored social institutions, fragmenting a once organic Muslim society, and cause Muslims to stray from God.

In the eyes of jihadists, the United States, the leading Western power, constitutes Islam's major enemy; they believed that striking at the World Trade Center and the Pentagon, symbols of American economic and military power, was fitting retaliation for American aggression against Muslims. It would demonstrate American weakness and the jihadists' resolve to destroy the infidels. Jihadists expected that the suicide bombers would be regarded by their coreligionists as martyrs; that the boldness of the strike and the ensuing publicity would incite and mobilize Muslims throughout the world to rise up and unite against Islam's enemies; and that al Qaeda would be seen as the vanguard in the global struggle for Islam's survival and return to its former glory. That a significant number of Muslims identified with al Qaeda's anti-Americanism was demonstrated immediately after 9/11 when in the streets of Arab countries people cheered and thanked Allah for answering their prayers, and numerous commentators maintained that America got what it deserved.

The worldwide holy war against the West that al Qaeda hoped for did not occur, and many Muslims are repelled by jihadist terrorism and reject al Qaeda's theocratic aspirations. Nevertheless, the threat remains: September 11 was followed by additional terrorist attacks in several lands and if other plots were not foiled or bungled the casualty toll would have been much greater. Moreover, jihadist movements, often acting independently of al Qaeda, have sprung up in many lands; support for militant Islam feeds on the perception that Muslims everywhere are victims of injustice and humiliation, that a foreign conspiracy accounts for Arab/Muslim failures, and that taking vengeance for these wrongs is a religious obligation. With the jihadist ideology inspiring Muslim youth worldwide, including the Muslim diaspora in Europe—doubtless the American presence in Iraq has drawn more young people to radical Islamist causes—it is likely that Westerners will continue to face terrorist attacks.

Radical Islamists are true believers fiercely committed to divinely sanctioned warfare against unbelievers. Regarding their conflict with the West as a clash of civilizations, they see themselves engaged in a holy war whose ultimate aim is the destruction of Western civilization, the reestablishment of Muslim power, and the imposing of religious law, shari'a, wherever Muslims hold sway. For inspiration and justification they turn back to Muhammad himself and to a selective reading of Islamic religious texts. Did not the Prophet spread the faith and create a unitary Islamic state through warfare? Does not the Qur'an instruct the faithful to wage war against non-Muslims in order to expand Islam's borders, propagate the faith and "kill the unbelievers wherever you find them" (Sura 9:5)? Does not Allah command the state to base its legal system on Islamic law and to enforce all the strictures of the faith? And to realize these goals, does not Islamic law hold that fighting Islam's enemies is the individual's highest duty, which will earn him a place in Paradise? Bin Laden believed that he was adhering to traditional Islam when in his famous fatwa to all Muslims (February 23, 1998) he proclaimed that in accordance with the will of Allah, individual Muslims had a holy duty to kill Americans, including civilians, wherever they could be found. In many ways contemporary jihadists are driven by the same imperialist ambitions—the quest for domination, subjugation, and holy war against the infidels—that energized the early Arab conquerors led by Muhammad and the caliphs. Far from being a perversion of Islam as some commentators, both Muslim and westerner, maintain, al Qaeda's religiously endorsed cosmic aim of world mastery finds inspiration in Islamic history and theology; and its long-term goals are shared by Salafism and Wahhabism, widespread modern fundamentalist Islamic movements that also call for the establishment of Allah's rule throughout the world.

Of course, moderate Muslims often draw different conclusions from reading their holy texts and scholarly commentaries of respected theologians over the centuries. One could find in these writings passages arguing that jihad should be waged only in self-defense or to redress injustice, that war should be the last resort, that suicide is prohibited, and that the killing of women and children is contrary to God's commands and Muhammad's teachings. The Qur'an sets strict rules for waging war, say Muslim moderates, whereas Islamists, who resort to and justify indiscriminate violence, respect no rules. David Dakake, an American Muslim writer and researcher maintains, as do other moderates, that the jihadists have betrayed the faith:

> [P]roperly understood, the traditional doctrine of jihad, leaves no room for militant acts like those perpetrated against the United States on September 11th. Those who carried out these crimes in the name of God and the Prophet, followed neither God nor the Prophet, but followed their own imaginings about "religion" without any serious understanding of the traditional sources of the Islamic faith. No textual justification for their acts can be found in the Qur'an, nor can one cite examples of such brutality and slaughter of innocents from the life of the Prophet or the military jihad of the early decades of Islam.[2]

Moderates maintain that Islamists have disfigured Islamic principles. Nevertheless, militant jihadists today did not emanate from a void: they consider themselves faithful Muslims, strike in the name of Islam, and find much in Islamic belief, history, and tradition that nurtures their ideology and fervor, despite their opponents' accusation of misinterpretation. And Muslim scholars have developed a convenient doctrine—abrogation—that enables militants to overrule the more peaceful and tolerant verses of the Qur'an. The doctrine of abrogation holds that Allah had revealed the Qur'an at different periods in Muhammad's life. Consequently some later revelations have abrogated and replaced earlier ones, a view that permits extremists to argue that the "verses of sword" have superseded the "peaceful" verses of the Qur'an. Finally, that Islamists both seek and obtain clerical approval for their terrorist operations shows the immanent connection between their ideology and historic Islam.

Analysts frequently view radical Islamism as a totalitarian movement—some refer to it as Islamofascism—in the tradition of communism and Nazism. Both Western ideologies offered a utopian vision of the future for which their adherents, committed idealists, ruthlessly crushed dissent and resorted to mass murder. Jihadists too see themselves engaged in an apocalyptic struggle to win the future. For them, the establishment of God's rule throughout the globe is the noblest of causes; without hesitation and with good conscience they will kill both Muslims and infidels—by the millions, if necessary—who block the realization of their holy mission. And once in power, political dissent will be treated as heresy and apostasy—crimes against God. Bassam Tibi, a German political scientist, a Muslim of Syrian background, and a student of Islamic history and culture, maintains that Islamism "embodies the foremost totalitarian movement of the twenty-first century—a movement based on a politicized religion." It shares with twentieth-century totalitarian movements

> the goal of imposing norms of beliefs and behaviour on all aspects of life, thus also denying any separation between the private and the public sphere. As a form of totalitarianism, Islamism plans to subordinate civil society to the comprehensive state apparatus directed by a totalising Shari'ah [Islamic law]. It also contains anti-Semitism, one of the components that [Hannah] Arendt identified as a fundamental feature of totalitarian ideologies..... [J]ihadist Islamists are men acting as 'true believers' in a totalitarian movement.[3]

Because radical Islamists adhere to a totalitarian and imperialist ideology with a global design and a global reach that has a proven capacity to attract followers and incite fanaticism, the fight of liberal democracy against jihadism may well be the decisive ideological conflict of the twenty-first century. And the stakes are high because, like twentieth-century totalitarian movements, jihadists aspire to impose a world order that will obliterate Western civilization's most precious ideals. And there can be no accommodation with an ideology that aims to shape the world in accordance with a rigid and uncompromising religious truth; sees Christians and Jews as immoral infidels who blaspheme God with their behavior and oppress Muslims with their power; and finds religious justification for mass murder. The struggle may well be difficult, protracted, and costly, for unlike traditional wars against enemy states with visible military forces and installations, this war confronts operatives and organizations that are hidden, elusive, ruthless—deliberately seeking out soft civilian targets—scattered throughout the world, and often protected by sympathizers, including local authorities. Many jihadists, veterans of the Afghan struggle against the Soviet Union and now the insurgency in Iraq, are well trained in the terrorist arts and have embraced a cult of killing and suicide, which they view as religious acts of triumphant joy and martyrdom that are a prelude to Paradise. Moreover, it seems that the madrassas and radical imams are recruiting a sufficient number of operatives to compensate for the jihadists' losses in Afghanistan and Iraq. And there is always the possibility—some analysts say there is only the slightest chance of this happening—that al Qaeda, or a terrorist franchise, will acquire a weapon of mass destruction which it will not hesitate to use, for the terrorist mind takes nihilistic delight in mass death and destruction.

However, it must be emphasized that the West is not engaged in a war against Islam, but against radical Islamism. Because jihadists also threaten to overthrow existing Muslim governments and to establish a repressive fundamentalist regime, which the majority of Muslims worldwide oppose, many analysts urge policy makers to woo Muslim moderates; to encourage religious scholars to denounce al Qaeda's indiscriminate murder of civilians as a desecration of true Islam; to strengthen ties with moderate Arab governments; and patiently to promote liberal-democratic attitudes and reforms in the Middle East. Mansour al-Nogaidan, a former Saudi Arabian jihadist, astutely assesses the essential problem in the Arab/Muslim world, but laments that his view, is "not a popular conviction and has attracted angry criticism, including death threats, from many sides." In effect, al-Nogaidan is calling for Muslims to do what Christians have done—incorporate into their religious tradition liberal interpretations of sacred texts and a tolerant attitude toward other religions:

> Islam needs a Reformation. It needs someone with the courage of Martin Luther. . . . Muslims are too rigid in our adherence to old, literal interpretations of the Koran. It's time for many verses—especially those having to do with relations between Islam and other religions—to be reinterpreted in favor of a more modern Islam. It's time to accept that God loves the faithful of all religions. It's time for Muslims to question our leaders and their strict teachings, to reach our own understanding of the prophet's words and to call for a bold renewal of our faith as a faith of goodwill, of peace and of light.[4]

To which it could be argued that the Middle East would also benefit from the secular, rational, and humanist outlook of the Enlightenment, which has become an integral part of modern Western civilization and is crucial to the shaping of the liberal-democratic tradition. But in a climate of opinion shaped to a large extent by powerful religious authorities, it is unlikely that many Muslim intellectuals dwelling in the Middle East will, in the manner of Voltaire and Diderot, apply a skeptical and critical spirit to traditions propagated and sanctioned by these authorities—traditions that stifle independent thought, freedom, and tolerance.

This anthology deals with the phenomenon of Islamism in theory and practice. The editors have chosen writings that reveal and analyze the jihadist worldview which motivates Islamic terrorists and justifies their war against those defined as Allah's enemies; that explore al Qaeda's aims and operations; that assess the results of the war against global terrorism; that analyze the mindset of suicide bombers and their handlers; that study the growth of jihadist organizations in the West; and that focus on the burgeoning, Nazi-like anti-Semitism among Muslims, which demonizes Jews and incites terrorist violence against them.

NOTES

1. Quoted in Robert S. Leiken and Steven Brooke, "The Moderate Muslim Brotherhood," *Foreign Affairs*, March/April 2007, p. 111.
2. David Dakake, "The Myth of Militant Islam," in Joseph E.B. Lumbard, ed., *Islam, Fundamentalism and the Betrayal of Tradition: Essays by Western Muslim Scholars* (Bloomington, IN: World Wisdom, 2004), p. 28.
3. Bassam Tibi, "The Totalitarianism of Jihadist Islamism and Its Challenge to Europe and Islam," *Totalitarian Movements and Political Religions* (March 2007), pp. 35–54. Also, <http://www. informaworld.com/smpp/section?content=a 772105385&fulltext=713240928>.
4. Mansour al-Nogaidan, "Losing My Jihadism," *Washington Post*, July 22, 2007, p. B01.

Part 1

JIHADISM: THEOLOGY AND IDEOLOGY

Religious scholars throughout Islamic history agree that jihad is an individual duty when an enemy attacks Muslim countries. With God's permission we call on everyone who believes in God and wants reward to comply with His will to kill Americans and seize their money wherever and whenever they find them. We also call on religious scholars, their leaders, their youth, and their soldiers, to launch the raid on the soldiers of Satan, the Americans, and whichever devil's supporters are allied with them, to rout those behind them so that they will not forget it.[1]

This excerpt from a "Declaration of the World Islamic Front for Jihad against the Jews and the Crusaders," written by Osama bin Laden in 1998 (see part 2, chapter 1), contains the essence of the worldview of Islamic extremists, particularly those who belong to or identify with al Qaeda. It reveals much of the motivation that drove the terrorists to hijack the planes on 9/11 and crash them into the Twin Towers and the Pentagon. The perpetrators of 9/11 believed that they were God's soldiers fighting a holy war against God's enemies, that they had a divine imperative to fight for the establishment of God's sovereignty on earth, that killing many infidels was serving God, and that sacrificing their life in the process would earn them God's gratitude and the blessings of Paradise.

This belief was based on their understanding of religious doctrines and traditions that began with Muhammad. The Prophet had conveyed to his followers their religious obligation to perform jihad, a complex term whose two essential meanings are an internal striving by an individual for moral self-improvement and a collective military struggle to defend Islam against its enemies and to extend Muslim power over other lands so that all people will be subject to God's laws as revealed to Muhammad. Historically, the doctrine of jihad held that the Islamic community (umma), the recipient of Allah's revelation and the "best community ever produced" (Sura 3: 106), is commanded to make Allah's directives supreme over the whole world. Either by conversion or conquest, infidels are destined to submit to Islamic jurisdiction. Westerners, who are repulsed by the Islamic concept of jihad and feel threatened by jihadist terrorists, generally interpret jihad as a Muslim's fanatical duty to engage in holy war against the perceived enemies of Islam. Seeking to defend their faith against critics who attack contemporary Islam as an incubator of terrorism, some Muslim intellectuals and religious authorities and Western apologists often respond by stressing Islam's peaceful, tolerant, and humanitarian characteristics, its command to win converts by preaching and persuasion. Central to their argument is the traditional distinction in Islam between the "Lesser Jihad" and the "Greater Jihad," first developed in the ninth century by a group of ascetics who formed the nucleus of the early mystical Sufi movement. An oft-quoted hadith text (that is, a text dealing with traditions about the life of Muhammad) relating to the concept of a spiritual Greater Jihad is as follows:

> A number of fighters came to the Messenger of Allah, and he said: "You have done well in coming from the 'lesser jihad' to the 'greater jihad.'" They said: "What is the 'greater jihad?'" He said: "For the servant (of God) to fight his passions."

The Greater Jihad then is an internal struggle by the individual to achieve dominance over his passions, to achieve a spiritual reformation, to lead a religious life, whereas the Lesser Jihad retains the military meaning of the term—armed struggle against infidels and apostates. Over the centuries, however, most classical theologians and jurists interpreted jihad as a military obligation. For centuries preceding the abolition of the caliphate in 1924, Muslim rulers invoked jihad primarily to wage wars of conquest that imams legitimized with religious edicts. As Bernard Lewis, a leading scholar of the Middle East, points out:

> For most of the fourteen centuries of recorded Muslim history, jihad was most commonly interpreted to mean armed struggle for the defense or advancement of Muslim power.... [T]he presumption is that the duty of jihad will continue, interrupted only by truces, until all the world either adopts the Muslim faith or submits to Muslim rule. Those who fight in the jihad qualify for rewards in both worlds—booty in this one, paradise in the next.[2]

And Nonie Darwish, an Egyptian American, is even more emphatic:

> After 9/11 many Muslims in the West reinterpreted the meaning of jihad as an inner struggle for self-improvement.... This "inner struggle" business is hogwash. In the Arab world there is only one meaning for jihad, and that is: a religious holy war against infidels. It is a fight for Allah's cause. Ask anyone in the Arab street what "Jihad for the sake of Allah's cause" means and he will say it means dying as a shahid [martyr] for the sake of spreading Islam. I have never heard of any discussion of inner struggle in

my thirty years living in the Middle East. Such nonsense is a PR ploy for Western consumption.[3]

Today, when militant Muslims identify themselves as jihadists, moral striving is not their principal concern; for them jihad means the personal duty of every Muslim to wage holy war against God's enemies—those who obstruct the establishment of an Islamic world community in which all the laws ordained by God are strictly enforced. These enemies of God include Muslim rulers, those so-called Muslims, really apostates and agents of the West, who do not make shari'a, Islamic law, authoritative in their own lands; Jews, "children of the Devil" who have planted their Zionist entity in the Muslim heartland; and Americans and their western allies, contemporary crusaders and infidels who occupy Muslim lands and propagate hateful liberal and secular values that undermine the sanctity of Islamic law—the only legitimate way of organizing a just society—and promote unbelief and immoral behavior. Jihadists seek to reverse the decline of Islamic power, which began in the Late Middle Ages, by liberating lands that were once part of the caliphate and are now under non-Muslim control—Kashmir, Spain, and Israel, among others.

Jihadist ideology is an integral part of historic Islam with roots that extend back to Muhammad and early Muslim theologians. (To be sure, militants today read the Qur'an selectively, searching only for those passages that support and legitimize their militant world-view and ignoring other passages that call for tolerance and coexistence with other faiths.) Jihadists view themselves as defenders of the true faith against its enemies and regard terrorism as a legitimate tactic in fulfillment of sacred obligation. As one Egyptian radical expressed it: "Islam is the religion of strength and the Muslim has the duty to be a terrorist, in the sense that he has to terrorize the enemies of Allah to represent peace and security to the faithful. Terrorism against the enemies of God is a duty in our religion. Whoever leaves jihad lives in humiliation."[4] This view is echoed by Ayman al Zawahiri (see part 2, chapter 2), often a spokesman for al Qaeda: "Waging jihad against the infidels is the basis of glory and honor, whereas abandoning it results in humiliation and debasement."[5] And jihadists concur with bin Laden that in waging war against the alliance of Jews and crusaders, "the most honorable death is to be killed in the way of Allah."[6] In May 2005 in a television lecture Ibrahim Mudayris, a senior Palestinian cleric, described the ultimate aim of militant jihadists: "We [Muslims] have ruled the world [in the past] and a day will come by Allah, when we shall rule the world [again]. The day will come and we shall rule America, Britain; we shall rule the entire world, except the Jews [who will meet a dire end]."[7]

Jihadist ideology calls for the extension of Islamic law, strictly interpreted and enforced, to all Muslim lands. An illustration of the type of society bin Laden and his cohorts envision is seen in Afghanistan under the Taliban, who ruled Afghanistan from 1996 to 2001. In seeking to impose Islamic law throughout the land, the Taliban outlawed movies, television, music, and the Internet; banned singing and dancing at weddings, an old Afghan tradition; prohibited decorating the walls of homes with photographs or pictures; commanded men to wear beards as a sign of piety; and placed strict prohibitions on women. The Taliban's religious police rigorously enforced these regulations. Executions and floggings in a former soccer stadium became regular public spectacles. The religious police beat, often brutally, women who did not wear the burqa—which covered the body from head to toe leaving only a narrow slit for the eyes—used cosmetics, or walked the streets without a male chaperone. Forbidden from working, many Afghan women were made destitute, and with schools for females closed, they were deprived of a future.

Al Qaeda maintains that it is acting in self-defense against the United States and its allies who, like westerners in the Middle Ages, are waging a crusade against the Muslim world and they point to specific grievances: American troops stationed in Saudi Arabia, the land of Muhammad; westerners fighting Muslims in Afghanistan and Iraq; American support for "the Zionist usurpers of Palestinian land" and so forth. But ultimately their aims are more theological, ideological, and sinister. What drives jihadists is an abhorrence of Western civilization, which they believe perverts their faith and way of life, and a fierce determination to establish Allah's will—a total truth that permits no dissent or alternative viewpoints—throughout the globe and, in the process, to destroy competing systems and ideologies. For this reason, it has been suggested that Islamic jihadism, like fascism and communism, is another totalitarian movement that threatens Western civilization's core values, if not its very existence.

NOTES

1. Bruce Lawrence, ed., *Messages to the World: The Statements of Osama bin Laden*, trans. James Howarth (New York: Verso, 2005), pp. 60–61.
2. Bernard Lewis, *The Crisis of Islam: Holy War and Unholy Terror* (New York: Random House, 2004), pp. 31–32.
3. Nonie Darwish, *Now They Call Me Infidel: Why I Renounced Jihad for America, Israel, and the War on Terror* (New York: Sentinel, 2006), p. 201.
4. Quoted in Lorenzo Vidino, *Al Qaeda in Europe: The New Battleground of International Jihad* (Amherst, NY: Prometheus Books, 2006), pp. 49–50.
5. Quoted in Raymond Ibrahim, ed. and trans., *The Al Qaeda Reader* (New York: Broadway Books, 2007), p. 161.
6. Efraim Karsh, *Islamic Imperialism: A History* (New Haven, CT: Yale University Press, 2006), p. 225.
7. Itamar Marcus and Barbara Crook, "Kill a Jew—Go to Heaven: The Perception of the Jew in Palestinian Society," *Jewish Political Studies Review*, Vol. 17, Nos. 3–4 (Fall 2005), p. 127.

1

"The Religious Sources of
Islamic Terrorism"

Shmuel Bar

Minimizing a religious explanation for Islamic terrorism, several analysts emphasize political and socioeconomic causes: the Arab-Israeli conflict, which Arabs view as an unendurable humiliation; the extension of Western political power and cultural influence into the Middle East, which is seen as still another humiliation; and the economic hardships that grip the Arab masses, which provide recruits for terrorist organizations. Shmuel Bar, a veteran of the Israeli intelligence community and a senior research fellow at an Israeli think-tank, recognizes the importance of these factors but maintains that they do "not do justice to the significance of the religious culture in which [Islamic terrorism] is rooted and nurtured," a culture in which there is no distinction between religion and politics. His essay examines the religious-ideological motivation for Islamic terrorism.

*   *   *

While terrorism—even in the form of suicide attacks—is not an Islamic phenomenon by definition, it cannot be ignored that the lion's share of terrorist acts and the most devastating of them in recent years have been perpetrated in the name of Islam. This fact has sparked a fundamental debate both in the West and within the Muslim world regarding the link between these acts and the teachings of Islam. Most Western analysts are hesitant to identify such acts with the bona fide teachings of one of the world's great religions and prefer to view them as a perversion of a religion that is essentially peace-loving and tolerant. Western leaders such as George W. Bush and Tony Blair have reiterated time and again that the war against terrorism has nothing to do with Islam. It is a war against evil.

The non-Islamic etiologies of this phenomenon include political causes (the Israeli-Arab conflict); cultural causes (rebellion against Western cultural colonialism); and social causes (alienation, poverty). While no public figure in the West would deny the imperative of fighting the war against terrorism, it is equally politically correct to add the codicil that, for the war to be won, these (justified) grievances pertaining to the root causes of terrorism should be addressed. A skeptic may note that many societies can put claim to similar grievances but have not given birth to religious-based ideologies that justify no-holds-barred terrorism. Nevertheless an interpretation which places the blame for terrorism on religious and cultural traits runs the risk of being branded as bigoted and Islamophobic.

The political motivation of the leaders of Islamist jihadist-type movements is not in doubt. A glance at the theatres where such movements flourished shows that most fed off their political—and usually military—encounter with the West. This was the case in India and in the Sudan in the nineteenth century and in Egypt and Palestine in the twentieth. The moral justification and levers of power for these movements, however, were for the most part not couched in political terms, but based on Islamic religious sources of authority and religious principles. By using these levers and appealing to deeply ingrained religious beliefs, the radical leaders succeed in motivating the Islamist terrorist, creating for him a social environment that provides approbation and a religious environment that provides moral and legal sanction for his actions. The success of radical Islamic organizations in the recruitment, posting, and ideological maintenance of sleeper activists (the 9/11 terrorists are a prime example) without their defecting or succumbing to the lure of Western civilization proves the deep ideological nature of the phenomenon.

Therefore, to treat Islamic terrorism as the consequence of political and socioeconomic factors alone would not do justice to the significance of the religious culture in which this phenomenon is rooted and nurtured. In order to comprehend the motivation for these acts and to draw up an effective strategy for a war against terrorism, it is necessary to understand the religious-ideological factors which are deeply embedded in Islam.

THE WELTANSCHAUUNG [WORLDVIEW] OF RADICAL ISLAM

Modern international Islamist terrorism is a natural offshoot of twentieth-century Islamic fundamentalism. The "Islamic Movement" emerged in the Arab world and British-ruled India as a response to the dismal state of Muslim society in those countries: social injustice, rejection of traditional mores, acceptance of foreign domination and culture. It perceives the malaise of modern Muslim societies as having strayed from the "straight path" and the solution to all ills in a return to the original mores of Islam. The problems addressed may be social or political: inequality, corruption, and oppression. But in traditional Islam—and certainly in the worldview of the Islamic fundamentalist—there is no separation between the political and the religious. Islam is, in essence, both religion and regime and no area of human activity is outside its remit. Be the nature of the problem as it may, "Islam is the solution."

The underlying element in the radical Islamist worldview is ahistoric and dichotomist: Perfection lies in the ways of the Prophet and the events of his time; therefore, religious innovations, philosophical relativism, and intellectual or political pluralism are anathema. In such a worldview, there can exist only two camps—*Dar al-Islam* ("The House of Islam"—i.e., the Muslim countries) and *Dar al–Harb* ("The House of War"—i.e., countries ruled by any regime but Islam)—that are pitted against each other until the final victory of Islam. These concepts are carried to their extreme conclusion by the radicals; however, they have deep roots in mainstream Islam.

While the trigger for "Islamic awakening" was frequently the meeting with the West, Islamic-motivated rebellions against colonial powers rarely involved individuals from other Muslim countries or broke out of the confines of the territories over which they were fighting. Until the 1980s, most fundamentalist movements such as the Muslim Brotherhood (*Ikhwan Muslimun*) were inward-looking; Western superiority was viewed as the result of Muslims having forsaken the teachings of the Prophet. Therefore, the remedy was, first, "re-Islamization" of Muslim society and restoration of an Islamic government, based on Islamic law (shari'ah). In this context, jihad was aimed mainly against "apostate" Muslim governments and societies, while the historic offensive jihad of the Muslim world against the infidels was put in abeyance (at least until the restoration of the caliphate).

Until the 1980s, attempts to mobilize Muslims all over the world for a jihad in one area of the world (Palestine, Kashmir) were unsuccessful. The Soviet invasion of Afghanistan was a watershed event, as it revived the concept of participation in jihad to evict an "infidel" occupier from a Muslim country as a "personal duty" for every capable Muslim. The basis of this duty derives from the "irreversibility" of Islamic identity both for individual Muslims (thus, capital punishment for "apostates"—e.g., Salman Rushdie) and for Muslim territories. Therefore, any land (Afghanistan, Palestine, Kashmir, Chechnya, Spain) that had once been under the sway of Islamic law may not revert to control by any other law. In such a case, it becomes the "personal duty" of all Muslims in the land to fight a jihad to liberate it. If they do not succeed, it becomes incumbent on any Muslim in a certain perimeter from that land to join the jihad and so forth. Accordingly, given the number of Muslim lands under "infidel occupation" and the length of time of those occupations, it is argued that it has become a personal duty for all Muslims to join the jihad. This duty—if taken seriously—is no less a religious imperative than the other five pillars of Islam (the statement of belief or *shahadah*, prayer, fasting, charity, and haj). It becomes a de facto (and in the eyes of some a de jure) sixth pillar; a Muslim who does not perform it will inherit hell.

Such a philosophy attributing centrality to the duty of jihad is not an innovation of modern radical Islam. The seventh-century Kharijite sect, infamous in Islamic history as a cause of Muslim civil war, took this position and implemented it. But the Kharijite doctrine was rejected as a heresy by medieval Islam. The novelty is the tacit acceptance by mainstream Islam of the basic building blocks of this "neo-Kharijite" school.

The Soviet defeat in Afghanistan and the subsequent fall of the Soviet Union were perceived as an eschatological sign, adumbrating the renewal of the jihad against the infidel world at large and the apocalyptical war between Islam and heresy which will result in the rule of Islam in the world. Along with the renewal of the jihad, the Islamist Weltanschauung, which emerged from the Afghani crucible, developed a Thanatophile ideology—in which death is idealized as a desired goal and not a necessary evil in war.

An offshoot of this philosophy poses a dilemma for theories of deterrence. The Islamic traditions of war allow the Muslim forces to retreat if their numerical strength is less than half that of the enemy. Other traditions go further and allow retreat only in the face of a tenfold superiority of the enemy. The reasoning is that the act of jihad is, by definition, an act of faith in Allah. By fighting a weaker or equal enemy, the Muslim is relying on his own strength and not on Allah; by entering the fray against all odds, the mujahed is proving his utter faith in Allah and will be rewarded accordingly.

The politics of Islamist radicalism has also bred a mentality of *bello ergo sum* (I fight, therefore I exist)—Islamic leaders are in constant need of popular jihads to boost their leadership status. Nothing succeeds like success: The attacks in the United States gave birth to a second wave of mujahidin who want to emulate their heroes. The perception of resolve on the part of the West is a critical factor in shaping the mood of the Muslim population toward radical ideas. Therefore, the manner by which the United States deals with the present crisis in Iraq is not unconnected to the future of the radical Islamic movement. In these circles, the American occupation of Iraq is likened to the Soviet invasion of Afghanistan; a sense of American failure would feed the apocalyptical ideology of jihad.

THE LEGALITY OF JIHAD

These beliefs are commonly viewed as typical of radical Islamic ideology, but few orthodox Islamic scholars would deny that they are deeply rooted in orthodox Islam or would dismiss the very ideology of jihad as a military struggle as foreign to the basic tenets of Islam.

Hence, much of the debate between radicals and nonradicals is not over the religious principles themselves, but over their implication for actual behavior as based on the detailed legal interpretation of those principles. This legal interpretation is the soul of the debate. Even among moderate Islamic scholars who condemn acts of terrorism (albeit with reservation so as not to include acts perpetrated against Israel in such a category), there is no agreement on *why* they should be condemned: Many modernists acknowledge the existence of a duty of jihad in Islam but call for an "Islamic

Protestantism" that would divest Islam of vestiges of anachronistic beliefs; conservative moderates find in traditional Islamic jurisprudence (*shari'ah*) legal justification to put the imperative of jihad in abeyance; others use linguistic analysis to point out that the etymology of the word jihad (*jahada*) actually means "to strive," does not mean "holy war" and does not necessarily have a military connotation.

The legalistic approach is not a barren preoccupation of scholars. The ideal Islamic regime is a nomocracy: The law is given and immutable, and it remains for the leaders of the ummah (the Islamic nation) to apply it on a day-to-day basis. Islam is not indifferent to any facet of human behavior; all possible acts potentially have a religious standing, ranging between "duty"; "recommend"; "optional"; "permitted"; "reprehensible"; and "forbidden." This taxonomy of human behavior has far-reaching importance for the believer: By performing all his religious duties, he will inherit paradise; by failing to do so ("sins of omission") or doing that which is forbidden ("sins of commission"), he will be condemned to hell. Therefore, such issues as the legitimacy of jihad—ostensibly deriving from the roots of Islam—cannot be decided by abstract morality—or by politics, but by meticulous legal analysis and ruling (*fatwa*) according to the shari'ah, performed by an authoritative Islamic scholar (*'alem, pl. 'ulama*).

The use of *fatwas* to call for violent action first became known in the West as a result of Ayatollah Khomeini's *fatwa* against Salman Rushdie, and again after Osama bin Laden's 1998 *fatwa* against the United States and Israel. But as a genuine instrument of religious deliberation, it has not received the attention it deserves. Analysts have frequently interpreted *fatwas* as no more than the cynical use of religious terminology in political propaganda. This interpretation does not do justice to the painstaking process of legal reasoning invested in these documents and the importance that their authors and their target audience genuinely accord to the religious truthfulness of their rulings.

The political strength of these *fatwas* has been time-tested in Muslim political society by rebels and insurgents from the Arabian Peninsula to Sudan, India, and Indonesia. At the same time, they have been used by Muslim regimes to bolster their Islamic credentials against external and domestic enemies and to legitimize their policies. This was done by the Sudanese mahdi in his rebellion against the British (1881–1885); by the Ottoman caliphate (December 1914) in World War I; by the Syrian regime against the rebellion in northern Syria (1981); and . . . by Egyptian President Anwar Sadat to legitimize his peace policies toward Israel.

The *fatwas* promulgated by sheikhs and 'ulama who stipulate that jihad is a "personal duty" play, therefore, a pivotal role in encouraging radicalism and in building the support infrastructure for radicals within the traditional Islamic community. While one may find many *fatwas* which advocate various manifestations of terrorism, fatwas which rule that those who perform these acts do not go to paradise but inherit hell are few and far between.

The questions relating to jihad which are referred to the religious scholars—relate to a number of issues:

The very definition, current existence, and area of application of the state of jihad. Is jihad one of the "pillars" or "roots" of Islam? Does it necessarily imply military war, or can it be perceived as a duty to spread Islam through preaching or even the moral struggle between one's soul and Satan? If the former, then what are the *necessary conditions for jihad*? Does a state of *jihad* currently exist between *Dar al-Islam* and *Dar al-Harl*. And how can one define Dar al-Islam today, in the absence of a caliphate? Is the rest of the world automatically defined as *Dar al-Harb* with which a state of jihad exists, or do the treaties and diplomatic relations which exist between Muslim countries and "infidel" countries (including the charter of the United Nations) change this?

Who must participate in jihad, and how? Is jihad a personal duty for each and every Muslim under all circumstances or a collective duty that can be performed only under the leadership of a leader of all Muslims? Is it incumbent on women? On minors? (According to Islamic law, in the case of a defensive jihad for the liberation of Islamic territory from infidel occupation, "a woman need not ask permission of her husband nor a child of his parents nor a slave of his master.") May a Muslim refrain from supporting his attacked brethren or obey a non-Muslim secular law which prohibits him from supporting other Muslims in their struggle?

How should the jihad be fought? The questions in this area relate, inter alia, to: (A) Is jihad by definition an act of conflict against the actual "infidels" or can it be defined as a spiritual struggle against the "evil inclination"? If it is the former, must it take the form of war (*Jihad fi-sabil Allah*) or can it be performed by way of preaching and proselytization (*da'awah*)? (B) Who is a legitimate target? Is it permissible to kill noncombatant civilians—women, children, elderly, and clerics; "protected" non-Muslims in Muslim countries—local non-Muslims or tourists whose visas may be interpreted as Islamic guarantees of passage; Muslim bystanders? (C) The legitimacy of suicide attacks (*istishhad*) as a form of jihad in the light of the severe prohibition on a Muslim taking his own life, on one hand, and the promise of rewards in the afterlife for the *shahid* who falls in a jihad on the other hand. (D) The weapons which may be used. For example, may a hijacked plane be used as a weapon as in the attacks of September 11 in the light of Islamic prohibitions on killing prisoners? (E) The status of a Muslim who aids the "infidels" against other Muslims. (F) The authority to implement capital punishment in the absence of a caliph.

How should jihad be funded? "Pocketbook jihad" is deeply entrenched in Islamic tradition. It is based on the injunction that one must fight jihad with his soul or with his tongue or with his money. Therefore, financial support of jihad is politically correct and even good for business for the wealthy supporter. The transfer of *zakat* (almsgiving) raised in a community for *jihad fi-sabil Allah* (i.e., jihad on Allah's path or military jihad) has wide religious and social legitimacy. The precepts of "war booty" call for a fifth to be rendered to the mujahidin. Acts that would otherwise be considered religiously prohibited are thus legitimized by the payment of such a "tax" for the sake of jihad. While there have been attempts to bring Muslim clerics to denounce acts of terrorism, none, to date, have condemned the donation of money for jihad.

THE DILEMMA OF THE MODERATE MUSLIM

It can be safely assumed that the great majority of Muslims in the world have no desire to join a jihad or to politicize their religion. However, it is also true that insofar as religious establishments in most of the Arabian Peninsula, in Iran, and in much of Egypt and North Africa are concerned, the radical ideology does not represent a marginal and extremist perversion of Islam but rather a genuine and increasingly mainstream interpretation. Even after 9/11, the sermons broadcast from Mecca cannot be easily distinguished from those of al Qaeda.

Facing the radical Weltanschauung, the moderate but orthodox Muslim has to grapple with two main dilemmas: the difficulty of refuting the legal–religious arguments of the radical interpretation and the aversion to—or even prohibition of—inciting an Islamic Kulturkampf[1] which would split the ranks of the *ummah*.

The first dilemma is not uniquely Islamic. It is characteristic of revelation-based religions that the less observant or less orthodox will hesitate to challenge fundamental dogmas out of fear of being branded slack or lapsed in their faith. They will prefer to pay their dues to the religious establishment, hoping that by doing so they are also buying their own freedom from coercion. On a deeper level, many believers who are not strict in observance may see their own lifestyle as a matter of convenience and not principle, while the extreme orthodox is the true believer to whom they defer.

This phenomenon is compounded in Islam by the fact that "Arab" Sunni Islam never went though a reform. Since the tenth century, Islam has lacked an accepted mechanism for relegating a tenet or text to ideological obsolescence. Until that time, such a mechanism—*ijtihad*—existed; *ijtihad* is the authorization of scholars to reach conclusions not only from existing interpretations and legal precedents, but from their own perusal of the texts. In the tenth century, the "gates of *ijtihad*" were closed for most of the Sunni world. It is still practiced in Shi'ite Islam and in Southeast Asia. Reformist traditions did appear in non-Arab Middle Eastern Muslim societies (Turkey, Iran) and in Southeast Asian Islam. Many Sufi (mystical) schools also have traditions of syncretism, reformism, and moderation. These traditions, however, have always suffered from a lack of wide legitimacy due to their non-Arab origins and have never been able to offer themselves as an acceptable alternative to ideologies born in the heartland of Islam and expressed in the tongue of the Prophet. In recent years, these societies have undergone a transformation and have adopted much of the Middle Eastern brand of

Islamic orthodoxy and have become, therefore, more susceptible to radical ideologies under the influence of Wahhabi missionaries, Iranian export of Islam, and the cross-pollination resulting from the globalization of ideas in the information age.

The second dilemma—the disinclination of moderates to confront the radicals—has frequently been attributed to violent intimidation (which, no doubt, exists), but it has an additional religious dimension. While the radicals are not averse to branding their adversaries as apostates, orthodox and moderate Muslims rarely resort to this weapon. Such an act—(accusing another Muslim of heresy by falsifying the roots of Islam, allowing that which is prohibited or forbidding that which is allowed) is not to be taken lightly; it contradicts the deep-rooted value that Islam places on unity among the believers and its aversion of *fitna* (communal discord). It is ironic that a religious mechanism which seems to have been created as a tool to preserve pluralism and prevent internal debates from deteriorating into civil war and mutual accusations of heresy (as occurred in Christian Europe) has become a tool in the hands of the radicals to drown out any criticism of them.

Consequently, even when pressure is put on Muslim communities, there exists a political asymmetry in favor of the radicals. Moderates are reluctant to come forward and to risk being accused of apostasy. For this very reason, many Muslim regimes in the Middle East and Asia are reluctant to crack down on the religious aspects of radical Islam and satisfy themselves with dealing with the political violence alone. By way of appeasement politics, they trade tolerance of jihad elsewhere for local calm. Thus, they lose ground to radicals in their societies.

THE WESTERN DILEMMA

It is a tendency in politically oriented Western society to assume that there is a rational pragmatic cause for acts of terrorism and that if the political grievance is addressed properly, the phenomenon will fade. However, when the roots are not political, it is naive to expect political gestures to change the hearts of radicals. Attempts to deal with the terrorist threat as if it were divorced from its intellectual, cultural, and religious fountainheads are doomed to failure. Counterterrorism begins on the religious-ideological level and must adopt appropriate methods. The cultural and religious sources of radical Islamic ideology must be addressed in order to develop a long-range strategy for coping with the terrorist threat to which they give birth.

However, in addressing this phenomenon, the West is at a severe disadvantage. Western concepts of civil rights along with legal, political, and cultural constraints preclude government intervention in the internal matters of organized religions; they make it difficult to prohibit or punish inflammatory sermons of imams in mosques (as Muslim regimes used to do on a regular basis) or to punish clerics for *fatwas* justifying terrorism. Furthermore, the legacy of colonialism deters Western governments from taking steps that may be construed as anti-Muslim or as signs of lingering colonialist ideology. This exposes the Western country combating the terrorist threat to criticism from within. Even most of the new and stringent terrorism prevention legislation that has been enacted in some countries leans mainly on investigatory powers (such as allowing for unlimited administrative arrests, etc.) and does not deal with prohibition of religion-based "ideological crimes" (as opposed to anti-Nazi and anti-racism laws, which are in force in many countries in Europe).

The regimes of the Middle East have proven their mettle in coercing religious establishments and even radical sheikhs to rule in a way commensurate with their interests. However, most of them show no inclination to join a global (i.e., "infidel") war against radical Islamic ideology. Hence, the prospect of enlisting Middle Eastern allies in the struggle against Islamic radicalism is bleak. Under these conditions, it will be difficult to curb the conversion of young Muslims in the West to the ideas of radicalism emanating from the safe houses of the Middle East. Even those who are not in direct contact with Middle Eastern sources of inspiration may absorb the ideology secondhand through interaction of Muslims from various origins in schools and on the Internet.

FIGHTING HELLFIRE
WITH HELLFIRE

Taking into account the above, is it possible—within the bounds of Western democratic value[s]—to implement a comprehensive strategy to combat Islamic terrorism at its ideological roots? First, such a strategy must be based on an acceptance of the fact that for the first time since the Crusades, Western civilization finds itself involved in a religious war; the conflict has been defined by the attacking side as such with the eschatological goal of the destruction of Western civilization. The goal of the West cannot be defense alone or military offense or democratization of the Middle East as a panacea. It must include a religious-ideological dimension: active pressure for religious reform in the Muslim world and pressure on the orthodox Islamic establishment in the West and the Middle East not only to disengage itself clearly from any justification of violence, but also to pit itself against the radical camp in a clear demarcation of boundaries.

Such disengagement cannot be accomplished by Western-style declarations of condemnation. It must include clear and binding legal rulings by religious authorities which contradict the axioms of the radical worldview and virtually "excommunicate" the radicals. In essence, the radical narrative, which promises paradise to those who perpetrate acts of terrorism, must be met by an equally legitimate religious force which guarantees hellfire for the same acts. Some elements of such rulings should be, inter alia:

• A call for renewal *of ijtihad* as the basis to reform Islamic dogmas and to relegate old dogmas to historic contexts.

- That there exists no state of jihad between Islam and the rest of the world (hence, jihad is not a personal duty).
- That the violation of the physical safety of a non-Muslim in a Muslim country is prohibited.
- That suicide bombings are clear acts of suicide, and therefore, their perpetrators are condemned to eternal hellfire.
- That moral or financial support of acts of terrorism is also *haram*.
- That a legal ruling claiming jihad is a duty derived from the roots of Islam is a falsification of the roots of Islam, and therefore, those who make such statements have performed acts of heresy.

Only by setting up a clear demarcation between orthodox and radical Islam can the radical elements be exorcized. The priority of solidarity within the Islamic world plays into the hands of the radicals. Only an Islamic Kulturkampf can redraw the boundaries between radical and moderate in favor of the latter. Such a struggle must be based on an in-depth understanding of the religious sources for justification of Islamist terrorism and a plan for the creation of a legitimate moderate counterbalance to the radical narrative in Islam. Such an alternative narrative should have a sound base in Islamic teachings, and its proponents should be Islamic scholars and leaders with wide legitimacy and accepted credentials. The "Middle-Easternization" of Asian Muslim communities should also be checked.

A strategy to cope with radical Islamic ideology cannot take shape without a reinterpretation of Western concepts of the boundaries of the freedoms of religion and speech, definitions of religious incitement, and criminal culpability of religious leaders for the acts of their flock as a result of their spiritual influence. Such a reinterpretation impinges on basic principles of Western civilization and law. Under the circumstances, it is the lesser evil.

NOTE

1. Kulturkampf (culture struggle) was the attempt in the 1870s by the newly unified Germany to curtail the power of the German Catholic church.

2

A MEDIEVAL THEORIST
OF JIHAD

Ibn Taymiyyah

From the onset of the religion, Muslims regarded jihad as a just war on behalf of God; warfare in the pursuit of personal power or national aggrandizement did not constitute jihad. Both the Qur'an and the hadith, the sayings attributed to Muhammad, explicitly prescribe jihad as an obligation for both the individual and the collective community. Muhammad glorified jihad and criticized those who did not participate in it, calling them "hypocrites" and "sick at heart," The Qur'an states: "Those who are killed in the path of God, He does not let their good deeds go for nothing." The following passages lauding jihad are from the hadith:

> He who draws his sword in the path of God has sworn allegiance to God.
> He who fights so that the word of God may prevail is on the path of God.
> He who when he dies has never campaigned or even intended to campaign dies in a kind of hypocrisy.
> In Islam there are three dwellings, the lower, the upper, and the uppermost.... The uppermost is the jihad in the cause of God which only the best of them attain.[1]

Present day Islamists who advocate jihad against the enemies of Islam often quote extensively Shaykh ul-Islaam Taqi al-Din Ahmad ibn Taymiyyah (1263–1328), a Syrian theologian who regarded jihad as a Muslim's religious and moral duty. During ibn Taymiyyah's lifetime much of the Muslim world was ruled by Mongol conquerors. The Mongol rulers had converted to Islam, but allowed traditional Mongol tribal law to be used alongside Islamic law. Asserting that Muslims must be governed only by Allah's commandments, ibn Taymiyyah denounced the Mongol rulers as apostates and called upon true Muslims to wage jihad against them. He also called for armed struggle against nonbelievers beyond the borders of Islam who endangered the Muslim community.

Contemporary jihadist ideologues refer to ibn Taymiyyah to legitimate their goals of overthrowing Muslim political leaders who do not govern in accordance with Islamic law; of waging war against foreign unbelievers who threaten the Muslim community; and of instilling in the Muslim masses the belief that jihad is a sacred obligation, while often ignoring or reinterpreting his opposition to attacks against non-combatant women and children.

The following is drawn from ibn Taymiyyah's discussion of jihad.

*   *   *

[Jihad] is the best voluntary [religious] act that man can perform....

...The [first] reason is that the benefit of jihad is general, extending not only to the person who participates in it but also to others, both in a religious and a temporal sense....[Second,] More than any other act [jihad] implies love and devotion for God, Who is exalted, trust in Him, the surrender of one's life and property to Him, patience, asceticism, remembrance of God and all kinds of other acts [of worship]. Any individual or community that participates in it, finds itself between two blissful outcomes: either victory and triumph or martyrdom and Paradise. [Third]...it is in jihad that one can live and die in ultimate happiness, both in this world and in the Hereafter. Abandoning it means losing entirely or partially both kinds of happiness....[J]ihad is religiously and temporally more beneficial than any other deed full of hardship....[T]he death of a martyr is easier than any other form of death. In fact, it is the best of all manners of dying....

If a rebellious group, although belonging to Islam, refuses to comply with clear and universally accepted commands, all Muslims agree that jihad must be waged against them, in order that the religion will be God's entirely....[It] is reported that [the Prophet said]:

> ...Towards the end of time a group will emerge, young of age and simple of minds, who will speak the most beautiful words, but whose faith does not go deeper than their throats. They will abandon the religion just like an arrow pierces and then abandons a game animal. Wherever you will find them you must kill them since those who kill them will be rewarded on the Day of Resurrection.

NOTE

1. Bernard Lewis, ed. and trans., *Islam from the Prophet Muhammad to the Capture of Constantinople* (New York: Oxford University Press, 1987), vol. 1, pp. 210–211.

3

THE JIHADISTS' MENTOR

Sayyid Qutb

There is widespread agreement that the Egyptian writer Sayyid Qutb (1906–1966) played a profoundly important theoretical and inspirational role in the development of contemporary Islamic jihadism. He has been called "the intellectual hero"[1] of the groups that united to form al Qaeda, many of whose leaders, including Ayman al Zawahiri, were his disciples. In his writings, he offered an Islamic solution to the crises besetting the contemporary world, particularly an expanded concept of jihad that would help bring about the triumph of Islam.

As a young boy, Qutb was immersed in the Qur'an; later he attended a modern secular college in Cairo. After graduation, he worked for the Egyptian Ministry of Education, and wrote novels, poems, and literary criticism. In the late 1940s, he came to the United States to study education at Colorado State College of Education (now University of Northern Colorado). After several years, he fled the United States, shocked, if not traumatized, by the social permissiveness and the sexual freedom he found in America.

When Qutb returned to Egypt, he joined the Egyptian Muslim Brotherhood, a Salafi organization, and soon became recognized as the leading theoretician of Islamism. Believing that through the ages Islam has become corrupt and decadent, the Salafi movement aspires to restore Islam to its original pure state: practicing the faith as did the Prophet and his immediate disciples. Salafis only accept the authority of the Qur'an and the hadiths, the accounts of the words and deeds of Muhammad.

The Muslim Brotherhood has played an important role in modern Egyptian history. At times members of the Brotherhood have engaged in violence and assassinations of government leaders in order to realize their Salafist goals; at other times the Brotherhood has adopted a more moderate face and demonstrated a willingness to postpone to some indefinite future the achievement of these goals. Successive Egyptian governments have alternated efforts to reach an accommodation with the Brotherhood with periods of repression.

After a failed attempt to assassinate him in 1954, the Egyptian leader, Gamal Abdel Nasser, executed leaders of the Brotherhood and imprisoned Qutb and several thousand other Brothers. Apart from two relatively brief periods of freedom, Qutb spent the rest of his life in prison. He and other leaders of the Brotherhood were executed in 1966.

During his years in prison, often under extremely harsh conditions, Qutb produced a large body of writing, including his impressive multi-volume commentary on the Qur'an, *In the Shade of the Qur'an*, which Paul Berman, a prominent American writer, has called "one of the most remarkable works of prison literature ever produced."[2] In his works, Qutb confronts some of the most profound problems of contemporary life for which he proposes an Islamic solution. The central problem of modern society, he maintains, is spiritual impoverishment that has caused deep unhappiness even among those who have most benefited from scientific progress and economic prosperity. The answer for Qutb is a revolutionary Islamic transformation based on the rule of God and divine law as codified in shari'a; such a restructuring of society would free people from human masters, human laws, and false values:

> Any system in which the final decisions are referred to human beings, and in which the sources of authority are human, deifies human beings by designating others than God as lords over men. This declaration [that sovereignty belongs to God alone] means that the usurped authority of God be returned to Him and the usurpers be thrown out—those who by themselves devise laws for others to follow, thus elevating themselves to the status of lords and reducing others to the status of slaves.[3]

Qutb condemns the Western liberal-democratic tradition for promoting secularism and restricting the sphere of religion that God intended to predominate over all human activities. Western democracy is a flawed and hateful system, he says, because it rejects the most crucial principle of life: only Allah's laws are the foundation of society and government. Democracy means government by the people, rather than the sovereignty of God; it means secular authorities making laws that are not divinely sanctioned; and it means a pluralist outlook that tolerates ideas and behavior that contradict Muslim principles. For Qutb, the West in general is a cesspool of injustice and human degradation:

> Look at this capitalism with its monopolies, its usury, and whatever else is unjust in it; at this individual freedom, devoid of human sympathy and responsibility for relatives except under the force of law; at this materialistic attitude which deadens the spirit; at this behavior, like animals, which you call "Free mixing of the sexes"; at this vulgarity which you call "emancipation of women"; at these cumbersome laws of marriage and divorce, which are contrary to the demands of practical life....[4]

Only a rejection of Western secularism and values can lead to the redemption of Islam.

He also rails against the Jews, describing them as wicked, cruel, murderous, and conspiratorial, and in the tradition of that proven forgery, the *Protocols of the Learned Elders of Zion* (see p. 202), with which he was familiar, he accuses them of having a master plan to dominate the world. The Jews, he said, are a threat to Islam today just as they were in the days of Muhammad. They are "launching a Zionist crusade against the very foundations of [Islam]...[T]he struggle between Islam and the Jews...will continue as it has because the Jews will be satisfied only with the destruction of the Muslim religion."[5] Qutb identifies the Jews with a broad cultural ecumenism that serves their "evil designs":

> The statement that "Culture is the human heritage" and that it has no country, nationality or religion is correct only in relation to science and technology....Beyond this limited meaning this statement about culture is one of the tricks played by world Jewry, whose purpose is to eliminate all limitations, especially the limitations imposed by faith and religion, so that the Jews may penetrate into the body politic of the whole world and then may be free to perpetrate their evil designs. At the top of the list of these activities is usury, the aim of which is that all the wealth of mankind end up in Jewish financial institutions which are run on interest.[6]

Qutb seeks the creation of a vanguard of true Muslims who would practice the religion as Salafists imagine it was practiced by Muhammad and his early followers. The vanguard would inspire a universal reform of Islam and the reestablishment of the caliphate. Much of this has been characterized as a traditional Salafi position.[7]

However, Qutb goes much further than his predecessors in his views of jihad. He redefines and broadens the concept to exclude those traditional limitations that would inhibit a global jihad. In particular, he confronts a traditional definition of jihad as defensive warfare: "If we insist on calling jihad a defensive movement then we must change the meaning of the word 'defense' and mean by it the 'defense of man' against those elements that limit his freedom." For Qutb freedom is liberating people from "servitude to anyone other than God."[8] Therefore, it would seem that any system but that of a true Islamic society, where civil law and shari'a are one is potentially subject to jihad. In effect, this justifies aggressive warfare against non-Muslims:

> Indeed Islam has the right to take the initiative. Islam is not the heritage of any particular race or country; this is God's religion and it is for the whole world. It has the right to destroy all obstacles in the form of institutions and traditions, which limit man's freedom of choice. It does not attack individuals nor does it force them to accept its beliefs; it attacks institutions and traditions to release human beings from their poisonous influences, which distort human nature and which curtail human freedom.[9]

Following in the tradition of Ibn Taymiyyah, he also expanded the concept of jihad to justify armed struggle against the leaders of nominally Muslim countries who were not governing as true Muslims, in effect challenging the religious injunction against *fitna*, the sowing of discord within Muslim society. The apostate rulers of these countries were unfit to govern, no better than the ignorant unbelievers who had resisted Muhammad, and they must be removed from power so that an authentic Muslim society dedicated to implementing and obeying all of God's rules and commands can be established.

Those constituting the vanguard he maintains must accept the necessity for jihad and prepare themselves for a martyr's death. He argues that martyrs don't satisfy the definition of death as "a total loss of function" because their blood has given "impetus to the cause," and even after their physical destruction they "remain an active force in shaping the life of their community and giving it direction."[10]

Qutb lived according to his principles. Prior to his final arrest, he was offered the chance to escape from Egypt and save his life, but he refused, choosing instead to give his estimated 3,000 followers an example of martyrdom. Many of these followers, most prominently Ayman al Zawahiri, were later involved in Egyptian terrorist movements and ultimately became part of al Qaeda.

Qutb's fundamentalism, warnings against the Western ideas and practices permeating Muslim society, call for jihad against both internal and external enemies of Islam, celebration of martyrdom, and anti-Semitic diatribes constitute the ideological foundations of contemporary Islamist radicalism. His 1964 book *Milestones* was specifically designed for the vanguard. Following is a brief excerpt from the chapter where Qutb confronts the issue of defensive jihad.

*   *   *

Those who say that Islamic Jihaad was merely for the defense of the "homeland of Islam" diminish the greatness of the Islamic way of life and consider it less important than their "homeland." This is not the Islamic point of view, and their view is a creation of the modern age and is completely alien to Islamic consciousness. What is acceptable to Islamic consciousness is the belief, the way of life which this belief prescribes, and the society which lives according to this way of life. The soil of the homeland has itself no value or weight. From the Islamic point of view, the only value which the soil can achieve is because on that soil God's authority is established and God's guidance is followed; and thus it becomes a fortress for the belief, a place for its way of life to be entitled the "homeland of Islam," a center for the movement for the total freedom of man.

Of course, in that case the defense of the "homeland of Islam" is the defense of the Islamic beliefs, the Islamic way of life and the Islamic community. However, defense is not the ultimate objective of the Islamic movement of Jihaad but is a means of establishing the divine authority within it so that it becomes the headquarters for the movement of Islam, which is then to be carried throughout the earth to the whole of mankind, as the object of this religion is all humanity and its sphere of action is the whole earth.

NOTES

1. Paul Berman, "The Philosopher of Islamic Terror," *The New York Times Magazine*, March 23, 2003, p. 26.
2. Ibid., p. 27.
3. Sayyid Qutb, *Milestones* (New Delhi, India: Millat Book Centre, n.d.), p. 58.
4. Ibid., p. 139.
5. Excerpted in Marvin Perry and Friedrich M. Schweitzer, eds., *Antisemitic Myths: A Historical and Contemporary Anthology* (Bloomington, IN: Indiana University Press, 2008), pp. 314–315.
6. Qutb, *Milestones*, p. 111.
7. Marc Sageman, *Understanding Terror Networks* (Philadelphia, PA: University of Pennsylvania Press, 2004), p. 11.
8. Quoted in Sageman, p. 12.
9. Qutb, *Milestones*, p. 75.
10. Quoted in Berman, p. 66.

4

"Islam Is Not a Religion of Pacifists"

Ayatollah Ruhollah Khomeini

Grand Ayatollah Ruhollah Khomeini (1902–1989), the leader of the revolution that overthrew the Shah of Iran in 1979, succeeded in establishing a theocratic state. Forbidding in manner, cunning in strategy, and merciless toward his enemies, Khomeini dominated the new Islamic state, his unsmiling face seemingly everywhere.

Ruhollah Khomeini was born into a family of Shi'ite mullahs in the small, dusty oasis town of Khomein—from which he later took his surname. He had a rigorous religious education, and as early as 1924, the young Khomeini signaled his interest in political events by writing an essay attacking the program of modernization and secularization that Rezah Shah, founder of the Pahlavi dynasty, was pursuing.

Khomeini married into a wealthy and respected family in 1930, and through gifts from the faithful and shrewd investments, he became quite prosperous in later years, although he was known for his lack of generosity and of the hospitality that was expected of senior clerics. By the mid-1930s he had begun to achieve recognition as a serious religious scholar.

After Reza Khan was forced to abdicate in 1941, his young son Mohammad-Reza became Shah. Khomeini, who was an aide to Iran's senior cleric, Grand Ayatollah Borujerdi, served on some occasions as intermediary between Borujerdi and the Shah. At first the young Shah seemed to build up Islam as a counterweight to communism, but ultimately he began to pursue policies of secularization and Westernization that were reminiscent of his father, and, also like his father, sought to neutralize the power of the mullahs in order to strengthen his personal rule.

Khomeini envisioned a politically activist role for the clergy, but he was inhibited by the classic Shi'ite position on government taken by Borujerdi, who maintained that only the martyred twelfth Imam, the so-called Hidden Imam, who is a central figure in Shi'a Islam, can offer perfect government. The Imam is believed to be in a state of "occultation," neither dead nor alive, but it is also believed that he will reveal himself sometime in the future. Traditionally Shi'ites had tolerated existing governments, even oppressive ones, waiting for the Hidden Imam to reveal himself and establish a utopia. This position was clearly challenged by Khomeini, who as early as 1961 advocated direct rule by the clergy, an innovation that had no precedent in Islam.

By the late 1950s, Khomeini had become an ayatollah, a preeminent Shi'ite religious authority, and when Borujerdi died in 1962 he sought to replace him, even flattering the Shah to earn support for his candidacy. But he was not a strong candidate and he was passed over. Apart from his political activism, Khomeini's love of poetry, and the mysticism in his complex theological lectures made him seem somewhat eccentric. This failure worked a profound change in his writing and preaching. Henceforth there was no mysticism, no poetry, but simple Manichean formulas of good versus evil.

As the Shah sought to distribute land to peasants, and pursued policies designed to emancipate women and to open positions in local government to non-Muslims, opposition to his rule grew and many people looked to Khomeini for leadership. In 1963, Khomeini, now a Grand Ayatollah, launched his campaign against the Shah. Shrewdly appealing to religious, nationalist, and anti-Western feelings, he bitterly criticized the Shah's ties to Israel and charged that Jews were planning to take over Iran; he opposed the Shah's plan to give women the vote; and he denounced the privileges given to American service personnel stationed in Iran.

Khomeini's strident opposition led to his arrest, triggering riots in Tehran and several other cities that resulted in numerous deaths. In 1964, he was released from prison but continued to attack the government and was arrested again and forced into exile in Turkey. In 1966, after quarreling with the Turkish authorities, he moved to the holy city of Najaf in Iraq. He resumed teaching and his radicalism attracted increasing numbers of anti-Shah students. Khomeini continued his denunciations of the Shah and called for his overthrow. Persisting in his appeals for the ouster of the Shah, he was expelled from Iraq in 1978, and he went to France, settling in a suburb of Paris for several months. Meanwhile, secret cells of Khomeini supporters had formed in Iran and there were riots in the streets. Clashes between the rioters and security forces resulted in the deaths of hundreds. Support for the Shah crumbled, as students, the middle class, merchants, workers and the army all began to abandon the regime, which had increasingly resorted to repressive measures. The Shah fled to the West in January 1979 and Khomeini returned to Iran two weeks later.

Revolutionary fervor gripped the country and vigilante groups and instantly created courts were responsible for the execution of hundreds of former officials in the Shah's government. Khomeini acted to establish his authority and created a state run by the clergy and governed according to Islamic law. Women were forced to wear the chador, a bulky black garment, alcohol and Western music were banned, a reformed penal system based on shari'a was established, and Khomeini's ideas came to dominate the schools and the media. In November 1979, a group of revolutionary students, in an action clearly sanctioned by Khomeini, seized the American embassy in Tehran and held fifty-two people hostage, initiating a crisis that was not resolved until the hostages were released a few minutes after Ronald Reagan was sworn in as President in January 1981.

Khomeini showed himself ruthless during the years of his rule, as thousands of opponents were imprisoned or executed. In foreign policy, he was an unrelenting opponent of both the United States and the Soviet Union and made provocative efforts to export his revolution to other Muslim countries in the region. From 1980 to 1988, Iraq and Iran were engaged in a bitter and costly war that was prolonged by Khomeini in the hope of overthrowing the Iraqi president Saddam Hussein.

In his last years, aged and ailing, Khomeini was still the undisputed leader of Iran and still capable of taking an action that had international impact. Several months before his death in 1989, Khomeini issued a fatwa condemning to death the writer Salman Rushdie for the "heresies" in his novel *Satanic Verses*. Rushdie was born a Sunni Muslim in India and theoretically was beyond Khomeini's authority. Nevertheless, threatened by fundamentalists from throughout the Muslim world, Rushdie was forced into hiding for years. It is an indication that the power and influence of Khomeini spread far beyond Iran, even to Sunni Muslims, despite the long history of conflict between the two branches of Islam.

In the selection below, originally published in 1942 and reprinted during the years that he was supreme leader of Iran, Khomeini takes an extreme and uncompromising view of jihad that seems typical of his later writing and preaching. Gone are the subtle distinctions and qualifications made by other Muslim thinkers, replaced by his unqualified glorification of the sword as "the key to Paradise," a view embraced by today's jihadists. In later writings Khomeini preached the virtues of martyrdom and extolled death as a continuation of life, teachings which also make up the jihadist ideology. The brackets were inserted by the translator.

*   *   *

There are two kinds of war in Islam: one is called Jihad [Holy War], which means the conquest of [other] countries in accordance with certain conditions. The other [type] is war to preserve the independence of the [Muslim] country and the repulsion of foreigners. Jihad or Holy War, which is for the conquest of [other] countries and kingdoms, becomes incumbent after the formation of the Islamic state in the presence of the Imam or in accordance with his command. Then Islam makes it incumbent on all adult males, provided they are not disabled and incapacitated, to prepare themselves for the conquest of [other] countries so that the writ of Islam is obeyed in every country in the world.

But world public opinion should know that Islamic conquest is not the same as conquests made by other rulers of the world. The latter want to conquer the world for their own personal profit, whereas Islam's conquest is aimed at serving the interests of the inhabitants of the globe as a whole. [Non-Islamic] conquerors want to rule the world so that they can spread through it every injustice and sexual indecency, whereas Islam wants to conquer the world in order to promote spiritual values, and to prepare mankind for justice and divine rule. [Non-Islamic] conquerors sacrifice the lives and possessions of the people to their own leisure and pleasure. But Islam does not allow its leaders and generals to enjoy themselves or to have a moment's leisure; in this way the lives and property of people can be protected and the bases of injustice destroyed in the world.

Islam's Holy War is a struggle against idolatry, sexual deviation, plunder, repression and cruelty. The war waged by [non-Islamic] conquerors, however, aims at promoting lust and animal pleasures. They care not if whole countries are wiped out and many families left homeless. But those who study Islamic Holy War will understand why Islam wants to conquer the whole world. All the countries conquered by Islam or to be conquered in the future will be marked for everlasting salvation. For they shall live under Light Celestial Law....

Those who know nothing of Islam pretend that Islam counsels against war. Those [who say this] are witless. Islam says: Kill all the unbelievers just as they would kill you all! Does this mean that Muslims should sit back until they are devoured by [the unbelievers]? Islam says: Kill them [the non-Muslims], put them to the sword and scatter [their armies]. Does this mean sitting back until [non-Muslims] overcome us? Islam says: Kill in the service of Allah those who may want to kill you! Does this mean that we should surrender [to the enemy]? Islam says: Whatever good there is exists thanks to the sword and in the shadow of the sword! People cannot be made obedient except with the sword! The sword is the key to Paradise, which can be opened only for Holy Warriors!

There are hundreds of other [Qur'anic] psalms and Hadiths [sayings of the Prophet] urging Muslims to value war and to fight. Does all that mean that Islam is a religion that prevents men from waging war? I spit upon those foolish souls who make such a claim.

5

MYTH IN THE SERVICE
OF JIHAD

David Cook

The jihadist fantasy of recreating and extending the medieval Muslim empire governed by a stringent interpretation of Islamic law is an expression of mythical thinking. Typical of the mythical mind, jihadists utilize martyrology and miracle stories that support and strengthen their commitment to the cause of global jihad. Certain recurrent themes, such as supernatural aid for the mujahid in battle, the miraculous purification of the body of a fallen warrior, and sudden visions of paradise, characterize these tales. Radical Islamists also interpret jihad in apocalyptic terms, relating their struggles to religious traditions about cataclysmic events that are expected to herald the advent of a new Muslim world order. One key figure in this scenario is the demonic Dajjal, a type of Antichrist frequently identified by radical Islamists with Jews and the West, who seeks to lead people away from God. The other key figure is the Mahdi, a messianic leader who will establish the dominance of a purified Islam. Radical Islamists, such as the Taliban, armed with a fundamentalist faith, often conceive of their mission in these messianic terms, a theme discussed in *Understanding Jihad* (2005), by David Cook, who teaches religious studies at Rice University.

* * *

The apocalyptic and/or messianic vision of the jihad is of obvious importance to the fighters. Without an explanation of its purpose, the process of jihad becomes less meaningful. Apocalyptic explanations justify to the believer the trials and tests of this world. Usually these events are explained as preparation for Paradise, separating the righteous from the sinners. This is in close accord with several verses from the Qur'an:

> Such are the times; we alternate them among the people, so that Allah may know who are the believers and choose martyrs from among you. Allah does not like the evildoers! And that Allah might purify the believers and annihilate

the unbelievers. Or did you suppose that you will enter Paradise, before Allah has known who were those of you who have struggled, and those who are steadfast? (3:140–142)

This process of separation is integral to the apocalyptic outlook and an important part of radical Islam. Therefore, it is equally important to construct an apocalyptic interpretation of events and to fit them into the eternal process of separation so that "true" Muslims will not lose hope (although ultimately an apocalyptist rationalizes losses on the part of the faithful by maintaining that they were never "truly" faithful).

Radical Muslims start their apocalyptic vision by citing hadiths to prove that jihad is a salvific action that will continue until the time of the Day of Resurrection....What distinguishes the saved from the damned is the willingness to fight for the sake of Islam. All other criteria are of lesser value—even worthless—according to this interpretation. During the course of this apocalyptic future, dramatic and cataclysmic events are expected to occur—indeed, the believers should want them to occur because they herald the passing of the old non-Muslim order and the beginning of the new.

There are two categories of apocalyptic signs: the lesser and the greater signs of the Hour. Lesser signs of the Hour are largely moral or social in nature, although some are political, natural (earthquakes and plagues), or cosmic. For the most part, radical Muslim apocalyptic writers agree that these events have already taken place or are too indistinct to ascertain. The greater signs of the Hour are the appearance of the Dajjal (the Muslim Antichrist), who will tempt the entire world to follow him in direct opposition to God; the appearance of Jesus, who will return from heaven in order to slay the Dajjal; and the appearance of the Mahdi, the Muslim messianic figure....

As one might surmise from the number of conspiracy theories in the, Muslim world, the Dajjal is a major figure in Muslim religious culture. Books and pamphlets about him regularly appear in the markets, and there are many websites on the Internet that discuss his identity. For many radical Muslims, the Dajjal is closely identified with the "world Jewish conspiracy" which is especially convenient since in the classical sources the Dajjal is said to be a Jew. To make the leap that the Dajjal is a social force or an anti-Muslim idea—such as the West, the "global Jewish conspiracy" or even the United Nations—is not difficult. The following tradition is most useful in this regard:

A group of my [Muhammad's] community will continue, fighting for the truth, victorious over those who oppose them, until the last of them fights the Antichrist.

As far as globalist radical Muslims are concerned, they are fulfilling this tradition in its entirety....

This is one trend in beliefs about the future. Another could be characterized as the messianic trend. The Muslim messianic figure, the Mahdi, has been the focus of expectation for Muslims for hundreds of years, and many dynasties have risen to power because of messianic slogans or claims to be the Mahdi. There are two basic frameworks for the appearance of the Mahdi: either he will appear in Mecca at the time of the hajj and lead a large number of Muslims to conquer the core lands of Islam and purify them, or else he will appear in Khurasan, the area that today includes parts of Iran, Central Asia, and Afghanistan.

The latter scenario is very convenient for globalist radical Muslims—or at least it was during the interval when the Taliban controlled Afghanistan. Since the Taliban's principal claim was that they imposed the *shari'a* in its entirety—a claim that radical Muslims supported and acclaimed—devoted themselves to the waging of jihad, and gave sanctuary to globalist radical Muslims such as Usama bin Ladin (in 1996), there was some substance to this idea. In 1996 Mulla 'Umar Muhammad Mujahid, the leader of the Taliban, took the title of *amir al-mu'minin*, a caliphal title. Since the abolition of the caliphate in 1924, many Muslims, including radical Muslims, have been seeking a manner by which a caliph could be elected. Thus there was a messianic component to the title, even though it was never accepted by the majority of Muslims.

However, beyond all doubt the primary messianic aspect of the Taliban state was the perpetuation of jihad. This dovetailed nicely with the radical Muslim critique of Muslim societies: they have lost their Islam, have been humiliated by the West (and the rest of the world), and occupy a subordinate position because they abandoned jihad. Since Afghanistan, as Khurasan, has powerful resonance with many Muslims because of the messianic expectations focused on that region, this gave the globalist radical Muslims associated with al-Qa'ida under the leadership of Bin Ladin additional moral authority to proclaim jihad and call for the purification of the present Muslim governments and elites.

In the end, the globalist radical Muslim vision of jihad is world domination. Islam must come to dominate the world in its entirety, in accordance with the radical Muslim interpretation of Qur'an 8:39, "And fight them, so that sedition [temptation] might end and the only religion will be that of Allah." Clearly this absolute vision does not speak for all Muslims, but it does have a resonance for many.

Part 2

AL QAEDA: ACTIVATING
JIHADISM

On September 11, 2001, nineteen Muslim Arabs, fifteen from Saudi Arabia, hijacked four planes: two of them crashed into the World Trade Center in New York, bringing down both towers; a third plane rammed into the Pentagon in Washington, DC, causing severe damage; and, the fourth plane, apparently headed for the White House, crashed in a field in Pennsylvania when passengers heroically attacked the hijackers. In the worst terrorist attack in history almost 3,000 people perished, exceeding the number of deaths in the Japanese surprise attack on Pearl Harbor. The meticulously planned operation was the work of al Qaeda, an international terrorist network of militant Muslims. In 1998, it was responsible for the deadly bombings of American embassies in Kenya and Tanzania, which killed hundreds, and in 2000, al Qaeda operatives detonated a bomb next to the U.S. destroyer *Cole* in the harbor of Aden, costing the lives of seventeen American sailors. Al Qaeda hoped that worldwide media coverage of the audacious attacks on 9/11 would gain it mass support in the Muslim world.

The leader of al Qaeda, Osama bin Laden, scion of a wealthy Saudi family, operated from Afghanistan with the protection of the radical fundamentalist Taliban, who ruled the country, establishing a repressive regime based on a rigid interpretation of Islamic law. When Taliban leaders refused to turn bin Laden over to the United States, President George W. Bush, supported by an international coalition, launched a military campaign whose ultimate goal was the destruction of international terrorism. The United States showed a fierce resolve unexpected by bin Laden, who thought that the Americans would not risk sending troops to fight in the forbidding Afghan terrain and against people who had defeated the Soviet Union. Or, if America did invade Afghanistan, he counted on Muslims throughout the world rising up against the United States for its attack on an Islamic country. By luring the United States into a global guerilla war, he hoped to overtax its military and demoralize the American people. Local Afghan forces opposed to the Taliban, assisted by American air power—which proved decisive—defeated the Taliban in a few weeks. But many of the Taliban took refuge in the lawless tribal regions of neighboring Pakistan where they established training camps, recruited followers, and crossed back into Afghanistan to wage guerilla war against the new government and its American supporters.

On numerous occasions, President Bush and his chief advisers declared that the attack on Afghanistan was directed against "evil-doers" and not against Muslims in general or their faith. However, bin Laden and his followers view the struggle against the United States as a jihad against the infidel. Bin Laden and other Arabs from Morocco to Yemen devoted to a militant Islam had fought in Afghanistan to drive out the Soviets. During that conflict, bin Laden and his cohorts drew up plans for the creation of an Islamic world-state governed by Islamic law, a revival of the medieval caliphate.

Muslims regard Arabia as their holy land; the prophet was born in Mecca and established the first Islamic state in Medina. In 1998, bin Laden told his followers that the stationing of American troops in Saudi Arabia, "the land of the two holy Mosques," demonstrated that America "had spearheaded a crusade against the Islamic nation." An absolutist and religious zealot who cannot tolerate pluralism, equal rights for women, and other basic democratic rights, bin Laden wants to drive westerners and Western values out of Islamic lands and use the state's power to impose a narrow and exclusive version of Islam on the Muslim world.

To be sure, many students of Islam believe that the actions of bin Laden and his followers violate such core Islamic teachings as the prohibition against killing innocent civilians. At the same time, however, terrorists find religious justification for their actions in Islamic traditions. The early followers of Muhammad, says Bernard Lewis, divided the world

> into two houses: the House of Islam, in which a Muslim government ruled and Muslim law prevailed, and the House of War, the rest of the world... ruled by infidels. Between the two, there was to be a perpetual state of war until the entire world either embraced Islam or submitted to the rule of the Muslim state.... For Osama bin Laden, 2001 marks the resumption of the war for the religious dominance of the world that began in the seventh century. For him and his followers, this is the moment of opportunity. Today America exemplifies the civilization that embodies the leadership of the House of War, and it... has become degenerate and demoralized, ready to be overthrown.[1]

Al Qaeda is inspired by classical Islam that justifies warfare against unbelievers and established a unitary state, the caliphate, which expanded Muslim power through conquest and imposed Islamic law over the Muslim community. It also draws on modern movements, Wahhabism and Salafism, which call for a return to a pure Islam that strictly adheres to the Prophet's teachings and want the state, eventually a restored caliphate, to enforce Islamic law.

The hatred of radical Muslims for the West shows that in an age of globalism the world is still divided by strong cultural traditions. It also reveals how the problems confronting the Middle East—authoritarian governments, the suppression of human rights, rampant corruption, mushrooming populations, high unemployment, and the ongoing Palestinian-Israeli conflict—have a global impact. All these factors have led many disillusioned young Muslims to place their hopes for a better life not in democratic reforms but in a radical Islam that promises to restore a glorious past and guarantee entrance to Paradise for jihadist martyrs. Fostering religious fanaticism and intolerance are the numerous religious schools, often financed by Saudi Arabia, that have been established in many parts of the Muslim world. In these schools youngsters are given little or no secular education and from an early age are indoctrinated with the tenets of radical Islam: rule by stringent Islamic law, hatred of the West, holy war against the infidel, the Jew as Devil, and the virtue of martyrdom for the faith.

NOTE

1. Bernard Lewis, "Revolt of Islam," *The New Yorker*, November 19, 2001, pp. 52, 62.

"Declaration of Jihad against Jews and Crusaders"

Osama bin Laden

Osama bin Laden, leader of al Qaeda and the world's best-known terrorist, was born in Saudi Arabia in 1957 into a large family of wealth and privilege. His father, Muhammad bin Laden, was a self-made billionaire of Yemeni origin whose construction business held a dominant position in the kingdom and who had established close personal relations with the Saudi royal family. Osama grew up in an atmosphere marked by a religious piety rooted in the fundamentalist Wahhabist tradition that is dominant in Saudi Arabia. At seventeen, he entered the Management and Economics School of King Abd al-Aziz University, where he was a somewhat mediocre business student. While at the university, he fell under the influence of two important Islamist religious scholars, Muhammad Qutb, the brother of Sayyid Qutb, and Abdallah Azzam, a Palestinian member of the Muslim Brotherhood who played an important theoretical and practical role in the development of the modern jihadist movement.

There is some question as to whether bin Laden received his diploma or left the university without a degree, but in any event he entered his father's construction empire and successfully managed several businesses, amassing a considerable personal fortune. By 1980, he was drawn to the cause of Afghanistan, where mujahideen, both Afghan and foreign, were fighting the communist-led and Soviet-supported government. He went to the Pakistan border city of Peshawar where he joined his former teacher Azzam in providing facilities and assistance for foreign, mainly Arab, mujahideen—often referred to as the "Afghan Arabs"—going to fight in Afghanistan.

Although there is some disagreement over bin Laden's exact role in the Afghan struggle, it is clear that he funded jihadist activities, personally participated in the fighting around the city of Jalalabad, and used his experience in construction to build bases and training facilities for the mujahideen, including the famous cave complex at Tora Bora. In 1988, with the Soviet defeat and withdrawal looming, bin Laden with several associates founded al Qaeda as an international jihadist movement. The term means "the base" or "the foundation" in Arabic and was commonly used by foreign volunteers in Afghanistan.

By 1990 bin Laden was back in Saudi Arabia, several months before Saddam Hussein's invasion of Kuwait precipitated the crisis that led to the first Gulf War. Bin Laden volunteered to lead a group of jihadist veterans of the war in Afghanistan, the so-called Afghan Arabs, against Saddam. His offer was refused by the Saudi government, which permitted American and other foreign forces to enter the kingdom. Bin Laden protested against this defilement of the holy land of Islam by the presence of infidel forces. His protests brought him house arrest, and he henceforth became an implacable foe of the Saudi government. Using his family influence to obtain travel documents, bin Laden returned to Afghanistan in 1991 and sought to mediate among the various factions struggling for control after the departure of the Soviets, fearing that that this civil war would have a negative impact on the jihadist movement elsewhere.

Bin Laden's efforts failed and he left Afghanistan for Sudan where he was offered protection by the military regime headed by a radical Islamist, Hassan al-Turabi. Bin Laden invested heavily in Sudan and involved the leadership of the country in his business ventures. He also arranged for settlement of the Afghan Arab mujahideen who followed him to Sudan and offered them employment. Among these Afghan Arabs was Ayman al Zawahiri, an Egyptian jihadist who had become a close associate of bin Laden by the late 1980s and would emerge as the second most important leader of al Qaeda. In Sudan, bin Laden was involved either directly or indirectly in jihadist activities, including plots to overthrow the Saudi monarchy, attacks on American peacekeepers in Somalia in 1993, the 1993 attack on the World Trade Center in New York, and an attempt to assassinate the Egyptian president Hosni Mubarak in 1994.

By 1994, the Saudi government stripped bin Laden of his citizenship, and the Sudanese government was pressured by the Saudis, the United States and Egypt to expel him and other militants. He left the country in 1996 and returned to Afghanistan, arriving there several months before the Taliban captured Kabul. Bin Laden established a close relationship with the new fundamentalist regime, which provided sanctuary and a base for him to organize his global jihadist activities. He in turn supported the Taliban with funds, as well as managerial and development expertise. It was only at this time that bin Laden achieved widespread notoriety as a leading terrorist. Both the 1998 bombings of the American embassies in Kenya and Tanzania, and the attack on the *U.S.S. Cole* in Yemen in 2000 were traced to al Qaeda. After the bombings of the American embassies, President Clinton launched a cruise missile attack on one of bin Laden's bases in Afghanistan in an unsuccessful attempt to kill him.

The American invasion of Afghanistan following 9/11 and the overthrow of the Taliban government deprived bin Laden of his sanctuary. By most accounts, he was almost captured at his Tora Bora cave complex but managed to slip away. He is presently believed to be somewhere in the mountainous tribal areas of Pakistan bordering Afghanistan.

Bin Laden's emergence as the world's leading terrorist owes much to his personal qualities. He has good managerial and organizational skills and has been willing to use his considerable personal wealth to realize his jihadist goals. His austere lifestyle and willingness to suffer physical privations and the risk of capture and death have earned him the admiration of many Muslims, including those who do not generally support terrorism. Describing bin Laden's first televised appearance after 9/11, Omar Saghi, a scholar of Islam, has written:

> The challenge he posed to America as an ascetic stripped of all worldly goods and hiding out in Afghanistan's miserable mountains was multiplied by the gaping breach that—as he delighted in emphasizing—separated him from the United States' predatory opulence.[1]

Bin Laden has been described as a brilliant polemicist who effectively uses the media to transmit his message. He has demonstrated a shrewd ability to appeal to and manipulate the hatreds, frustrations, and anger in the Muslim world. His skill in exploiting the media and Al Qaeda's effective use of technology and modern business techniques point to a frequently observed paradox: Bin Laden promotes a rigid, narrow fundamentalism whose roots are found in the distant past, and yet he and his organization employ modern means to realize this medieval vision.

Bin laden is not a religious scholar, but he is immersed in Islamic religious traditions. This last point is crucial. His frequent references to passages in the Qur'an and other religious texts to support his jihadist goals have struck a resonant chord in the Muslim world.

Political scientist Robert S. Snyder has characterized bin Laden as a "civilizational revolutionary," a term that distinguishes him from radicals calling for a revolution within their own country and classic Marxists, who support a global working-class revolution.[2] According to this interpretation, bin Laden's revolutionary unit is neither a nation nor a class, but an entire civilization—the Islamic civilization of the Middle East and beyond. Regarding national borders as Western imperialist creations that serve to divide Muslims, he focuses on the *umma*, the world community of Muslims, as his revolutionary unit. And for him a principal symbol of Islamic civilization is the caliphate that he aims to restore, perhaps with the expectation that he would become caliph. Restoration of the caliphate is only a prelude to the reconquest of all lands that were once under Muslim rule. Ultimately bin Laden envisions a future where the entire world will live under Islamic law.

Snyder's analysis has the advantage of highlighting bin Laden's opposition to national jihads aimed at a particular country, one whose rulers fundamentalists view as "apostates." He sought to change the national focus of such groups as Egyptian Islamic Jihad headed by Ayman

al Zawahiri, and ultimately prevailed as Zawahiri merged his group with
al Qaeda.

For bin Laden, the United States is the principal target of the global
jihad movement. His litany of accusations includes the familiar charges
that the United States supports Israel's efforts to crush the Palestinians,
that it is killing Muslims in Iraq and represses them elsewhere, and that it
defiles the "land of the two holy Mosques" by stationing troops in Saudi
Arabia. He also bitterly attacks Jews, who are thought to control the policies of the United States. In response to those jihadists who focus on overturning the regime in a particular Muslim country, bin Laden maintains
that corrupt apostate regimes are kept in power by American support;
therefore, attacking the "far enemy" is the most effective way of stripping
present Muslim rulers of their power and imposing Islamic law in these
lands.

By attacking the United States on 9/11, bin Laden hoped to trigger a
military response that would radicalize the Muslims of the Middle East
against America, leading to the weakening or toppling of moderate, pro-
Western Arab regimes and the ascendancy of al Qaeda. With a confidence
born of the victory by the mujahideen over the Soviets, he expected that
the United States would be trapped in a guerrilla war in Afghanistan and
would soon flee in humiliation. He did not anticipate his having to flee
Afghanistan; nor did the United States' invasion of that al Qaeda strong-
hold elicit the violent response in the Muslim world he expected. But it
has been argued that the current war in Iraq, a war begun at least in part
as a response to the threat of terrorism in a post-9/11 world, has served as
an effective recruitment tool for al Qaeda jihadists, while greatly exacerbating anti-American sentiment in the region and weakening moderate
Arab governments.

In February 1998, some three-and-a-half years before 9/11, bin Laden
formed the World Islamic Front in Afghanistan, and in the Front's name
issued a *fatwa*, or religious decree, proclaiming a jihad against "Crusaders
and Jews." The five signatories include Ayman al Zawahiri, who by then
had become bin Laden's closest associate. The declaration focuses on three
charges against the "Judeo-Crusader alliance." First, there is the ongoing
"occupation" of Saudi Arabia by American forces, who are accused of
defiling this holy land and turning it into a base for attacking neighboring
Muslim lands. Second, bin Laden and his colleagues charge the United
States with devastating Iraq in a "vicious" war and continuing to inflict
suffering on the Iraqi people. (The reference is obviously to America's
leadership of the coalition that fought the first Gulf War in 1991 in
response to Saddam Hussein's invasion of Kuwait and to the subsequent imposition of sanctions by the UN.) Finally, these actions by the
United States serve to distract attention from the continuing occupation of Jerusalem and the "murder" of Muslims by Israel. The declaration,
reproduced below, closes with an appeal to all true Muslims "to kill
Americans and seize their money wherever they find them." The bombings

of the American embassies in Kenya and Tanzania that same year have been viewed as bin Laden's first step in implementing the principles of this declaration.

* * *

Praise be to God, revealer of the Book, controller of the clouds, defeater of factionalism, who says in His Book: "When the forbidden months are over, wherever you find the polytheists, kill them, seize them, besiege them, ambush them." Prayers and peace be upon our Prophet Muhammad bin Abdallah, who said: "I have been sent with a sword in my hands so that only God may be worshiped, God who placed my livelihood under the shadow of my spear and who condemns those who disobey my orders to servility and humiliation."

Ever since God made the Arabian Peninsula flat, created desert in it and surrounded it with seas, it has never suffered such a calamity as these Crusader hordes that have spread through it like locusts, consuming its wealth and destroying its fertility. All this at a time when nations have joined forces against the Muslims as if fighting over a bowl of food. When the matter is this grave and support is scarce, we must discuss current events and agree collectively on how best to settle the issue.

There is now no longer any debate about three well acknowledged and commonly agreed facts that require no further proof, but we will repeat them so that people remember them. They are as follows:

Firstly, for over seven years America has occupied the holiest parts of the Islamic lands, the Arabian peninsula, plundering its wealth, dictating to its leaders, humiliating its people, terrorizing its neighbours and turning its bases there into a spearhead with which to fight the neighbouring Muslim peoples. Some might have disputed the reality of this occupation before, but all the people of the Arabian Peninsula have now acknowledged it. There is no clearer proof than America's excessive aggression against the people of Iraq, using the Peninsula as a base. It is true that all its leaders have rejected such use of their lands, but they are powerless.

Secondly, despite the great devastation inflicted upon the Iraqi people at the hands of the Judeo-Crusader alliance, and despite the terrible number of deaths—over one million—despite all this, the Americans are trying to repeat these horrific massacres again, as if they are not satisfied with the long period of sanctions after the vicious war, or with all the fragmentation and destruction.

Today they come to annihilate what is left of this people and humiliate their Muslim neighbours.

Thirdly, while these wars are being waged by the Americans for religious and economic purposes, they also serve the interests of the petty Jewish state, diverting attention from its occupation of Jerusalem and its murder of Muslims there. There is no better proof of this than their eagerness to destroy Iraq, the strongest neighbouring Arab state, and their efforts to fragment all the states in the region, like Iraq, Saudi Arabia, Egypt, and Sudan, into paper mini-states whose weakness and disunity will guarantee Israel's survival and the continuation of the brutal Crusader occupation of the Peninsula.

All these American crimes and sins are a clear proclamation of war against God, his Messenger, and the Muslims. Religious scholars throughout Islamic history have agreed that jihad is an individual duty when an enemy attacks Muslim countries. This was related by the Imam ibn Qudama in "The Resource," by Imam al-Kisa'i in "The Marvels," by al-Qurtubi in his exegesis, and by the Sheikh of Islam when he states in his chronicles that "As for fighting to repel an enemy, which is the strongest way to defend freedom and religion, it is agreed that this is a duty. After faith, there is no greater duty than fighting an enemy who is corrupting religion and the world."

On this basis, and in accordance with God's will, we pronounce to all Muslims the following judgment: To kill the American and their allies—civilians and military—is an individual duty incumbent upon every Muslim in all countries, in order to liberate the al-Aqsa Mosque [in Jerusalem] and the Holy Mosque [in Mecca] from their grip, so that their armies leave all the territory of Islam, defeated, broken, and unable to threaten any Muslim. This is in accordance with the words of God Almighty: "Fight the idolaters at any time, if they first fight you;" "Fight them until there is no more persecution and until worship is devoted to God;" "Why should you not fight in God's cause and for those oppressed men, women, and children who cry out: 'Lord, rescue us from this town whose people are oppressors! By Your grace, give us a protector and a helper!'"

With God's permission we call on everyone who believes in God and wants reward to comply with His will to kill the Americans and seize their money wherever and whenever they find them. We also call on the religious scholars, their leaders, their youth, and their soldiers, to launch the raid on the soldiers of Satan, the Americans, and whichever devil's supporters are allied with them, to rout those behind them so that they will not forget it.

God Almighty said: "Believers, respond to God and His Messenger when he calls you to that which gives you life. Know that God comes between a man and his heart, and that you will be gathered to Him."

God Almighty said: "Believers, why, when it is said to you, 'Go and fight in God's way,' do you dig your heels into the earth? Do you prefer this world to the life to come? How small the enjoyment of this world is, compared with the life to come! If you do not go out and fight, God will punish you severely and put others in your place, but you cannot harm Him in any way: God has power over all things."

God Almighty also said: "Do not lose heart or despair—if you are true believers you will have the upper hand."

NOTES

1. Quoted in Malise Ruthven, "The Rise of Muslim Terrorists," *The New York Review of Books* (May 29, 2008), p. 33.
2. Robert S. Snyder, "Hating America: Bin Laden as a Civilizational Revolutionary," *Review of Politics*, Vol. 65, No. 4 (Fall 2003), 325–349.

2

KNIGHTS UNDER THE PROPHET'S BANNER

Ayman al Zawahiri

Ayman al Zawahiri, the second most important leader of al Qaeda, has in recent years become the public face and voice of the organization. He has appeared on more tapes and issued more public statements than Osama bin Laden. Although the internal dynamics of the organization and the current condition of bin Laden are largely unknown, Zawahiri, a veteran jihadist and al Qaeda's theoretician, sometimes seems to be the person in charge.

Born in Egypt in 1951 to a middle-class family of professionals and scholars, Zawahiri was caught up in the fervor of Islamic fundamentalism early in his life. In 1966, at age fifteen, he formed a cell that was part of the Muslim Brotherhood (see part 1, chapter 3, p. 23). At that time, his focus was on Egyptian issues, and he supported the Brotherhood's Salafi program to introduce rule by shari'a. By the late 1970s, his cell had joined three others to form Egyptian Islamic Jihad (EIJ), an organization that he would ultimately come to lead. Meanwhile, he had graduated from medical school and earned a master's degree in surgery. In 1980, Zawahiri went to Pakistan as a doctor to assist the Afghan mujahideen fighting against the Soviets. He worked in the border city of Peshawar and made several trips into Afghanistan. Further radicalized by this experience, he returned to Egypt in 1981.

Bitterly opposed to the peace treaty with Israel signed by Anwar Sadat, Zawahiri entered into a conspiracy to kill the Egyptian leadership and ignite a revolution. Although most of the leadership of EIJ was arrested in a crackdown after the government learned about the plan in February 1981, Zawahiri remained free. When Sadat was assassinated in October 1981, Zawahiri, who was suspected of having had prior knowledge of the plot, was arrested along with hundreds of other Islamist radicals. He was tortured, tried, and imprisoned for three years. The trial of the radicals received wide coverage by the international press. Zawahiri, who served as unofficial spokesman for his fellow defendants, used the courtroom as a forum to denounce Zionism and communism.

He emerged from prison even more radicalized and in 1985 made his way back to Peshawar where he sought to reform EIJ. However his ideas clashed with those of Abdallah Azzam, bin Laden's mentor and spiritual guide of the Afghan Arabs (see part 2, chapter 1) over the purpose of jihad. Holding to a traditional view of jihad, Azzam sought to recover Muslim lands that had fallen into the hands of the infidel—these included his native Palestine, parts of the Soviet Union, and even southern Spain. Opposed to Muslims fighting other Muslims, he rejected the plans of Zawahiri and EIJ for jihad against the Egyptian government. Azzam's murder in 1989 has never been solved, but suspicion has fallen on EIJ and Zawahiri.

Meanwhile Zawahiri had established a close relationship with bin Laden and the newly formed al Qaeda. After the conclusion of the Soviet-Afghan war in 1992, Zawahiri followed bin Laden to Sudan where he planned a series of terrorist attacks in Egypt and conspired in several failed efforts to murder Egyptian leaders. This led to crackdowns by the Egyptian government and arrests of militants that further weakened EIJ. Moreover, the pressure put on the Sudanese government to stop providing sanctuary to militants, forced bin Laden and Zawahiri to leave Sudan. Bin Laden returned to Afghanistan in 1996 and Zawahiri joined him a year later.

Zawahiri's alliance with bin Laden was limiting his ability to direct the weakened EIJ. Bin Laden's insistence on concentrating jihad on the "far enemy," the United States, rather than on an apostate Muslim state, ran counter to the original goals of EIJ, and Zawahari faced strong criticism from within the organization. When American agents seized EIJ members in Azerbaijan in 1998 and closed a cell in Albania that same year, Zawahiri issued a statement promising revenge. The day after the statement was issued, American embassies were bombed in Kenya and Tanzania. Nevertheless, EIJ continued to weaken and in 2001 Zawahiri merged the organization with al Qaeda.

There is evidence that even before the formal merger of the two organizations, Zawahiri had begun to play an important operational role in al Qaeda. He appears to have taken part in planning the attack on the *U.S.S. Cole* in 2000, and to have also been involved in the planning for 9/11. Zawahiri had used suicide bombers in the operations against the Egyptian government that he organized from his Sudanese sanctuary and also initiated the practice of making martyrdom videos. Several months after 9/11 he appeared on a tape with bin Laden, claiming responsibility for the attacks and showing footage from a martyrdom video of one of the hijackers.

There is strong reason to believe that both Zawahiri and bin Laden are currently in the mountainous tribal areas of Pakistan bordering Afghanistan.

In 2006, Zawahiri appeared on a videotape, where he claimed responsibility for the 2005 bombings in the London transportation system, and he has subsequently appeared on other videotapes threatening the West with more destructive attacks.

In 2001, Zawahiri wrote *Knights Under the Prophet's Banner,* which he intended for "two kinds of people. The first is the intellectual group, the second the mujahideen group." The core of the book is a discussion of the goals, targets, and strategy of the jihadist movement, presented in a style that he himself has described as "clear and simple." He is characteristically unyielding in his opposition to defined enemies both within and without the Muslim world and coolly calculating when he discusses strategy for inflicting the maximum damage by terrorist actions.

In the following excerpt, Zawahiri defines the enemies of Islam as the West in general and the United States and Israel in particular, along with Russia, which merits inclusion apparently because of the struggle in Chechnya. These enemies are aided by such "tools" as the United Nations, the international media, and rulers of Muslim countries. The only solution is jihad because efforts to achieve Islamist aims peacefully are doomed to failure by the "contempt" shown for Islam by the "new Jewish Crusade." The struggle must be worldwide, but the establishment of a fundamentalist Muslim state on some territory can serve as a base for further advances toward the ultimate goal of restoration of the caliphate. This may take long to achieve, but temporary setbacks should not discourage the faithful.

Zawahiri stresses the importance of gaining the support of the Muslim masses and suggests that one wing of the jihadist movement be devoted to rallying the people through preaching and the provision of educational and charitable services. Specifically, he believes that Palestine is the one cause that has been "firing up the feelings of the Muslim nation from Morocco to Indonesia for the past 50 years." The masses have already demonstrated that they are ready to support the mujahideen in struggles to liberate Islamic lands from control of the infidel as in Chechnya and Afghanistan. The jihad movement therefore should proclaim a jihad for Palestine that would rally the Muslim world.

Jihad in Palestine will also allow the movement to demonstrate the "treason" of the moderate rulers in Muslim countries as well as those religious scholars and writers who support them. Without completely renouncing his previous commitment to the creation of a Salafist Egypt, Zawahiri, however, cautions that the struggle against "apostate" rulers in a specific country will be long and difficult, especially since these rulers are protected by the power of the West. Therefore, the battle must be brought home to the enemies of Islam, principally the Americans and the Jews. Zawahiri points out that small groups, using relatively simple means can inflict frightening damage. The mujahideen should concentrate on inflicting the maximum casualties, choose targets and weapons that would have the greatest impact, and concentrate on "martyrdom operations." Excerpts from *Knights Under the Prophet's Banner* follow.

* * *

A. The universality of the battle:

The western forces that are hostile to Islam have clearly identified their enemy. They refer to it as the Islamic fundamentalism. They are joined in this by their old enemy, Russia. They have adopted a number of tools to fight Islam, including:

1. The United Nations.
2. The friendly rulers of the Muslim peoples.
3. The multinational corporations.
4. The international communications and data exchange systems.
5. The international news agencies and satellite media channels.
6. The international relief agencies, which are being used as a cover for espionage, proselytizing, coup planning, and the transfer of weapons.

In the face of this alliance, a fundamentalist coalition is taking shape. It is made up of the jihad movements in the various lands of Islam. It represents a growing power that is rallying under the banner of jihad for the sake of God and operating outside the scope of the new world order. It is free of the servitude for the dominating western empire. It promises destruction and ruin for the new Crusades against the lands of Islam. It is ready for revenge against the heads of the world's gathering of infidels, the United States, Russia, and Israel. It is anxious to seek retribution for the blood of the martyrs, the grief of the mothers, the deprivation of the orphans, the suffering of the detainees, and the sores of the tortured people throughout the land of Islam, from Eastern Turkestan to Andalusia (Islamic state in Spain)....

B. There is no solution
without jihad:

With the emergence of this new batch of Islamists, who have been missing from the nation for a long time, a new awareness is increasingly developing among the sons of Islam, who are eager to uphold it, namely, that there is no solution without jihad....

Particularly helpful in reaching the conclusion that there is no solution without jihad were the brutality and arbitrary nature of the new Jewish Crusade that treats the Islamic nation with extreme contempt. As a result, the Muslims in general and the Arabs in particular are left with nothing that is dear to them. We have become like orphans in a banquet for the villains (Arabic proverb).

2. CONFIRMED DUTIES:

A. The Islamic movement in general, and the jihad movements in particular, must train themselves and their members on perseverance, patience, steadfastness, and adherence to firm principles. The leadership must set an example for the members to follow. This is the key to victory. "O ye who believe. Endure, outdo all others in endurance, be ready, and observe your duty to Allah, in order that ye may succeed." (Koranic verse)

If signs of relaxation and retreat start to show on the leadership, the movement must find ways to straighten out its leadership and not to permit it to deviate from the line of jihad.

MOBILIZING THE FUNDAMENTALIST MOVEMENT

B. The mobilization (tajyyish) of the nation, its participation in the struggle, and caution against the struggle of the elite with the authority:

The jihad movement must come closer to the masses, defend their honor, fend off injustice and lead them to the path of guidance and victory. It must step forward in the arena of sacrifice and excel to get its message across in a way that makes the right accessible to all seekers and that makes access to the origin and facts of religion simple and free of the complexities of terminology and the intricacies of composition.

The jihad movement must dedicate one of its wings to work with the masses, preach, provide services for the Muslim people, and share their concerns through all available avenues for charity and educational work. We must not leave a single area unoccupied. We must win the people's confidence, respect, and affection. The people will not love us unless they felt that we love them, care about them, and are ready to defend them.

In short, in waging the battle the jihad movement must be in the middle, or ahead, of the nation. It must be extremely careful not to get isolated from its nation or engage the government in the battle of the elite against the authority.

We must not blame the nation for not responding or not living up to the task. Instead, we must blame ourselves for failing to deliver the message, show compassion, and sacrifice.

The jihad movement must be eager to make room for the Muslim nation to participate with it in the jihad for the sake of empowerment (al-tamkin). The Muslim nation will not participate with it unless the slogans of the mujahideen are understood by the masses of the Muslim nation.

The one slogan that has been well understood by the nation and to which it has been responding for the past 50 years is the call for the jihad against Israel. In addition to this slogan, the nation in this decade is geared against the U.S. presence. It has responded favorably to the call for the jihad against the Americans.

A single look at the history of the mujahideen in Afghanistan, Palestine, and Chechnya will show that the jihad movement has moved to the center of the leadership of the nation when it adopted the slogan of liberating the nation from its external enemies and when it portrayed it as a battle of Islam against infidelity and infidels....

The jihad movement's opportunity to lead the nation toward jihad to liberate Palestine is now doubled. All the secular currents that paid lip service to the issue of Palestine and competed with the Islamic movement to lead the nation in this regard are now exposed before the Muslim nation following their recognition of Israel's existence and adoption of negotiations and compliance with the international resolutions to liberate what is left, or permitted by Israel, of Palestine. These currents differ among themselves on the amount of crumbs thrown by Israel to the Muslim and the Arabs.

The fact that must be acknowledged is that the issue of Palestine is the cause that has been firing up the feelings of the Muslim nation from Morocco to Indonesia for the past 50 years. In addition, it is a rallying point for all the Arabs, be they believers or non-believers, good or evil....

[Rulers of Muslim lands] have allied themselves with the enemies or God against His supporters and antagonized the mujahideen, because of their Islam and jihad, in favor of the Jewish and Christian enemies of the nation. They have committed a violation of monotheism by supporting the infidels against the Muslims.

Tracking down the Americans and the Jews is not impossible. Killing them with a single bullet, a stab, or a device made up of a popular mix of explosives or hitting them with an iron rod is not impossible. Burning down their property with Molotov Cocktails is not difficult. With the available means, small groups could prove to be a frightening horror for the Americans and the Jews.

C. The Islamic movement in general and the jihad movement in particular must launch a battle for orienting the nation by:

- Exposing the rulers who are fighting Islam.
- Highlighting the importance of loyalty to the faithful and relinquishment of the infidels in the Muslim creed.
- Holding every Muslim responsible for defending Islam, its sanctities, nation, and homeland.
- Cautioning against the ulema of the sultan [pro-government clerics] and reminding the nation of the virtues of the ulema of jihad and the imams of sacrifice and the need for the nation to defend, protect, honor, and follow them.

- Exposing the extent of aggression against our creed and sanctities, and the plundering of our wealth.

D. Adherence to the goal of establishing the Muslim state in the heart of the Islamic world:

The jihad movement must adopt its plan on the basis of controlling a piece of land in the heart of the Islamic world on which it could establish and protect the state of Islam and launch its battle to restore the rational caliphate based on the traditions of the prophet.

Toward a Fundamentalist Base in the Heart of the Islamic World

Armies achieve victory only when the infantry takes hold of land. Likewise, the mujahid Islamic movement will not triumph against the world coalition unless it possesses a fundamentalist base in the heart of the Islamic world. All the means and plans that we have reviewed for mobilizing the nation will remain up in the air without a tangible gain or benefit unless they lead to the establishment of the state of caliphate in the heart of the Islamic world....

The establishment of a Muslim state in the heart of the Islamic world is not an easy goal or an objective that is close at hand. But it constitutes the hope of the Muslim nation to reinstate its fallen caliphate and regain its lost glory.

E. If the goal of the jihad movement in the heart of the Islamic world in general and Egypt in particular is to cause change and establish an Islamic state, it must not precipitate collision or be impatient about victory.

The jihad movement must patiently build its structure until it is well established. It must pool enough resources and supporters and devise enough plans to fight the battle at the time and arena that it chooses....

Striking at the Americans and the Jews

Thus, if the unjust forces drag us into a battle at a time that we do not want, we must respond in the arena that we choose; namely, to strike at the Americans and the Jews in our countries. By this, we win three times:

First by dealing the blow to the great master, which is hiding from our strikes behind its agent.

Second, by winning over the nation when we choose a target that it favors, one that it sympathizes with those who hit it.

Third, by exposing the regime before the Muslim people when this regime attacks us to defend its U.S. and Jewish masters, thus showing its ugly face, the face of the hired policeman who is faithfully serving the occupiers and the enemies of the Muslim nation.

F. It is a long road of
jihad and sacrifice.

If our goal is comprehensive change and if our path, as the Koran and our history have shown us, is a long road of jihad and sacrifices, we must not despair of repeated strikes and recurring calamities. We must never lay down our arms, regardless of the casualties or sacrifices.

We must realize that countries do not fall all of a sudden. They fall by pushing and overcoming.

Moving the Battle
to the Enemy

G. The Islamic movement and its jihad
vanguards, and actually the entire Islamic nation,
must involve the major criminals.

This includes the United States, Russia, and Israel in the battle and do not let them run the battle between the jihad movement and our governments in safety. They must pay the price, and pay dearly for that matter. . . .

Therefore, we must move the battle to the enemy's grounds to burn the hands of those who ignite fire in our countries. . . .

Choosing the Targets and
Concentrating on the
Martyrdom of Operations

I. Changing the methods of strikes:

The mujahid Islamic movement must escalate its methods of strikes and tools of resisting the enemies to keep up with the tremendous increase in the number of its enemies, the quality of their weapons, their destructive powers, their disregard for all taboos, and disrespect for the customs of wars and conflicts. In this regard, we concentrate on the following:

1. The need to inflict the maximum casualties against the opponent, for this is the language understood by the west, no matter how much time and effort such operations take.
2. The need to concentrate on the method of martyrdom operations as the most successful way of inflicting damage against the opponent and the least costly to the mujahideen in terms of casualties.
3. The targets as well as the type and method of weapons used must be chosen to have an impact on the structure of the enemy and deter it enough to stop its brutality, arrogance, and disregard for all taboos and customs. It must restore the struggle to its real size.
4. To re-emphasize what we have already explained, we reiterate that focusing on the domestic enemy alone will not be feasible at this stage.

M. The battle is for every Muslim

An important point that must be underlined is that this battle, which we must wage to defend our creed, Muslim nation, sanctities, honor, dues, wealth, and power, is a battle facing every Muslim, young or old.

It is a battle that is broad enough to affect every one of us at home, work, in his children or dignity.

In order for the masses to move, they need the following:

1. A leadership that they could trust, follow, and understand.
2. A clear enemy to strike at.
3. The shackles of fear and the impediments of weakness in the souls must be broken.

These needs demonstrate to us the serious effects of the so-called initiative to end the violence and similar calls that seek to distort the image of the leadership and take the nation back to the prison of weakness and fear.

To illustrate this danger, let us ask ourselves this question: What will we tell the future generations about our achievements?

Are we going to tell them that we carried arms against our enemies then dropped them and asked them to accept our surrender?

N. What jihad value could the future generation benefit from such conduct?

We must get our message across to the masses of the nation and break the media siege imposed on the jihad movement. This is an independent battle that we must launch side by side with the military battle.

Liberating the Muslim nation, confronting the enemies of Islam, and launching jihad against them require a Muslim authority, established on a Muslim land, that raises the banner of jihad and rallies the Muslims around it. Without achieving this goal our actions will mean nothing more than mere and repeated disturbances that will not lead to the aspired goal, which is the restoration of the caliphate and the dismissal of the invaders from the land of Islam.

This goal must remain the basic objective of the Islamic jihad movement, regardless of the sacrifices and the time involved.

3

ISLAMIC IMPERIALISM

Efraim Karsh

Pointing to American intervention in Afghanistan and Iraq, Muslims frequently condemn the United States as an arrogant imperialist power seeking to take control of Muslim lands. According to this scenario, Western attempts to dominate Muslims began with the First Crusade at the end of the eleventh century, were renewed in the nineteenth and early twentieth centuries when Europeans extended their hegemony over much of North Africa and the Middle East, and continues today with the United States and Israel being the main victimizers of Arabs and other Muslims. Not only in the Muslim world but also in Europe, where the term imperialism now has ugly connotations, the accusation that Arabs are long suffering victims of Western aggression has garnered much sympathy for Arabs and disdain for the United States. It could of course be argued that the United States never intended to occupy and rule Iraq and Afghanistan and that Israel is faced with enemies implacably opposed to its existence. And from a broad historical perspective, shouldn't Arab imperialism also enter the equation as Efraim Karsh, a leading authority on the Middle East, suggests? Muhammad instructed his followers to establish a new world order, says Karsh, in which all nations would embrace Islam or submit to Islamic rule; just such an imperialist vision led to the Arab conquest of neighboring lands. Thus from its inception, says Karsh, Islam was inextricably tied to conquest and expansion. Over the centuries, Islamic theologians and rulers retained this millenarian vision of a universal Islamic empire, and it remains alive today in al Qaeda's fantasy of a restored caliphate and world domination. The principal reason why America is reviled by al Qaeda and many of its sympathizers, Karsh maintains, is because it is perceived as the major obstacle to the establishment of a world community of Allah's faithful. These ideas are treated by Karsh in the following excerpt from *Islamic Imperialism* (2006).

* * *

The 9/11 atrocities afford the starkest demonstration of the global scope of bin Laden's imperialist ambitions. In his 1996 proclamation of jihad he had vowed "to re-establish the greatness of this umma," a pledge he reiterated shortly after 9/11 by quoting from Muhammad's farewell address: "I was ordered to fight the people until they say there is no god but Allah." For his part Zawahiri defined the jihad's objective as nothing short of "the restoration of the caliphate and the dismissal of the invaders from the land of Islam....It is the hope of the Muslim nation to restore its fallen caliphate and regain its lost glory."

In his first-ever televised interview in March 1997, with CNN's Peter Arnett, bin Laden defined the objective of his jihad as "driv[ing] the Americans away from all Muslim countries," rather than from Saudi Arabia alone. "The cause of the reaction must be sought and the act that has triggered this reaction must be eliminated," he said. "The reaction came as a result of the US aggressive policy toward the entire Muslim world and not just toward the Arabian Peninsula....So, the driving-away jihad against the US does not stop with its withdrawal from the Arabian Peninsula, but rather it must desist from aggressive intervention against Muslims in the whole world."

What is the precise nature of this "aggressive intervention?" Superficially, it is the ongoing U.S.-orchestrated "butchering" of the world's 1.2 billion-strong Muslim community—"in Palestine, in Iraq, in Somalia, in southern Sudan, in Kashmir, in the Philippines, in Bosnia, in Chechnya, and in Assam." At a deeper level, bin Laden's words echo the standard anti-Western indictment, which attributes Islam's current dismal position to the post–World War I dismemberment of the last Islamic great power, the Ottoman Empire. The 9/11 attacks are therefore a heroic retribution for this historical injustice that targeted "the main enemy who divided the umma into small and little countries and pushed it, for the last few decades, into a state of confusion." "What America is tasting now is only a copy of what we have tasted," bin Laden proudly announced in a videotaped message shortly after the attacks. "Our Islamic nation has been tasting the same for more than eighty years, of humiliation and disgrace, its sons killed and their blood spilled, its sanctities desecrated." Now, for the first time, "the sword fell upon America."

But the story does not end here. Bin Laden's historical reckoning extends well beyond the Ottoman calamity. As he sees it, his jihad against the "Jewish-crusader alliance" is the natural extension of Islam's millenarian struggle for world domination, dating back to the Prophet Muhammad. "We left our country on a jihad in the path of Allah," bin Laden told the al-Jazeera satellite television channel in 1999. "And it is for the sake of Allah, praise and glory be upon Him, that we made this blessed Hijra to facilitate the institutionalization of the Shari'a." The use of the term "Hijra" to describe al-Qaeda's activities is not accidental. Just as Muhammad was forced to flee his native town of Mecca in order to be able to fight for the worldwide spread of Islam, so bin Laden, a fellow native of the Hijaz, fashions himself as Allah's servant expelled from his homeland by an apostate regime, only to use his exile as a springboard for a holy war in the path of Allah.

In this respect, the "blessed attacks" against the "head of world infidelity" have fully achieved their objectives. They have not only "removed the disgrace that befell our nation" and taught the United States a lesson it will never forget, but have also exposed the incredible fragility of this "modern-day Hubal" (an idol worshiped by pre-Islamic Arabian pagans), thus setting in train a chain of events that, runs the rhetoric, will eventually result in Islam's worldwide triumph. "When people see a strong horse and a weak horse, by nature, they will like the strong horse," bin Laden told a Saudi cleric visiting him in his Afghan hideout shortly after 9/11.

> In Holland, at one of the centers, the number of people who accepted Islam during the days that followed the operations was more than the people who accepted Islam in the last eleven years. I heard someone on Islamic radio who owns a school in America say: "We don't have time to keep up with the demands of those who are asking about Islamic books to learn about Islam." This event made people think [about Islam] which benefited Islam greatly.

Bin Laden was keenly aware that, despite these gains, the latest phase in this millenarian struggle for world mastery had only just begun and was bound to be hazardous and prolonged. Yet he had no doubt regarding its ultimate outcome: the triumph of Islam and the consequent destruction of the United States, just as Islam's victory in Afghanistan triggered the disintegration of the Soviet Union. "The Soviet Union entered Afghanistan in the last week of 1979, and with Allah's help their flag was folded a few years later and thrown in the trash, and there was nothing left to call the Soviet Union," bin Laden told ABC correspondent John Miller in May 1998. "We anticipate a black future for America. Instead of remaining the United States, it shall end up separated states [sic] and shall have to carry the bodies of its sons back to America." He reiterated this apocalyptic prediction after 9/11. "God willing, the end of America is close," he prophesied in a videotaped interview shown by al-Jazeera on December 12, 2001. "Its end is not dependent on the survival of this slave to God. Regardless if Osama is killed or survives, the awakening has started, praised be God. This was the fruit of these operations."...

Neither have all Muslims reconciled themselves to the loss of Islam's colonies beyond the Middle East. At a 1980s meeting in Pakistan with representatives of the seven Afghan resistance parties, a group of American officers and diplomats were surprised to see a huge map on which large parts of what was then Soviet Central Asia and China's Xinjiang Province were labeled "Temporarily Occupied Muslim Territory." Chatting with English-speaking mujahidun after the meeting, an American diplomat asked about this labeling and was told, in perfect seriousness: "Yes, Inshallah [God willing], the region will soon be won back for Islam one day."

This yearning for lost imperial dominions has by no means been confined to Asia. To this day many Arabs and Muslims unabashedly pine for the restoration of Spain and consider their 1492 expulsion from the country a grave historical injustice, as if they were Spain's rightful owners and not former colonial occupiers of a remote foreign land, thousands of miles from their ancestral homeland. Edward Said[1] applauded Andalusia's colonialist legacy as "the ideal that should be moving our efforts now," while Osama bin Laden noted "the tragedy of Andalusia" after the 9/11 attacks, and the perpetrators of the March 2004 Madrid bombings, in which hundreds of people were murdered, mentioned revenge for the loss of Spain as one of the atrocity's "root causes."

Even countries that have never been under Islam's imperial rule have become legitimate targets for Islamic domination. As Europe's Muslim population grew rapidly in the late twentieth century through immigration, higher rates of child birth, and conversion (in France one in ten people is a Muslim and a reported fifty thousand Christians convert to Islam every year; in Brussels Muhammad has been the most popular name for male babies for some years; in Britain attendance at mosques is higher than in the Church of England), prophecies of Islam's eventual triumph over the West have become commonplace. Since the late 1980s various Islamist movements in France, notably the Union des Organizations Islamiques de France (UOIF), have begun to view the growing number of French Muslims as a sign that the country has become a part of the House of Islam. This message has been echoed by the creation of an extensive European network of mosques, schools, and Islamic charities by the Muslim Brothers over the past fifty years....

In the autumn of 2003, the German public was shocked to learn of the racist and anti-Western messages inculcated in young Muslim children inside Saudi-funded mosques and schools when a journalist infiltrated the King Fahd Academy in Bonn and videotaped classroom teaching. Americans were similarly taken aback by a series of exposés of the supremacist teachings of Islamic schools across the United States, which, among other things, disparaged Christianity and Judaism and alienated children from Western society and culture. In fact, one needs to look no further than the Muslim Brothers' English-language internet homepage, which notes the restoration of the caliphate and the "mastering [of] the world with Islam" as the organization's primary goals.

Even such moderate Islamic scholars as Dr. Zaki Badawi, longtime director of the Islamic Cultural Center in London, a hub of interfaith dialogue, were not deterred from acknowledging the persistence of Islam's imperial dream, albeit in far more tempered language. "Islam endeavors to expand in Britain," he said. "Islam is a universal religion. It aims to bring its message to all corners of the earth. It hopes that one day the whole of humanity will be one Muslim community."

Dr. Yusuf Qaradawi, a spiritual guide of the Muslim Brothers and one of today's most influential Islamic thinkers, whose views are promulgated to millions of Muslims worldwide through the media and the internet, gave this sweeping vision theological grounding. "The Prophet Muhammad was asked: 'What city will be conquered first, Constantinople or Romiyya?' " he wrote on December 2, 2002, citing a well-known hadith:

> He answered: 'The city of Hirqil [Emperor Hercalius, that is, Constantinople] will be conquered first'.... Romiyya is the city called today Rome, the capital of Italy. The city of Hirqil was conquered by the young 23-year-old Ottoman [sultan] Muhammad bin Morad, known in history as Mohammad the Conqueror, in 1453 [CE]. The other city, Romiyya, remains, and we hope and believe [that it too will be conquered]. This means that Islam will return to Europe as a conqueror and victor, after being expelled from it twice-once from the South, from Andalusia, and a second time from the East, when it knocked several times on the door of Athens.

This goal need not necessarily be pursued by the sword; it can be achieved through demographic growth and steady conversion of the local populations by "an army or preachers and teachers who will present Islam in all languages and in all dialects." But should peaceful means prove insufficient, physical force can readily be brought to bear....

Osama bin Laden and other Islamists's war is not against America per se, but is rather the most recent manifestation of the millenarian jihad for a universal Islamic empire (or umma). This is a vision by no means confined to an extremist fringe of Islam, as illustrated by the overwhelming support for the 9/11 attacks throughout the Arab and Islamic worlds.

In the historical imagination of many Muslims and Arabs, bin Laden represents nothing short of the new incarnation of Saladin. The House of Islam's war for world mastery is a traditional, indeed venerable, quest that is far from over. Only when the political elites of the Middle East and the Muslim world reconcile themselves to the reality of state nationalism, forswear pan-Arab and pan-Islamic imperialist dreams, and make Islam a matter of private faith rather than a tool of political ambition will the inhabitants of these regions at last be able to look forward to a better future free of would-be Saladins.

NOTE

1. Edward Said (1935–2003), a Palestinian-born American scholar of literature and literary theory who is best known for his advocacy of the Palestinian cause.

4

KNOWING THE ENEMY: JIHADIST IDEOLOGY AND THE WAR ON TERROR

Mary R. Habeck

Analysts have suggested several reasons why bin Laden ordered the attacks on 9/11. The jihadists believed that American society, with its materialism, sexual freedom, and female equality, was the essence of evil and condemned by God; it was also weak and ready to collapse. They expected the strikes on 9/11 would bring such internal unrest and division that the American government would be unable to function. Adding to the chaos would be retaliatory attacks on American Muslims by enraged citizens. Bin Laden fantasized that images of beaten and killed Muslims on American streets would draw hundreds of thousands of enraged Muslims throughout the world to his cause. And if America responded to the suicide attacks by massive air raids on Muslim lands, as bin Laden half expected, then the entire Muslim world would erupt in a global jihad under his leadership.

Bin Laden has defended 9/11, terrorist attacks in general, and the killing of innocent civilians by defining the attacks as a defensive response to Western aggression in Muslim lands and selectively citing religious texts and favored religious authorities. He has also suggested that far from being innocent victims, the people who perished on 9/11 were part of either the military or financial network that supports Western aggression.

In the following excerpt from *Knowing the Enemy: Jihadist Ideology and the War on Terror* (2006), Mary Habeck, who teaches at the School of Advanced International Studies, Johns Hopkins University, shows the relationship between bin Laden's jihadist ideology and the attacks on 9/11.

*   *   *

THEORY

It should now obvious why the United States had to be attacked on September 11. Inspired by their distinctive ideology, certain extremists decided that the United States had to be destroyed. There are two central innovations in the ideology that allow—even demand—the destruction of the United States and the murder of thousands of innocents: an aberrant definition of tawhid [the central Muslim belief in the one God], and a concentration on violence as the core of their religion. Unlike the vast majority of the Islamic world, the extremists give tawhid political implications and use it to justify all their violent acts. They assert that tawhid means God alone has sovereignty and His laws alone—as laid out in the Qur'an and hadith and by certain traditional jurists—are normative. Thus the only acceptable society for the jihadis is a government that applies the tenets of Islamic law in a way that they believe is correct. Based on this definition of tawhid, the extremists argue that democracy, liberalism, human rights, personal freedom, international law, and international institutions are illegal, illegitimate, and sinful. Because it grants sovereignty to the people and allows them to make laws for their society rather than depending entirely on the God-given legal system of Islam, democracy is the focus for jihadist critiques. The United States is recognized by the jihadis as the center of liberalism and democracy, a center that is willing to spread its ideas and challenge other ways of organizing society, and thus must be destroyed along with democracy itself. The antidemocratic rhetoric of Zarqawi[1] and bin Ladin is not, then, just a reaction to U.S. policies, but rather a reflection of their own most deeply held religio-political views of the world.

Violence also permeates jihadist thought. In their reading of history, the conflict between the United States and Islam is part of a universal struggle between good and evil, truth and falsehood, belief and infidelity, that began with the first human beings and will continue until the end of time. A literal clash of civilizations is taking place around the world and, in the end, only one system can survive: Muslims must rid the earth of democracy or else the supporters of democracy (especially the United States, but the entire "West" as well) will destroy true Islam. Jihadis do not believe that this is a theoretical or ideological struggle that can be played out peacefully; rather, the existence of a political or legal system with provisions that transgress the bounds of the shari'a is an act of aggression against Islam that must be dealt with through revolutionary force.

Because history is dominated by the struggle between good and evil, jihadis assert that all Muslims are called by God to participate in the fight—physically if at all possible, or at least by word or financially—acting as God's sword on earth to deal with the evildoers and their wicked way of life. Muslims who answer the call to fight must do so solely to win God's pleasure so that, in the end, it does not matter if the holy warrior accomplishes anything positive through his violence and incitement to violence: intentions alone count. If a mujahid is killed while slaughtering innocent civilians or soldiers on the field of battle, and he acted with pure intentions, he will be guaranteed a welcome into a paradise of unimaginable delights! At the end of time the jihadis envision a world ruled solely by their version of Islam, a world in which "the religion will be for God alone." Thus the jihadis believe that they are more than small groups of violent people who have murdered thousands of men, women, and children. Instead they are honored participants in a cosmic drama, one that will decide the fate of the world and that will ultimately end with the victory of the good, the virtuous, and the true believers.

In addition to fighting evil for God's pleasure, al-Qaida had more mundane short and long-term objectives for the 9/11 assault, objectives that have been articulated by its leaders and that they have lived out. In the short term, al-Qaida wanted to energize a war effort that they began during the early nineties, convince a larger number of Muslims to join their cause, and frighten the United States into leaving all Islamic lands. Al-Qaida's longer term goals included converting all Muslims to their version of Islam, expanding the only legitimate Islamic state (Afghanistan) until it contained any lands that had ever been ruled by Islamic law, and, finally, taking the war beyond the borders of even this expansive state until the entire world was ruled by their extremist Islam. In pursuit of these ends, they believed that the murder of thousands of innocent civilians—including Muslims—was not only legally justified but commanded by God Himself. The jihadist war is thus, in many ways, a struggle over who will control the future of Islam: will this ancient religion become associated with the hatred and violence of the jihadis, or the more tolerant vision proposed by moderate, liberal, and traditional Muslims?

PRACTICE

Yet al Qaida failed to achieve two of their short-term goals on September 11. The greater Islamic world did not rise, take up the sword, and join their cause, while the United States decided to become more involved in Islamic lands rather than retreating behind its borders. Both of these developments have created dilemmas for the leaders of al-Qaida and allied groups, although the reaction (or lack thereof) of the vast majority of the Islamic world has been the greater blow. Everything that 'Usama bin Ladin and other jihadis have hoped to achieve depends upon recruiting new mujahidun and expanding the war. Since 9/11, jihadis have established a theoretical explanation for this seminal failure by returning to their ideological roots—particularly the works of Sayyid Qutb and their views of history as a series of repetitious events. There are several templates that bin Ladin and other extremists use to understand the current conflict—the struggle against Pharaoh (the archetypical tyrant), the Mongol conquest, and the eternal battle of good and evil—but the most important template, and the one to which the jihadis always return, is the war against the crusaders. Jihadist discussions of these Western incursions have always talked about the aggression committed against the Islamic world, but since the war in Afghanistan the emphasis has changed to the response of the Islamic world to the crusader offensive: confused, erratic, and lacking unity. The result was a series of wars that lasted for centuries and included serious defeats for the believers. Jihadis have therefore argued that their supporters should not be discouraged by the lack of a mass uprising by the umma, and should instead have the perseverance, patience, and unity commanded by God. This is a war that could last two hundred years, but eventually Islam will produce another Salah al-Din who will rouse the Islamic world, unite the Muslims against their enemies, and drive them from the lands of their community.

But there is another jihadist explanation for the apathy of the greater Islamic world to their cause: they believe that they alone are the true believers. They disparage any Muslims who will not participate in their jihad as "sinners" or "hypocrites," or at least think of them as sheep who have been led astray by evil ulama and the tyrant rulers....

....They understand that they must appeal to ordinary Muslims to join their cause if they are going to win their lengthy war against the "crusaders and Jews." Yet, at the same time, they believe that ideological and religious purity is necessary for their cause, and this purity demands that they regard as enemies any Muslims who do not actively support them. Different jihadist groups have dealt with this dilemma in various ways. The most common response is to attempt to win over Muslims to their cause through da'wa: calling ordinary Muslims "back" to true Islam. Like Wahhab, the extremists have decided that they should direct the majority of their missionary activity at erring Muslims and not at the unbelieving world. The result has been a concentration on preaching the jihadist version of Islam to Muslims in extremist mosques as well as through Internet sites, magazines, pamphlets, and privately published books, all directed at converting fellow Muslims to their way of thinking and acting....

How, then, should the world respond to the jihadis and their revolutionary ideology? As should be obvious from this discussion, the extremists themselves are not interested in dialogue, compromise, or participation in a political process to attain their ends. For ideological reasons, they have chosen to use violence rather than peaceful means to resolve their problems and achieve their objectives. The ultimate goals of the jihadis are likewise so radical—to force the rest of the world to live under their version of Islamic law—that there is no way to agree to them without sacrificing every other society on the planet. The United States and other countries must then find reasonable strategies that will exploit the failures of the jihadis, stop the extremists from carrying out violent attacks, minimize the appeal of their beliefs, and eventually end their war with the world.

NOTE

1. Abu Musab al-Zarqawi was the leader of al Qaeda in Iraq until he was killed by American forces in June 2006.

5

"Jihadist Strategies in the War on Terrorism"

Mary R. Habeck

In this second selection by Mary R. Habeck, a lecture on November 4, 2004, sponsored by the Heritage Foundation, she argues that the jihadists "have strategies that are rational, systematic, and followed rigorously," and that they consciously base these strategies on the precedents set by Muhammad.

*　*　*

I am going to be talking about a group of people who are generally known as fundamentalists, extremists, or (as I have grown to call them) "jihadis." The term jihad suggests what they believe their lives are about—holy war that is directed against people they believe are their enemies and the enemies of their way of life.

Yet there is more to what they are doing than simple warfare. In fact, I believe they are involved in a war that has a definite strategy behind it, not simply the sort of random attacks that people talk about all the time. However, if you watch the news it is really hard to see that. You look at the news and you see Muslims being killed, you see churches being attacked, you see Jews being killed. You see all sorts of people being targeted and attacked, and in some cases those attacks seem to be counterproductive. After all, it does not make sense to kill the Muslims that you are trying to win over to your side of the argument. It does not make sense to target churches or other places of worship when all this does is win sympathy for the victims of these attacks.

There are also things like the Madrid attack, which, while it seemed to attain their ends, was accompanied by a second plan for a second attack on April 2—an attack that, if it had been carried out, would have had nothing to do with the elections, or with Spanish participation in Iraq.[1] In fact, it could not have been sold as anything except an apparently random attack—a counterproductive attack on the Spanish. It might have convinced the

Spanish themselves to get re-involved in Iraq, or at least (in some way) with the war on terrorism.

However, I am going to argue that, in fact, this is not true. These are not random attacks; they are not entirely counterproductive. They do have strategies that are rational, systematic, and followed rigorously. Unlike other groups—such as the Anarchists of the late 19th and early 20th century (which really did seem to carry out pretty random attacks), or the Communists (whose pragmatism allowed them to pretty much get away with anything as long as they could make some sort of argument that it was helping the cause)—these new terrorists believe that they have an ideology that is so important that it must be followed rigorously. There are many different groups and each one of them is carrying out its own rational systematic strategy.

To understand each attack, therefore, you have to get into the mindset of the group that carried out that attack and not try to make broad generalizations about jihadis, extremists, or fundamentalists. These are very different people and very different groups with very different arguments about how they should be carrying out their warfare. To understand their arguments and attacks you have to understand their ideology, and in some cases understand theological arguments that they are having with the rest of the Islamic world.

LEVELS OF STRATEGY

I am going to differentiate in this talk between four different levels of strategy or tactics. First, there are grand strategies; then there are military strategies; operations (or operational art, as some people call it); and then there are tactics. I am only going to be talking about the first two levels here—that is, grand strategies and military strategies.

Grand strategy is basically the same for almost every jihadi group. This is, I think, the only place where you can say that there is something unifying these groups and holding them together. The objective is, almost across the board, the same. They want to restore the greatness of their vision of Islam by defeating every rival to its power. The means by which they are going to attempt this are also the same and fit into this grand strategic vision. They are hoping to create an Islamic state. They all argue about what that means and how it is going to be created, but somewhere they want to create an Islamic state. They also want to defeat all of their rivals through military means—that is, through violence of some sort. Additionally, they hope to win over the rest of the Islamic world to their vision of what Islam is about and how to restore Islam to greatness.

Those three things are the same across the board. If you take a look at these extremist groups, they all agree, at least on those basic principles. The result of this grand strategic vision is that they must take on an immense number of enemies. They must take on, in fact, what they call "The West" (or as some of them say, "the Jewish crusaders"); "the agent rulers" (that is, the rulers in almost every single one of the Muslim states); "the apostates and the heretics," (which means any Muslim that doesn't agree with them as well as the Shi'a groups—because most of the groups I'll be talking about are Sunni). They also have to take on what they call "oppressors," but this is a term that they use in a very specific way and has little to do with the socialist or leftist use of this term. For instance, "oppressors" include all the Hindus in the world.

The military strategies, unlike this grand strategic vision, seem more random. However, the extremists do not attack all of these groups simultaneously. They have, in fact, prioritized which one of these groups has to be attacked first, second, and third; which is the most important; which is the most dangerous; how they are going to carry out these attacks. In other words, they have definite strategies, but differing definite strategies, even about how to carry out these military attacks. Behind the seeming randomness then, even of the military strategies, there are a few basic principles which will help you to understand, when you see on the news that this or that group has carried out an attack on X, Y, or Z, why they might have chosen them and why they might be choosing another group next.

TURNING TO THE PAST

Generally, these military strategies are based on something extremists call the "Method of Mohammad." This term comes from a lot of interpretation of the Qur'an and Hadith, but it also comes from something called the Sirah, which are not well known in the West, but are very widely known in the Islamic world. The Sirah are essentially sacralized biographies of Mohammad's life. They tell the story of Mohammad in chronological fashion and provide the kind of historical background and continuous narrative that is missing from both the Qur'an and the Hadith.

In the Sirah, Mohammad is portrayed as the perfect man. Because he is the perfect man, he will have the perfect method for applying Islam. In fact, some believe that his early successes were miraculous—so miraculous that they could only have been supported and helped by God. Therefore, the logic goes, if followers want to experience the same successes, they have to follow his footsteps exactly, precisely following the "Method of Mohammad." In other words, the strategies that I am going to look at today were taken from an attempt to recreate, precisely, Mohammad's life and what he did in order to make Islam successful 1,400 years ago.

The First Stage. What is this method? It begins where Mohammad began, which was in the city of Mecca, a place that was hostile to his message and that persecuted the early Muslims. This was the place where he began what was called the Da'wah—the call to Islam, the call to repent, to turn to God, and to follow the commandments of God. There was no violence allowed at this stage. Mohammad created a very small group, a jama'a which met in secret for fear of persecution, but was slowly inculcated into Islam as a way of life. It became, in fact, a small vanguard with an "Amir"—a leader. In this case, that meant Mohammad.

As you can see, this easily translates into the modern world—the creation of a small vanguard that will lead the rest of the world to the light of Islam (or at least some people's vision of Islam). This vanguard will not, at first, practice violence, but will instead be inculcated into the true Islam, and what the true Islam entails for their lives. It consists of "true believers," a small vanguard that always has a leader. There is a Hadith from the traditions of Mohammad that says, "Wherever there are three Muslims, there must be an Amir." There must be a leader and they take this literally. Wherever there are three of these extremists together, they truly believe that one of them must be the Amir. Notice also, that in their vision, this is done in secrecy. Therefore, you are allowed to do this in secrecy, away from the prying eyes of the unbelieving world. That is the first stage.

The Second Stage. The second stage in Mohammad's life and in their method is the Hijrah, the migration away from Mecca (an unbelieving place) to Medina (a place that was more accepting and open to the message of Islam). Once there is a dedicated vanguard, in other words, you have to migrate away from the unbelieving society to someplace where there is already an Islamic society or you must create one yourself, because that is what Mohammad was forced to do (i.e., use a small vanguard to create the perfect Islamic society). Therefore the argument is, "We must do exactly the same thing. The vanguard of true believers must migrate away from the unbelieving society to someplace that is either more open to our ideas, where there is already an Islamic society, or we must create one of our own to become stronger."

The Hijrah is taken so seriously that there are several groups that have named themselves after those people who immigrated—the Muhajiroon. They call themselves this in several different countries. Osama bin Laden talked about this stage and believed that when he was leaving Saudi Arabia to go first to Sudan, and then to Afghanistan, he was taking part in this stage of the "Method of Mohammad." He believed he was migrating away from the unbelieving Saudi Arabia to the perfect Islamic state in Afghanistan. Other groups have been no less certain about this. Some have migrated within an Islamic country (for instance, within Egypt or within Algeria) to set up their own mini-Islamic state in those countries.

The Third Stage. The third stage is Medina, a stage that includes the creation of an Islamic state and the permission to use violence. Almost immediately after Mohammad arrived in Medina, he set up, with the help of his small vanguard of dedicated believers, an Islamic state that would implement the new creed of Islam fully. Today there are various places that might act as that Islamic state. And several extremist groups believe that you must create an Islamic state before you can proceed to the next part of the Medinan state, which is *jihad*.

In this part of the third stage, the belief goes, Muslims are allowed to take part in violence for the sake of Islam. This is what happened in

Mohammad's life. It was at Medina that he was first allowed to use violence against the unbelievers, those who had been oppressing him, those who had been persecuting him, and then gradually those people against whom he was allowed to carry out this warfare included most of the unbelievers in the Arab peninsula.

Many of the groups that we hear about on the news believe that they have created this Islamic state and that they are now allowed to carry out this jihad against people in the West and elsewhere. It is here that you find the biggest split among these groups and the strategies that they are willing to follow because once you have decided to carry out violence, the question becomes who exactly you should be carrying this violence out against.

WHO ARE THE TARGETS?

There are basically three different strategies that have been adopted by these groups. If you look at all the groups out there and who they have decided to attack, the targets fit into one of these three groups.

The first group has decided that we need to attack the "near enemy" first, followed by the "far enemy." The second group has decided to attack the "greater unbelief" first, followed by the "lesser unbelief." The third group has decided to attack the "apostates" first, followed by the "unbelievers." All of these come from the "Method of Mohammad." All of them can be read into the Qur'an, the Hadith, and the Sirah.

The "Near Enemy"

Who is the "near enemy" and who is the "far enemy"? This is where you have people disagreeing. When Mohammad was deciding who he was first going to confront with violence, he was surrounded by people who did not support him, and it was those people he was first forced to engage with violence—those people who lived directly around him. Later, he was allowed to carry out violence elsewhere in order to spread the message of Islam.

Who is today's "near enemy" according to these groups that use this particular strategy? It is anyone in the Islamic lands—those who have occupied Islamic lands, those who have taken away Islamic territory, and even the rulers of some of these countries who call themselves Muslims. It encompasses those enemies that are directly inside these countries. They must be taken on first and defeated, and then afterwards, we can spread the message of Islam—without violence if possible, but with violence if necessary—to the rest of the world.

The "Greater Unbelief"

The second strategy attacks the "greater unbelief" first, followed by the "lesser unbelief." The "greater unbelief becomes that major enemy that has worn many guises over the centuries and which was embodied first by the

Romans, then by the Greeks, and finally by the United States. The U.S. is considered that "greater unbelief" that must be taken on and defeated, whether its citizens are in Islamic countries or elsewhere: Once they are defeated, it is believed, all the rest of the "unbelievers" will fall into line. Terrorists then believe they can take on the "lesser unbelief"—all the other enemies of their vision of Islam—after the U.S. is gone.

The "Apostates"

The third strategy attacks the "apostates" first, followed by other "unbelievers." The "apostates," as I mentioned, include the heretics within the Muslim world (e.g., the Shi'a). There are groups that are dedicated to the idea of a systematic, rational strategy to first defeat all the apostates, whether they are the rulers like Pakistani President Pervez Musharraf or whether they are groups of people who follow a vision of Islam that terrorists do not agree with (such as the Shi'a, the Ahmadi or others). The idea is to defeat them first and then go outside of these Islamic countries and take on the rest of the "unbelievers."

If you look at what is going on in the world today, every single one of these terrorist groups subscribes to one of these strategies and uses it in order to pinpoint who and when they will attack.

AFTER THE JIHAD

After his triumphal stay in Medina, Mohammad was able to leave and return to Mecca and take the city without a fight. It became a part of the Islamic state without a fight or a battle—the doors were open and he was welcomed in.

These people also believe the same thing. They believe that once they begin this jihad and once they set up this Islamic state and carry this fight to the "unbelievers," that all of the places that have been the centers of unbelief in the Islamic world (especially Saudi Arabia) will open up and become part of their Islamic state. The belief insists that one by one, they will all join with the extremists as they show success in other countries.

These strategies define what is happening in the world today. If you look at the attacks that are going on, this is how you can tell precisely which group you are dealing with and which strategy they are following. Listen to what they are saying. I have been amazed by the things they are willing to say, the things they are willing to put on a Web site (in what are called khutab—the preaching on Friday afternoon). Throughout the Islamic world you have people who are willing to say exactly what they believe, even if they are in the most extremist vein. You do not have to translate, decode, or decrypt these things—they are perfectly willing to share their strategies with the rest of the world.

RECENT ATTACKS EXPLAINED

I encourage you to take a look at these English jihadi sites and see for yourself. It now makes sense why Madrid was attacked on March 11. After all, the terrorists had been talking about that attack long before anything had happened in Iraq (and long before Spain had decided to go to Iraq). The jihadis were talking about carrying out some sort of huge attack on Spain.

Why? Because Spain has been occupying "Islamic land" for the past 600–700 years. These terrorists believe that they are actually beginning with the "near enemy" by taking on Spain and occupying Andalusia. They believed that by carrying out these attacks they would win over the Muslims within Spain and North Africa, who would then join up with them to return Andalusia to the Islamic fold. From this standpoint, it also makes sense that they do not care about other Muslims being killed. To people with this mindset everyone who does not agree with them is an apostate or a heretic. Otherwise, they would have joined up with them. Therefore, it does not matter if other Muslims are killed because in the long run they believe the grand strategic vision and military strategies will eventually bring success.

Using this logic, it makes sense to attack the United States, because if you can destroy the United States (the "greater unbelief"), then terrorists who follow this particular strategy believe they will not only have eliminated their greatest enemy, but will then be able to return in triumph to Saudi Arabia, Egypt, and elsewhere and win over the rest of the Islamic world without a fight.

NOTE

1. The terrorist attack on commuter trains in Madrid on March 11, 2004, occurred shortly before the Spanish elections. The governing party lost to the Socialists, who quickly withdrew the Spanish forces that were part of the American-led coalition in Iraq.

6

"WHAT AL-QAIDA REALLY WANTS: THE FUTURE OF TERRORISM"

Yassin Musharbash

While in prison in his native Jordan, journalist Fouad Hussein met Abu Musab al-Zarqawi, the future head of al Qaeda in Iraq, and Abu Muhammad al-Maqdisi, a prominent theorist of the global jihadist movement. He has also corresponded with key figures of the terrorist network. Utilizing these sources, Husssein published a book, still untranslated, detailing what is purported to be al Qaeda's master plan—a chilling seven-stage process that culminates in a universal Islamic state in twenty years. In the following selection published on August 12, 2005, in the English online edition of *Der Spiegel*, Germany's most popular news weekly, Yassin Musharbash, a Jordanian-born German journalist, summarizes Hussein's conclusions.

* * *

There must be something particularly trustworthy about the Jordanian journalist Fouad Hussein. After all, he has managed to get some of the most sought after terrorists to open up to him. Maybe it helped that they spent time together in prison many years ago—when Hussein was a political prisoner he successfully negotiated for Abu Musab al-Zarqawi to be released from solitary confinement. Or is it because of the honest and direct way in which he puts his ideas onto paper? Whatever the reason, the result is that a film, which Hussein, made about al-Zarqawi, has even been shown on al-Qaida affiliated Web sites. "That showed me that they at least felt understood," the journalist says.

Even for an Arab journalist it is no easy matter getting in touch with al-Qaida's inner circle. Nevertheless, Hussein, who is based in Amman, Jordan, has succeeded in turning his correspondence with the terrorists into a remarkable book: "al-Zarqawi—al-Qaida's Second Generation."

If you meet Hussein, as you might when he is relaxing in Amman's Café Vienna, you see he is calm and laidback, without any of the glamour of a secret service spy. But what this small, slim man has to report is nothing less than the world's most dangerous terrorist network's plan of action: al-Qaida's strategy for the next two decades. It is both frightening and absurd, a lunatic plan conceived by fanatics who live in their own world, but who continually manage to break into the real world with their brutal acts of violence.

One of Hussein's most sensational sources for the book, according to what he told SPIEGEL Online, was Seif al-Adl. The Egyptian terrorist, who is suspected of taking part in the attacks on the American Embassies in Dar es Salaam and Nairobi in 1998, has a ransom of US $5 million on his head from the FBI. Secret services suspect that al-Adl is now in Iran.

To prove that he really has had contact to al-Adl, Hussein includes in the first two pages of the book a copy of a handwritten letter the wanted man sent to the author. In the original document, which is 15 pages long, al-Adl describes the disagreements between al-Zarqawi and Osama bin Laden during the Afghanistan war. "Statements from Seif al-Adl have also crept into the chapter on al-Qaida's strategy," explains Fouad Hussein.

AN ISLAMIC CALIPHATE IN SEVEN EASY STEPS

In the introduction, the Jordanian journalist writes, "I interviewed a whole range of al-Qaida members with different ideologies to get an idea of how the war between the terrorists and Washington would develop in the future." What he then describes between pages 202 and 213 is a scenario, proof both of the terrorists' blindness as well as their brutal single-mindedness. In seven phases the terror network hopes to establish an Islamic caliphate, which the West will then be too weak to fight.

- **The First Phase**. Known as "the awakening"—this has already been carried out and was supposed to have lasted from 2000 to 2003, or more precisely from the terrorist attacks of September 11, 2001 in New York and Washington to the fall of Baghdad in 2003. The aim of the attacks of 9/11 was to provoke the US into declaring war on the Islamic world and thereby "awakening" Muslims. "The first phase was judged by the strategists and masterminds behind al-Qaida as very successful," writes Hussein. "The battle field was opened up and the Americans and their allies became a closer and easier target." The terrorist network is also reported as being satisfied that its message can now be heard "everywhere."
- **The Second Phase**. "Opening Eyes" is, according to Hussein's definition, the period we are now in and should last until 2006. Hussein says the terrorists hope to make the western conspiracy aware of the "Islamic community." Hussein believes this is [the] phase in which al-Qaida wants an organization to develop into a movement. The network is banking on recruiting young men during this period. Iraq should become the center

for all global operations, with an "army" set up there and bases established in other Arabic states.

- **The Third Phase**. This is described as "Arising and Standing Up" and should last from 2007 to 2010. "There will be a focus on Syria," prophesies Hussein, based on what his sources told him. The fighting cadres are supposedly already prepared and some are in Iraq. Attacks on Turkey and—even more explosive—in Israel are predicted. Al Qaeda's masterminds hope that attacks on Israel will help the terrorist group become a recognized organization. The author also believes that countries neighboring Iraq, such as Jordan, are also in danger.

- **The Fourth Phase**. Between 2010 and 2013, Hussein writes that al-Qaida will aim to bring about the collapse of the hated Arabic governments. The estimate is that "the creeping loss of the regimes' power will lead to a steady growth in strength within al-Qaida." At the same time attacks will be carried out against oil suppliers and the US economy will be targeted using cyber terrorism.

- **The Fifth Phase**. This will be the point at which an Islamic state, or caliphate, can be declared. The plan is that by this time, between 2013 and 2016, Western influence in the Islamic world will be so reduced and Israel weakened so much, that resistance will not be feared. Al-Qaida hopes that by then the Islamic state will be able to bring about a new world order.

- **The Sixth Phase**. Hussein believes that from 2016 onwards there will be a period of "total confrontation." As soon as the caliphate has been declared, the "Islamic army" will instigate the "fight between the believers and the non-believers" which has so often been predicted by Osama bin Laden.

- **The Seventh Phase**. This final stage is described as "definitive victory." Hussein writes that in the terrorists' eyes, because the rest of the world will be so beaten down by the "one and a-half million Muslims,"[1] the caliphate will undoubtedly succeed. This phase should be completed by 2020, although the war shouldn't last longer than two years.

A SERIOUS PLAN?

But just how serious is this scenario? "Al-Qaida makes no compromises," says the book's author Fouad Hussein. He obviously believes that this seven-point plan could well become the guiding principle for a whole range of al-Qaida fighters. Hussein is far from an hysterical alarmist—in fact he is seen as a serious journalist and his Zarqawi book is better than most of the reports in Arabic on the subject. Only last year, the journalist made a film, which was received with great interest and was shown on the German-French TV channel arte. In it he provided deep insights into al-Qaida's Internet propaganda machine.

Nevertheless, there is no way the scenario he depicts can be seen as a plan which al-Qaida can follow step by step. The terrorist network just doesn't work like that anymore. The significance of the central leadership has diminished and its direct commands have lost a great deal of importance. The supposed master plan for the years 2000 to 2020 reads in parts more like a group of ideas cobbled together in retrospect, than something planned and presented in advance. And not to mention the terrorist agenda is simply unworkable: the idea that al-Qaida could set up a caliphate in the entire Islamic world is absurd. The 20-year plan is based mainly on religious ideas. It hardly has anything to do with reality—especially phases four to seven.

But that doesn't mean that we should simply discount everything that Hussein has uncovered. A few of the steps in the agenda are plausible. The idea that Syria will become a focus for the Mujahedin is regarded by experts as highly likely. "Close ranks, concentrate on getting more recruits, set up cells," was the call to the "Mujahedin in Syria" which appeared on one Web site at the beginning of August. From the point of view of the jihadists, Israel and Turkey are also fairly logical targets for an escalation of the confrontation. "Al-Qaida views every fight as a victory, because for so long Muslims didn't have any weapons at all," says Hussein. He may not be far off. As for Jordan, al-Qaida leaders such as al-Zarqawi, have already made attacks on the country. They have also stated on numerous occasions that Jerusalem is the real target.

Equally, the idea that in the future al-Qaida could increasingly become a movement that attracts young frustrated men, is hardly a theory plucked out of thin air. The terror network puts a lot of effort into its propaganda—assumedly in order to expand its support base.

ATTACKS ON THE WEST: A MEANS TO AN END

What is interesting is that major attacks against the West are not even mentioned by Fouad Hussein. Terrorism here cannot be ignored—but it seems these attacks simply supplement the larger aim of setting up an Islamic caliphate. Attacks such as those in New York, Madrid and London would in this case not be ends in themselves, but rather means to a achieve a larger purpose—steps in a process of increasing insecurity in the West.

Nowadays, it is harder than ever to truly understand al-Qaida: the organization has degenerated into branches and loosely connected cells, related groups are taken in, and people who hardly had anything to do with al-Qaida before, now carry out attacks in its name. It is hard to imagine orders, which come right from the top because Osama bin Laden spends all his time struggling to survive. At the same time, the division between foot soldiers in the organization and sympathizers is becoming increasingly blurred. It is all too easy to fall prey to disinformation—al-Qaida also excels in this area. Even Hussein's scenario should be judged skeptically.

His book should therefore be read for what it really is: an attempt to second guess how al-Qaida terrorists think, what they really want and how they propose to get there.

NOTE

1. The author may be referring to the total number of Muslims in the world, which is estimated at 1.2 billion.

Part 3

THE WAR ON TERROR:
SEIZING THE INITIATIVE

Before September 11, al Qaeda operated in Muslim lands from Indonesia to Morocco usually with little fear of government interference and received huge sums from wealthy Arabs in the Persian Gulf region and from worldwide Muslim organizations purporting to be raising funds only for charitable purposes. Al Qaeda members also found a haven in western European lands where they coordinated their operations generally unrestrained by the authorities. After September 11, the destruction of al Qaeda training camps in Afghanistan; American pressure on other lands that had harbored terrorists; the tracking down, capture, and killing of al Qaeda leaders; and the rigorous international efforts to destabilize al Qaeda's vast financial network weakened the terrorist organization. But thousands of al Qaeda fighters crossed from Afghanistan into the lawless tribal border region of Pakistan where they have regrouped—establishing training camps, recruiting new fighters, and planning new operations The seething discontent in the Muslim world, doubtlessly exacerbated by the conflict in Iraq, provides al Qaeda with recruits, including suicide bombers eager to inflict maximum casualties on civilians, even if doing so means blowing themselves up.

Several al Qaeda operations have been thwarted since 9/11, including attempts to explode airplanes. But terrorists, either loosely or directly affiliated with al Qaeda, succeeded in other operations, most of them suicide bombings that killed and wounded thousands of innocents. These terrorist attacks included bombings of night clubs and restaurants in Bali, Indonesia, frequented by Australian tourists; a series of truck-bomb explosions in Istanbul, Turkey, that wrecked two Jewish synagogues, the British consulate, and a British bank; several suicide attacks in Saudi Arabia directed principally at employees of foreign concerns; suicide bombings of resorts in Egypt and hotels in Amman, Jordan; and suicide attacks in Britain and Spain that caused considerable loss of life (see part 5). And, of course, al Qaeda operatives in Iraq, many of them suicide bombers, have contributed greatly to the ongoing violence in the country, attacking American forces and killing thousands of civilians in heavily trafficked areas. These operatives are often part of the homegrown, foreign-led Sunni terrorist group Al Qaeda in Iraq.

But here too al Qaeda has suffered reversals. In June 2006 the Jordanian-born leader of Al Qaeda in Iraq, Abu Musab al-Zarqawi was killed by an

American air strike. By early 2008 joint American and Iraqi offensives had driven al Qaeda operatives out of their strongholds and greatly reduced the number of civilian and military casualties inflicted by these insurgemts.

Nevertheless, with al Qaeda cells located in some sixty countries, with many affiliated groups and freelancers inspired by bin Laden's ideology and eager to attack Western interests and with bin Laden still unaccounted for, international terrorism remains a threat to world stability. Moreover, despite the seizure of al Qaeda's assets, local cells continue to receive substantial funds from wealthy Arab donors, from money collected from the faithful purportedly for charitable causes, and from criminal activities. Nor do terrorist undertakings require great sums of money. The bombing in Bali cost less than $35,000, the London transit bombings less than $500, and the September 11 attacks under $500,000.

The events of September 11 may have signaled a new type of warfare for a new century. Free and open societies like the United States are vulnerable to attack, less from states that are deterred by America's might—as in the cold war—than by stateless conspiratorial groups employing modern computers, communications, and difficult to trace financial operations to organize and finance terrorism. Such groups are not deterred by America's arsenal. And there is the fearful prospect that a rogue state will supply these groups with biological, chemical, and eventually nuclear weapons to wage war by proxy.

The challenges posed by radical Islam and the war on terror confront American policy-makers with hard and painful choices, as the war in Iraq and the tensions with Iran demonstrate. America's hope of creating a democratic Iraq that would serve as a beacon in the Middle East and defuse the terrorist threat has not materialized despite the considerable expenditure of American life and treasure. Iraq has become a transnational recruiting and training center for Muslim jihadists tied to al Qaeda. It is likely that this development will facilitate the growth of an international network of armed, trained, and militant anti-American Islamists. And Iran, headed by fundamentalists who refer to the United States as the "Great Satan" and have financed and armed terrorists in the region and beyond, has an ongoing nuclear energy program with the potential for developing nuclear weapons. It appears that for the foreseeable future, Islamic radicalism will be a major concern of the Western world, particularly the United States.

Recently, however, there have been a few encouraging signs within the Islamist world. Some radical religious scholars, former jihadists and sympathizers have now turned against al Qaeda, charging that the jihad practiced by bin Laden and his associates violates Islamic teachings, kills people indiscriminately, including many Muslims, and has failed to achieve any of al Qaeda's political objectives. The sentiments expressed by Sheikh Salman al Oudah, a Saudi religious scholar who criticized bin Laden on a popular Middle East television network, appears to be attracting a wide audience:

> My brother Osama, how much blood has been spilt? How many innocent people, elderly.and women have been killed...in the name of Al Qaeda?

Will you be happy to meet God Almighty carrying the burdens of these hundreds of thousands or millions [of victims] on your back?[1]

A major theoretician of jihad known as Dr. Fadl, a surgeon, was once an associate of Zawahiri and a leader of Egyptian Islamic jihad, as well as a member of the group that founded al Qaeda with bin Laden in 1988. He is renowned for his expertise in shari'a and has been characterized as the "ideological godfather of Al Qaeda."[2] From his prison in Egypt, in November 2007, Fadl issued the first segment of a new book *Rationalizing Jihad in Egypt and the World* that, along with a subsequent interview in an Egyptian newspaper, caused a sensation in the Arab world as he seemed to reject much of what he had formerly written about jihad. Fadl now writes that "there is no such thing in Islam as ends justifying means" and denounces indiscriminate bombing "such as blowing up of hotels, buildings, and public transportation," that will kill innocent people. He characterizes Zawahiri and bin Laden as "extremely immoral" and is strongly critical of 9/11 as not only counter-productive—"What good is it if you destroy one of your enemy's buildings and he destroys one of your countries?"—but as a sinful betrayal of a country that had granted the hijackers a visa, which he considers a contract of protection.[3]

This opposition holds out some hope that in addition to the efforts by the West to combat Islamic terrorism, the global jihadist movement will be seriously weakened from within as disillusioned former supporters reject the extremism of al Qaeda.

NOTES

1. Cited in Peter Bergen and Paul Cruickshank, "The Unraveling: Al Qaeda's Revolt Against bin Laden," *The New Republic*, June 11, 2008, p. 17.
2. Ibid., p. 18.
3. Lawrence Wright, "The Rebellion Within: An Al Qaeda Mastermind Questions Terrorism," *The New Yorker*, June 11, 2008, pp. 46–47.

1

"COUNTERTERRORISM: THE CHANGING FACE OF TERROR"

Daniel Benjamin

Daniel Benjamin, scholar and journalist, has written extensively on Islamic terrorism and has held important positions with foreign policy think tanks. On June 13, 2006, he testified before the Senate Foreign Relations Committee. Among the important topics he treated are the emergence of Muslim "self-starter" terrorists who are drawn to bin Laden's ideas, but have little or no connection to al Qaeda; the spread of jihadist violence to different parts of the world; and the need for the United States and its allies to gain the support of moderates by promoting positive and peaceful change in the Muslim world. Following is Benjamin's prepared statement for the Committee.

* * *

Mr. Chairman, Distinguished Members of the Senate Foreign Relations Committee: I want to thank you for the opportunity to appear before you today to discuss the issue of the evolution of the terrorist threat. With the fifth anniversary of the attacks of September 11 approaching this is an appropriate moment for reflection on this issue. The terrorist threat we face today is vastly changed from the one that existed on that late summer day. Recent events also point to the necessity of a review of this kind: The killing last week of Abu Musab al-Zarqawi [head of Al Qaeda in Iraq] represents a signal achievement in the war on terror—in my view, the most important such blow we have delivered since al Qaeda was run out of Afghanistan in late 2001 and early 2002. But it is exactly this kind of dramatic yet fundamentally tactical achievement that invites misinterpretation of where we are in the struggle against radical Islamist violence. I am therefore pleased that you have scheduled this hearing and others that will follow so that we can try to discern where we stand in this conflict and what needs to be done.

Today, the United States faces an unnerving paradox: For all the tactical success—the terrorists arrested, plots foiled, networks disrupted—that have been achieved, our strategic position continues to slip. The ideology of jihad is spreading: A new generation of terrorists is emerging with few ties to al Qaeda but a worldview soaked in Osama bin Laden's hatred of the West, and new areas of the globe are increasingly falling under the shadow of this growing threat. Al Qaeda, of course, still exists, and we would be foolish to assume that the group, however degraded its capabilities may be, will cease to threaten us. Al Qaeda's operatives likely remain the most capable ones in the field. A terrorist organization is not an army, and while an army ceases to be effective once it has lost a certain number of its units, a terrorist group can cause grievous damage if only one or two cells can operate undetected. It is not necessary to spell out the implications of this further, and I would rather devote the time remaining to what has changed in the last five years.

In particular, I would like to address my comments to three new types of terrorists we face and to the changing geography of terror. I do so mindful that we too often try to apply a system of rigid categorization that is inappropriate to the phenomenon of contemporary terror. The first group that should be noted is the self-starters, also often called "home-grown." We have become familiar with them through such attacks as 2004 bombings in Madrid, the 2005 bombings in London, the murder of Dutch artist Theo van Gogh by a young Dutch Muslim militant also in 2005.[1] These are individuals who may have very little connection to al Qaeda or other preexisting groups, but they have been won over by the ideas of Usama bin Laden and his followers. These terrorists are self-recruited and often self-trained, using the vast wealth of instructional materials available on the Internet. Self-starters have appeared not only in Europe but also in Morocco, where they carried out a string of bombings in Casablanca, and in Pakistan, a country with a well-established jihadist infrastructure which some of the new recruits deemed insufficiently aggressive.

It is possible that the string of attacks in Egypt's Sinai Peninsula is also the work of self-starters, but we do not have sufficient intelligence at this point to say. The most recent, and, from an American perspective, most worrisome development is the disruption just this month of a conspiracy involving self-starters in Canada. As has widely been noted, the seventeen people involved sought to acquire three times as much ammonium nitrate as Timothy McVeigh used to destroy the Murragh Building in Oklahoma City. We have in the past too often paid heed to the conspiracies that succeeded and not sufficiently to those that failed. The condition of the Muslim community in Canada is far more like it is in the United States than it is in Europe, and therefore Toronto carries one powerful message: A self-starter conspiracy on American soil is a real possibility. It is true that as a group, the self-starters have a less experience and are less skilled than, say, those who have gone through al Qaeda training camps. However, we have seen a significant number of highly educated individuals show up in these cells. If only a small percentage of these groups manage to carry out attacks, we could therefore see a considerable amount of damage and casualties. Moreover, we should not make the mistake of believing that terrorists who begin as self-starters will not find the connections, training and resources they seek. Herein lies the danger of overemphasizing the new categories, as I mentioned before. Spanish officials have hinted that there was a Zarqawi link to the Madrid bombings. It appears that some of the London bombers traveled to Pakistan for training and evidently some of the Toronto suspects had links to others linked to Zarqawi. We could well see a re-networking of the threat, which could well mean a further increase in the level of danger we face.

Two other groups of terrorists are worth mentioning, both centered in Iraq: The first group consists of the foreign fighters who traveled there to fight against U.S. and coalition forces. Contrary to the expectations voiced by the administration at the outset of the war, those who came to Iraq did not represent the global remnants of al Qaeda after its eviction from Afghanistan. On the contrary, studies by the Israeli expert Reuven Paz and the Saudi scholar Nawaf Obeid both demonstrate that the foreign fighters are over-whelmingly young Muslims with no background in Islamist activism. That is, they represent another pool of the recently radicalized. Although U.S. offi-cials have repeatedly argued over the last three years that the Jordanian-born Zarqawi and his band of foreign fighters represented a very small percentage of the insurgents in Iraq, their violence drove the insurgency—especially the large-scale attacks, such as the attack on the Golden Mosque [revered by Shi'ites] last February that gave the country a powerful push toward an all-out civil war. Perhaps with the death of Zarqawi, the threat posed by the foreign fighters in Iraq will be diminished. It is undoubtedly good news that the most capable terrorist operative in the world is no longer on the scene.... We do not know how many of these foreign fighters remain, or how many have begun to wind their way home. What we can say, however, is that they could become the vanguard of a new generation of jihadists, much as the veterans of the fighting in Afghanistan in the 1980s and 1990s were the founding generation of al Qaeda.

One last group that deserves attention is comprised of Iraqi jihadists who have emerged from the turmoil of the last three years. In such groups as Ansar al Sunna and the Islamic Army of Iraq there are thousand of militants with a jihadist outlook—according to some reputable sources, there could be more than 15,000 in their ranks. They will likely have a durable sanctuary in al-Anbar province in western Iraq.[2] U.S. troops have fought repeated cam-paigns in this region, whether on the Syrian border or in cities such as Ramadi. Yet terrorist attacks have often increased because the militants shrewdly move out of town when troops arrive and return after they depart. They will be rooted out only when there is a capable Iraqi intelligence service. Since that service is likely to be dominated by Shiites and Kurds, there are not going to be many operatives able to work in the hostile environment of al-Anbar. It is too early to say what the long-term orientation of these Iraqi jihadists will be—will they focus their violence solely on the fledgling regime in Baghdad, or will some of them join the global jihad and seek to export violence beyond their borders? Chances are they will be principally focused on Iraq, but even so, the November 2005 bombings of three hotels in Amman suggest that some will have other targets in mind. It is true that those attacks were ordered by Zarqawi, but the operatives themselves were Iraqi. The attacks were the first successful ones in Jordan and the most stunning demonstration of the spillover effect of the turmoil in Iraq. Even if relatively small numbers opt for the global fight, it could make a significant difference to the terrorists' capabilities as has been seen by the actions of very small numbers of individuals involved in the Madrid and London bombings.

Some Iraqis doubtless will have motivation for attacks outside Iraq: Although three hotels were hit, there was a fourth bomber—an Iraqi woman named Sajida Mubarak Atrous al-Rishawi, whose device failed to detonate. Afterward, she explained that she had undertaken the suicide mission as an act of vengeance for the deaths of three of her brothers, who had died fighting American forces. Her statement carried a grim suggestion of how the devastation of Iraq may come back to haunt us through the growth of an indigenous Iraqi jihadist movement. The most conservative tallies of Iraqi civilian deaths, which have been compiled by the Iraq Body Count Web site, puts the toll at around 40,000. We can probably expect more Sajidas in our future.

Let me turn to the issue of the geography of jihad: Here the picture is one of metastasis. I have already mentioned Toronto. Not long ago in Australia, a major dragnet wrapped up at least 18 conspirators who appear to have been plotting an attack on the country's one nuclear power plant. In South Asia—especially in Bangladesh—the incidence of jihadist violence has grown dramatically. In Southeast Asia, a number of regional conflicts in such places as the southern Philippines and southern Thailand continue to raise fears of wider jihadist activity. In the Caucasus, the incidence of jihadist violence continues to be deeply alarming. Two regions in particular cause great concern. The first is Europe, and I want to thank Senator Allen for allowing me to testify in April on this issue. With more than 30 major failed plots across the continent in roughly five years, Europe has become a central battlefield. Much of Europe's problem owes to the fact that the individual Muslim's identity is sharply tested there. Most of the continent's Muslims arrived in the 1950s and 1960s as workers to fill postwar Europe's labor shortage, and they stayed on in countries that, for the most part, neither expected nor wanted to integrate them into their societies. It soon became apparent, however, that there was no easy way to send these workers back or to stanch the flow of family members seeking reunification with loved ones—let alone to stop them from having children.

As a result Europe has sleepwalked into an awkward multiculturalism. Its Muslim residents, many of them now citizens, live for the most part in ghetto-like segregation, receive second-rate schooling, suffer much higher unemployment than the general population, and those who do work are more likely than their Christian counterparts to have low-wage, deadend jobs. (For an intimation of the size of the pool of potential recruits, we need only think back to last year's riots in France. The young Muslims who took to the streets were not motivated by jihadist ideology, but they clearly presented an obviously ripe target for recruitment.) It is against this backdrop that we have seen the emergence of many of the self-starter groups as well as the dramatic expansion of a network of operatives associated with Zarqawi. How the Jordanian terrorist's death will affect this network is difficult to predict, but at a minimum, there are now convinced jihadists with terrorist connections in approximately forty countries.

The second area for concern is the Middle East. Contrary to popular belief, radical Islamism had been largely suppressed or wiped out in the region in the 1990s, but it is now resurgent. We have witnessed a series of bloody attacks in Egypt's Sinai Peninsula, and there are reports now of al Qaeda activists in Gaza. Kuwait, a country with no history of jihadist violence, experienced running gun battles between authorities and militants and discovered plotters within its own military. Recent visitors to Lebanon speak of a significant spike in jihadist activity. Syria, a country that waged a campaign of extermination against Islamists in the early 1980s, has seen Sunni radicalism reemerge. Qatar experienced its first vehicle bombing. Saudi Arabia suffered a series of bombings and attacks, and while the authorities have gained the upper hand against al Qaeda in the Arabian Peninsula, the group continues to exist. The discovery of Iraqi-style bombs in the kingdom may well be a harbinger of worse to come once veterans of the fighting to the north return home—Saudi Arabia has contributed the largest number of foreign fighters to the Iraqi insurgency. The potential for increasing volatility and destabilization is growing in the region, and that ought to be a cause for great concern. Why have we seen the overall growth in the threat?

The chief reason for this failure is at the level of strategy and it concerns a misunderstanding of the ideological nature of jihadist terror. Although U.S. government officials have often spoken of the terrorists' ideology of hatred, our policies have had the inadvertent effect of confirming for some Muslims the essentials of the bin Laden argument. It is worth reiterating the jihadists' fundamental storyline. At the heart of it is a belief, handed down from the revolutionary Egyptian Islamist writer Sayyid Qutb, that the West is the preordained enemy of Islam. In its most barebones formulation, the ideology holds that America and its allies seek to occupy Muslims' lands, steal their oil wealth and destroy their faith. Radical Islamists interpret much of history through this prism: the drawing of borders in the Middle East after World War I was aimed at dividing Muslims and destroying their historic unity.

The creation of Israel was another step in this direction since it, too, placed a western foothold in the region and was designed to weaken and subjugate Muslim nations. The U.S. deployment to Saudi Arabia and the invasion of Iraq in Operation Desert Storm marked another stage in this tale of woe. Radical Islamists believe, moreover, that United States supports the autocrats of the Muslim world as a way of keeping the believers down and undermining the faith. Thus, through the 2003 invasion of Iraq, we gave the radicals a shot in the arm, handing them a tableau that they could point to as confirmation of their argument. Polling in Muslim nations over the last three years has shown that America's image has plummeted to historic lows. Although most Muslims will not turn to violence, in this environment, it appears that more are turning in that direction than might otherwise be the case. It is clear that Iraq was a major part of the motivation of the Madrid and London bombers as well as Mohammed Bouyeri, the murderer of Theo van Gogh. In countries such as Pakistan, it is also clear that anti-Americanism grounded in the invasion of Iraq is increasingly being used as a tool of mobilization for radicals. The missteps of the occupation of Iraq opened a new "field of jihad" for militants who were more than eager to take on U.S. forces in the Arab heartland. For the radicals, killing Americans is the essential task; by doing so, they demonstrate that they are the only ones determined to stand up for Muslim dignities. Through their violence, they have also created a drama of the faith that disaffected Muslims around the world can watch on television and the Internet. Thus, the jihadist movement's show of its determination to confront American and coalition forces as well as those of the fledgling Iraqi regime has boosted its attractiveness.

However benign our intentions were in going into Iraq to liberate the populace there of an evil dictatorship, in the context of the culture of grievance that exists in much of the Muslim world, the extremists have benefited from our missteps and their narrative has had a profound resonance. Again, terrorism is a game of small numbers, and a small number of recruits can make a great difference. The events of the last few years have helped the jihadist movement sign up those recruits.

Mr. Chairman, the United States and its allies have shown great skill in tactical counterterrorism, as the killing of Zarqawi has reminded us. But the skillful application of force and the expert use of intelligence and law enforcement techniques alone will not allow us to prevail in the war on terror. Of course, they are essential, and they have surely saved the lives of many innocents in many countries around the world. Yet at the level of strategy, we are nowhere near where we should be. It is a central tenet of counterinsurgency that success depends on separating moderates from extremists, and thereby tilting the balance our way. At the core of this challenge is a competition of narratives between radical Islamists and the West.

I have summarized our enemies' story. I think most of us intuitively know what ours should be—that the United States and its allies are a benign power that seeks to help all who wish to modernize their societies and improve their material conditions so long as they play by the international rules of the road. Part of that story is that we harbor no enmity for any religion or race or ethnic group but instead recognize that our future depends in no small measure on improvements of conditions for people around the world. Unfortunately, that story is not coming through. We are indeed in a battle for hearts and minds, and we are not winning. For too many Muslims, our actions, especially in Iraq, are at odds with our professed values. We are also blamed by the radicals—but also many moderates—for the persistence of the autocratic regimes of the Middle East. Until we have policies that match our rhetoric and demonstrate our willingness to support positive and peaceful change in the Muslim world, we will not win over the moderates we need. This is why we can at once succeed tactically but slip strategically, with ever graver consequences. A recognition of this situation points the way to the necessary discussion of how to forge that strategy, and that, I believe is where we must go next and without delay. Thank you very much for the opportunity to speak here today.

NOTES

1. Theo van Gogh was murdered in November 2004.
2. The increase ("surge") of American forces in Iraq in 2007 and the cooperation of local Sunni tribes repelled by al Qaeda's brutality and extremism have greatly improved the situation in al-Anbar province since this was written.

2

"What to Do? A Global Strategy"

9/11 Commission Report

On November 27, 2002, Congress and President George W. Bush created the National Commission on Terrorist Attacks Upon the United States to investigate the attacks of 9/11. The Commission of ten members, five Republicans and five Democrats, was chaired by Thomas H. Kean, former governor of New Jersey, with Lee H. Hamilton, formerly a member of Congress from Indiana, as vice chair. The Commission's widely anticipated report was published in 2004. It is by general consensus the single most authoritative document on 9/11. The report starts with a detailed description of the events on 9/11, followed by a lengthy description and analysis of the background to the attacks, and closes with a series of recommendations for a global strategy and for reorganizing the Federal government to combat terrorism. Some of the recommendations have been implemented; others continue to be seriously discussed. The excerpt below, drawn from the section on global strategy, consists of several policy recommendations for combating terrorism.

* * *

ATTACK TERRORISTS AND THEIR ORGANIZATIONS

The U.S. government joined by other governments around the world is working through intelligence, law enforcement, military, financial, and diplomatic channels to identify, disrupt, capture, or kill individual terrorists. This effort was going on before 9/11 and it continues on a vastly enlarged scale. But to catch terrorists, a U.S. or foreign agency needs to be able to find and reach them.

NO SANCTUARIES...

To find a sanctuary, terrorist organizations have fled to some of the least governed, most lawless places in the world. The intelligence community has prepared a world map that highlights possible terrorist havens....

Recommendation: The U.S. government must identify and prioritize actual or potential terrorist sanctuaries. For each, it should have a realistic strategy to keep possible terrorists insecure and on the run, using all elements of national power. We should reach out, listen to, and work with other countries that can help....

PREVENT THE CONTINUED GROWTH OF ISLAMIST TERRORISM

...In short, the United States has to help defeat an ideology, not just a group of people, and we must do so under difficult circumstances. How can the United States and its friends help moderate Muslims combat the extremist ideas?

Recommendation: The U.S. government must define what the message is, what it stands for. We should offer an example of moral leadership in the world, committed to treat people humanely, abide by the rule of law, and be generous and caring to our neighbors. America and Muslim friends can agree on respect for human dignity and opportunity. To Muslim parents, terrorists like Bin Ladin have nothing to offer their children but visions of violence and death. America and its friends have a crucial advantage—we can offer these parents a vision that might give their children a better future. If we heed the views of thoughtful leaders in the Arab and Muslim world, a moderate consensus can be found.

That vision of the future should stress life over death: individual educational and economic opportunity. This vision includes widespread political participation and contempt for indiscriminate violence. It includes respect for the rule of law, openness in discussing differences, and tolerance for opposing points of view.

Recommendation: Where Muslim governments, even those who are friends, do not respect these principles, the United States must stand for a better future. One of the lessons of the long Cold War was that short-term gains in cooperating with the most repressive and brutal governments were too often outweighed by long-term setbacks for America's stature and interests....

The United States must do more to communicate its message. Reflecting on Bin Ladin's success in reaching Muslim audiences, Richard Holbrooke[1] wondered, "How can a man in a cave outcommunicate the world's leading communications society?" Deputy Secretary of State Richard Armitage worried to us that Americans have been "exporting our fears and our anger," not our vision of opportunity and hope.

Recommendation: Just as we did in the Cold War, we need to defend our ideals abroad vigorously. America does stand up for its values. The United States defended, and still defends, Muslims against tyrants and criminals in Somalia, Bosnia, Kosovo, Afghanistan, and Iraq. If the United States does not act aggressively to define itself in the Islamic world, the extremists will gladly do the job for us.

• *Recognizing that Arab and Muslim audiences rely on satellite television and radio, the government has begun some promising initiatives in television and radio broadcasting to the Arab world, Iran, and Afghanistan. These efforts are beginning to reach large audiences. The Broadcasting Board of Governors has asked for much larger resources. It should get them.*
• *The United States should rebuild the scholarship, exchange, and library programs that reach out to young people and offer them knowledge and hope. Where such assistance is provided, it should be identified as coming from the citizens of the United States....*

Recommendation: A comprehensive U.S. strategy to counter terrorism should include economic policies that encourage development, more open societies, and opportunities for people to improve the lives of their families and to enhance prospects for their children's future.

TURNING A NATIONAL STRATEGY INTO A COALITION STRATEGY

Practically every aspect of U.S. counterterrorism strategy relies, on international cooperation. Since 9/11, these contacts concerning military, law-enforcement, intelligence, travel and customs, and financial matters have expanded so dramatically, and often in an ad hoc way, that it is difficult to track these efforts much less integrate them.

Recommendation: The United States should engage other nations in developing a comprehensive coalition strategy against Islamist terrorism. There are several multilateral institutions in which such issues should be addressed. But the most important policies should be discussed and coordinated in a flexible contact group of leading coalition governments. This is a good place, for example, to develop joint strategies for targeting terrorist travel, or for hammering out a common strategy for the places where terrorists may be finding sanctuary.

PROLIFERATION OF WEAPONS OF MASS DESTRUCTION

The greatest danger of another catastrophic attack in the United States will materialize if the world's most dangerous terrorists acquire the world's most dangerous weapons. As we note in chapter 2, al Qaeda has tried to acquire or make nuclear weapons for at least ten years. In chapter 4, we mentioned officials worriedly discussing, in 1998, reports that Bin Ladin's associates thought their leader was intent on carrying out a "Hiroshima."

These ambitions continue. In the public portion of his February 2004 worldwide threat assessment to Congress, DCI [Director of Central Intelligence] [George] Tenet noted that Bin Ladin considered the acquisition of weapons of mass destruction to be a "religious obligation." He warned that al Qaeda "continues to pursue its strategic goal of obtaining a nuclear capability." Tenet added that "more than two dozen other terrorist groups are pursuing CBRN [chemical, biological, radiological, and nuclear] materials."

A nuclear bomb can be built with a relatively small amount of nuclear material. A trained nuclear engineer with an amount of highly enriched uranium or plutonium about the size of a grapefruit or an orange, together with commercially available material, could fashion a nuclear device that would fit in a van like the one Ramzi Yousef parked in the garage of the World Trade Center in 1993. Such a bomb would level Lower Manhattan.

The coalition strategies we have discussed to combat Islamist terrorism should therefore be combined with a parallel, vital effort to prevent and counter the proliferation of weapons of mass destruction (WMD). We recommend several initiatives in this area.

Strengthen Counterproliferation Efforts. While efforts to shut down Libya's illegal nuclear program have been generally successful, Pakistan's illicit trade and the nuclear smuggling networks of Pakistani scientist A.Q. Khan have revealed that the spread of nuclear weapons is a problem of global dimensions. Attempts to deal with Iran's nuclear program are still underway. Therefore, the United States should work with the international community to develop laws and an international legal regime with universal jurisdiction to enable the capture, interdiction, and prosecution of such smugglers by any state in the world where they do not disclose their activities.

Expand the Proliferation Security Initiative. In May 2003, the Bush administration announced the Proliferation Security Initiative (PSI): nations in a willing partnership combining their national capabilities to use military, economic, and diplomatic tools to interdict threatening shipments of WMD and missile-related technology.

The PSI can be more effective if it uses intelligence and planning resources of the NATO alliance. Moreover, PSI membership should be open to non-NATO countries. Russia and China should be encouraged to participate.

Support the Cooperative Threat Reduction Program. Outside experts are deeply worried about the U.S., government's commitment and approach to securing the weapons and highly dangerous materials still scattered in Russia and other countries of the Soviet Union. The government's main instrument in this area, the Cooperative Threat Reduction Program (usually referred to as "Nunn-Lugar," after the senators who sponsored the legislation in 1991), is now in need of expansion, improvement, and resources. The U.S. government has recently redoubled its international commitments to support this program, and we recommend that the United States do all it can, if Russia and other countries will do their part. The government should weigh the value of this investment against the catastrophic cost America would face should such weapons find their way to the terrorists who are so anxious to acquire them.

Recommendation: Our report shows that al Qaeda has tried to acquire or make weapons of mass destruction for at least ten years. There is no doubt the United States would be a prime target. Preventing the proliferation of these weapons warrants a maximum effort—by strengthening counterproliferation efforts, expanding the Proliferation Security Initiative, and supporting the Cooperative Threat Reduction program.

TARGETING TERRORIST MONEY....

Recommendation: Vigorous efforts to track terrorist financing must remain front and center in U.S. counterterrorism efforts. The government has recognized that information about terrorist money helps us to understand their networks, search them out, and disrupt their operations. Intelligence and law enforcement have targeted the relatively small number of financial facilitators—individuals al Qaeda relied on for their ability to raise and deliver money—at the core of al Qaeda's revenue stream. These efforts have worked. The death or capture of several important facilitators has decreased the amount of money available to al Qaeda and has increased its costs and difficulty in raising and moving that money. Captures have additionally provided a windfall of intelligence that can be used to continue the cycle of disruption.

NOTE

1. Richard Holbrooke is a prominent American diplomat who is best known for having brokered the Dayton Peace Accords (1995) that brought an end to the civil war in Bosnia.

3

AL QAEDA RESURGENT

Bruce Hoffman

The failure of al Qaeda to launch a new terrorist attack on American soil since 9/11 has led some analysts to maintain that the United States is winning the war on terror. They point to several ways in which the United States and its allies have severely impaired the ability of al Qaeda to direct a global jihadist network. The crushing of the Taliban regime in Afghanistan has deprived al Qaeda of a secure training facility. Counterterrorist operations, including continuous monitoring of the jihadists' electronic communications, have led to the death or capture of several thousand jihadists, disrupted al Qaeda's financial networks, and limited bin Laden's ability to build and command a global organization. According to some analysts, bin Ladin's operational role is now insignificant. Forensic psychiatrist and terrorism expert Marc Sageman has written of the diminishing importance of "al Qaeda Central" and the growing threat posed by the "leaderless jihad" of a scattered network of loosely-knit cells formed by Muslim youths living in the West.[1]

Rejecting this position is Bruce Hoffman, whose book *Inside Terrorism*, published in 1998 and revised and expanded in 2006, established him as a leading authority on terrorism and counterterrorism.[2] In the following testimony submitted to the House Armed Services Subcommittee on Terrorism, Unconventional Threats and Capabilities, on February 14, 2007, Hoffman argues that al Qaeda "is marshalling its forces to continue the epic struggle begun more than ten years ago." Supporting Hoffman's position of a revitalized al Qaeda is the disclosure by American counterintelligence officials that al Qaeda has established training camps in the tribal regions of Pakistan near the Afghan border, where it enjoys sanctuary, and that graduates of these camps are fighting Americans in Afghanistan and Iraq.

*   *   *

Five and half years ago, nineteen terrorists hijacked four airplanes and changed the course of history. Just as we underestimated al Qaeda then, we risk repeating the same mistake now. Al Qaeda today is frequently spoken of as if it is in retreat: a broken and beaten organization, its leadership living in caves, cut off somewhere in remotest Waziristan; incapable of mounting further attacks on its own and instead having devolved operational authority either to its various affiliates and associates or to entirely organically produced, homegrown, terrorist entities. Isolated and demoralized, al Qaeda is thus imagined to have been reduced to a purely symbolic role, inspiring copycat terrorist groups, perhaps, but lacking any operational capability of its own—a toothless tiger.

"Al Qaeda," President Bush declared last October, "is on the run." But al Qaeda in fact is on the march. It has regrouped and reorganized from the setbacks meted out to it by the United States and our coalition partners and allies during the initial phases of the global war on terrorism (GWOT) and is marshalling its forces to continue the epic struggle begun more than ten years ago. More than ever, al Qaeda's revival reminds us of our continued failure to heed advice of the Chinese strategist Sun Tzu. "If you know the enemy and know yourself," he famously advised centuries ago, "you need not fear the results of a hundred battles." Yet, if there has been one consistent theme in both America's war on terrorism and our melancholy involvement in Iraq, it is our serial failure to fulfill Sun Tzu's timeless admonition. The Bush administration's new strategy to "surge" 21,000 American troops into Iraq is the latest fundamental misreading of our enemy's mindset and intentions.

AL QAEDA TODAY: EVOLUTION, ADAPTATION, AND ADJUSTMENT

Al Qaeda's obituary has already been written often since 9/11. "Al-Qa'ida's Top Primed To Collapse, U.S. Says," trumpeted a *Washington Post* headline two weeks after Khalid Sheikh Mohammed, the mastermind behind the 9/11 attacks, was arrested in March 2003. "I believe the tide has turned in terms of al-Qa'ida," Congressmen Porter J. Goss, then-chairman of the U.S. House of Representatives Intelligence Committee and himself a former CIA case officer who became its director a year later, was quoted. "We've got them nailed," an unidentified intelligence expert was quoted, who still more expansively declared, "we're close to dismantling them." These upbeat assessments continued the following month with the nearly bloodless capture of Baghdad and the failure of al Qaeda to make good on threats of renewed attacks in retaliation for invasion. Citing Administration sources, an article in the *Washington Times* on 24 April 2003 reported the prevailing view in official Washington that al Qaeda's "failure to carry out a successful strike during the U.S.-led military campaign to topple Saddam Hussein has raised questions about their ability to carry out major new attacks." Despite major terrorist attacks in Jakarta and Istanbul during the latter half of that same year and the escalating insurgency in Iraq, this optimism carried into 2004. "The Al Qaida of the 9/11 period is under catastrophic stress," Ambassador Cofer Black, at the time the U.S. State Department's Counter-Terrorism Coordinator, declared. "They are being hunted down, their days are numbered." Then came the Madrid bombings six weeks later and the deaths of 191 persons. The most accurate assessment, perhaps, was therefore the one offered by al Qaeda itself. "The Americans," Thabet bin Qais, a spokesperson for the movement said in May 2003, "only have predications and old intelligence left. It will take them a long time to understand the new form of al-Qaida." Four years later we are indeed still struggling to understand the changing character and nature of al Qaeda and the shifting dimensions of the terrorist threat as it has evolved since 9/11.

Al Qaeda in fact is now functioning exactly as its founder and leader, Usama bin Laden envisioned it. On the one hand, true to the meaning of the Arabic word for the "base of operation" or "foundation"—meaning the base or foundation from which worldwide Islamic revolution can be waged (or, as other translations have it, the "precept" or "method")—and thus simultaneously inspiring, motivating and animating, radicalized Muslims to join the movement's fight. While, on the other, continuing to exercise its core operational and command and control capabilities: directing the implementing [of] terrorist attacks.

The al Qaeda of today combines, as it always has, both a "bottom up" approach—encouraging independent thought and action from low (or lower-) level operatives—and a "top down" one—issuing orders and still coordinating a far-flung terrorist enterprise with both highly synchronized and autonomous moving parts. Mixing and matching organizational and operational styles whether dictated by particular missions or imposed by circumstances, the al Qaeda movement, accordingly, can perhaps most usefully be conceptualized as comprising four distinct, though not mutually exclusive, dimensions. In descending order of sophistication, they are:

1. *Al Qaeda Central.* This category comprises the remnants of the pre-9/11 al Qaeda organization. Although its core leadership includes some of the familiar, established commanders of the past, there are a number of new players who have advanced through the ranks as a result of the death or capture of key al Qaeda senior-level managers. . . . It is believed that this hardcore remains centered in or around the Afghanistan and Pakistan borders and continues to exert actual coordination, if not some direct command and control capability, in terms of commissioning attacks, directing surveillance and collating reconnaissance, planning operations, and approving their execution.

This category comes closest to the al Qaeda operational template or model evident in the 1998 East Africa embassy bombings and 9/11 attacks. Such high value, "spectacular" attacks are entrusted only to al Qaeda's professional cadre: the most dedicated, committed and absolutely reliable element of the movement. Previous patterns suggest that these "professional" terrorists are deployed in predetermined and carefully selected teams. They will also have been provided with very specific targeting instructions. In some cases, such as the East Africa bombings, they may establish contact with, and enlist the assistance of, local sympathizers and supporters. This will be solely for logistical and other attack-support purposes or to enlist these locals to actually execute the attack(s). The operation, however, will be planned and directed by the "professional" element with the locals clearly subordinate and playing strictly a supporting role (albeit a critical one).

2. *Al Qaeda Affiliates and Associates.* This category embraces formally estab-lished insurgent or terrorist groups that over the years have benefited from bin Laden's largess and/or spiritual guidance and/or have received training, arms, money and other assistance from al Qaeda. Among the recipients of this assistance have been terrorist groups and insurgent forces in Uzbekistan and Indonesia, Morocco and the Philippines, Bosnia and Kashmir, among other places. By supporting these groups, bin Laden's intentions were three-fold. First, he sought to co-opt these movements' mostly local agendas and channel their efforts towards the cause of global jihad. Second, he hoped to create a jihadi "critical mass" from these geographically scattered, disparate movements that would one day coalesce into a single, unstoppable force. And, third, he wanted to foster a dependent relationship whereby as a quid pro quo for prior al Qaeda support, these movements would either under-take attacks at al Qaeda's behest or provide essential local, logistical and other support to facilitate strikes by the al Qaeda "professional" cadre noted above....

3. *Al Qaeda Locals.* These are dispersed cells of al Qaeda adherents who have or have had some direct connection with al Qaeda—no matter how tenuous or evanescent. They appear to fall into two subcategories.

One category comprises persons who have had some prior terrorism experience—having been blooded in battle as part of some previous jihadi campaign in Algeria, the Balkans, Chechnya, and perhaps more recently in Iraq, and may have trained in some al Qaeda facility whether in Afghanistan or Yemen or the Sudan before 9/11. Specific examples of this adversary include Ahmed Ressam, who was arrested in December 1999 at Port Angeles, Washington State, shortly after he had entered the U.S. from Canada. Ressam, for instance, had a prior background in terrorism, having belonged to Algeria's Armed Islamic Group (GIA). After being recruited to al Qaeda, he was provided with a modicum of basic terrorist training in Afghanistan. In contrast to the professional cadre detailed above, however, Ressam was given very non-specific, virtually open-ended targeting instruc-tions before being dispatched to North America. Also, unlike the well-funded professional cadre, Ressam was given only $12,000 in "seed money" and instructed to raise the rest of his operational funds from petty thievery. He was also told by KSM[3] to recruit members for his terrorist cell from among the expatriate Muslim communities in Canada and the U.S. The al Qaeda operative, Andrew Rowe, a British national and Muslim convert, convicted for his involvement in the 2003 al Qaeda plot to attack London's Heathrow Airport is another example of this category.

The other category, as is described in the detailed discussion of the 7/7 London attacks below, conforms to the profile of the four British Muslims responsible for the 2005 bombings of mass transit targets in London. In contrast to Ressam and Rowe, none of the four London bombers had previously fought in any of the contemporary, iconic Muslim conflicts (e.g., Algeria, Chechnya, Kashmir, Bosnia, Afghanistan, etc.) nor is there conclusive evidence of their having received any training in an al Qaeda camp in Afghanistan, Yemen, or the Sudan prior to 9/11. Rather, the ringleader of the London cell—Mohammed Siddique Khan, and an accomplice, Shahzad Tanweer, were brought to Pakistan for training and then returned to their homeland with both an attack plan and the knowledge to implement it. They then recruited others locally as needed, into the cell and undertook a relatively simple, but nonetheless sophisticated and highly consequential attack. In both the above categories, however, the terrorists will have some link with al Qaeda....

4. *Al Qaeda Network.* These are homegrown Islamic radicals—from North Africa, the Middle East, and South and Southeast Asia—as well as local converts to Islam mostly living in Europe, Africa, and perhaps Latin America and North America as well, who have no direct connection with al Qaeda (or any other identifiable terrorist group), but nonetheless are prepared to carry out attacks in solidarity with or support of al Qaeda's radical jihadi agenda. Like the "al Qaeda Locals" they too are motivated by a shared sense of enmity and grievance felt towards the United States and West in general and their host-nations in particular. In this specific instance, however, the relationship with al Qaeda is more inspirational than actual, abetted by profound rage over the U.S. invasion and occupation of Iraq and the oppression of Muslims in Palestine, Kashmir, Chechnya, and elsewhere. Critically, these persons are neither directly members of a known, organized terrorist group nor necessarily even a very cohesive entity unto themselves. Examples of this category, which comprises small collections of like-minded locals who gravitate towards one [another] to plan and mount terrorist attacks completely independent of any direction provided by al Qaeda, include the so-called Hofstad Group in the Netherlands, a member of whom (Mohammed Bouyeri) murdered the Dutch filmmaker Theo Van Gogh in Amsterdam in November 2004, and the so-called, trolley bombers: the two Lebanese nationals who placed bombs, that failed to explode, on two German commuter trains near Dortmund and Koblenz in July 2006.

The most salient threat posed by the above categories, however, continues to come from al Qaeda Central and from its affiliates and associates. However, an additional and equally challenging threat is now posed by less discernible and more unpredictable entities drawn from the vast Muslim Diaspora in Europe. As far back as 2001, the Netherlands' intelligence and security service had detected increased terrorist recruitment efforts among Muslim youth living in the Netherlands whom it was previously assumed had been completely assimilated into Dutch society and culture. Thus, representatives of Muslim extremist organizations—including, presumably, al Qaeda—had already succeeded in embedding themselves in, and drawing new sources of support from, receptive elements within established Diaspora communities. In this way, new recruits could be drawn into the movement who likely had not previously come under the scrutiny of local or national law enforcement agencies. Indeed, according to a BBC News documentary report broadcast in July 2006, Khan, the London bombing cell's ringleader, may have acted precisely as such an al Qaeda "talent spotter": trawling Britain's Muslim communities during the summer of 2001—literally weeks before 9/11—trying to attract new recruits to the movement....

This adversary, comprising hitherto unknown cells, is difficult, if not impossible, to effectively profile....Although the members of these terrorist cells may be marginalized individuals working in menial jobs from the lower socio-economic strata of society, some with long criminal records or histories of juvenile delinquency; others may well come from solidly middle and upper-middle-class backgrounds with university and perhaps even graduate degrees and prior passions for cars, sports, rock music, and other completely secular, material interests. For example, in the case of radicalized British Muslims, since 9/11 we have seen terrorists of South Asian and North African descent as well as those hailing both from the Middle East and Caribbean. They have included life-long devout Muslims as well as recent converts, persons from the margins of society who made a living as thieves or from drug dealing and students at the London School Economics and the University of London, two of the UK's premiere universities. What they will have in common is a combination of a deep commitment to their faith—often recently re-discovered; admiration of bin Laden for the cathartic blow struck against America on 9/11; hatred of the U.S. and the West; and, a profoundly shared sense of alienation from their host countries. "There appear to be a number of common features to this grooming," the report of the Intelligence and Security Committee of the UK House of Commons concluded.

> In the early stages, group conversation may be around being a good Muslim and staying away from drugs and crime, with no hint of an extremist agenda. Gradually individuals may be exposed to propaganda about perceived injustices to Muslims across the world with international conflict involving Muslims interpreted as examples of widespread war against Islam; leaders of the Muslim world perceived as corrupt and non-Islamic; with some domestic policies added as "evidence" of a persecuted Islam; and conspiracy theories abounding. They will then move on to what the extremists claim is religious justification for violent jihad in the Quran and the Hadith....and—if suicide attacks are the intention—the importance of martyrdom in demonstrating commitment to Islam and the rewards in Paradise for martyrs; before directly inviting an individual to engage in terrorism. *There is little evidence of over compulsion. The extremists appear rather to rely on the development of individual commitment and group bonding and solidarity* [my emphasis].

These new recruits are the anonymous cogs in the worldwide al Qaeda enterprise and include both long-standing residents and new immigrants found across in Europe, but specifically in countries with large expatriate

Muslim populations such as Britain, Spain, France, Germany, Italy, the Netherlands, and Belgium.

Indeed, ongoing investigations increasingly suggest that recent terrorist threats and attacks—the August 2006 plot to blow up 10 planes inflight from Britain and crash them into American cities, the July 2005 suicide bus and subways bombings in London, and the two separate operations foiled in Britain during 2004 involving on the one hand, bombings of a shopping center or nightclub and on the other simultaneous suicide attacks on economic targets in lower Manhattan, Newark, New Jersey, and Washington, DC—were all in fact coordinated in some way by al Qaeda, and not (as commonly assumed) cooked up by homegrown terror groups.

Thus, al Qaeda's goal remains as it has always been: to inspire radicalized Muslims across the globe to join the movement's holy fight. Not only does al Qaeda retain its core operational and command-and-control capabilities, it has shown remarkable resiliency and a stubborn capacity for renewal and regeneration. Even though its personnel may be dispersed, al Qaeda remains a hierarchal organization: capable of ordering, planning and implementing bold terrorist strikes.

The widely perceived current threat from less discernible and more unpredictable entities drawn from the vast Muslim Diaspora in Europe, moreover, actually represents the fruition of strategic decisions made by al Qaeda a decade ago. As far back as 1999, British authorities knew of al Qaeda's years long subversive activities among that country's Muslim community: believing that some 3,000 British Muslims had already left and returned to the country after receiving terrorist training at al Qaeda camps in Afghanistan, Pakistan, Yemen, and elsewhere. Three years later, the Netherlands' intelligence and security service called attention to increased terrorist recruitment efforts among assimilated Dutch Muslim youths. And, a senior official in Spain's Interior Ministry recently told me that authorities in that country now suspect that upwards of a thousand Muslims living there also received training in overseas al Qaeda camps before 9/11. In this way, new recruits from these countries have been drawn into the movement who had not previously come under scrutiny or suspicion. The threat thus is not only one of jihadi radicalization, but of deliberate, longstanding al Qaeda subversion.

Consider what we have learned since the 2005 London bombings and how new evidence about the attack's genesis completely dispels the prevailing assumption that entirely organic, "homegrown" threats posed by indigenous radicals acting on their own have superseded that of al Qaeda. Initially, British authorities concluded that the attacks were the work of disaffected British Muslims, self-radicalized and self-selected and operating purely within the country. We have subsequently learned, however, that the London cell's ringleader, Mohammed Siddique Khan, and a fellow bomber, Shahzad Tanweer, both visited Pakistani terrorist camps between November 2004 and February 2005—where it is now believed that they were trained by al Qaeda operatives....

Both men also recorded "Martyrdom" videos while in Pakistan that were subsequently released in September 2005 and then on the first anniversary of the bombings by al Qaeda's perennially active communications department, "Al Sahab [the Clouds] for Media Production." On those tapes, Ayman al Zawahiri also claims credit for the London attack in the name of al Qaeda: an admission that at the time was mostly dismissed given that it challenged the conventional wisdom that al Qaeda was no longer capable of such operations.

In addition, following the bombings, when Khan's photograph was a staple of nightly British newscasts and on the front page of daily newspapers, a reliable source working for Britain's security service claimed to have seen Khan at an al Qaeda camp in Afghanistan in either 1999 or 2000. Finally, as previously noted, a BBC documentary broadcast last July reported that during the summer of 2001 Khan was seen attempting to attract recruits from Britain's Muslim community for al Qaeda. He was accompanied, moreover, by two other British Muslims who would later stage a suicide bombing in Israel in April 2003. And, only a month before that attack, Khan himself visited Israel—taking the same route via Jordan that the bombers would soon follow—in what may have been a practice or dry-run for the operation.

The London bombing's pedigree, moreover, is familiar. Exactly a year earlier, British and American authorities had thwarted the aforementioned plot by a London-based al Qaeda cell led by Dhiren Barot (aka "Issa al-Hindi" and "Issa al-Britani") to simultaneously carry out suicide attacks on the New York Stock Exchange and the CitiGroup Building in midtown Manhattan, the Prudential Center in Newark, New Jersey, and the International Monetary Fund and the World Bank headquarters in Washington, DC. The trail in this operation similarly led back to Pakistan. It emerged that a protégé of the 9/11 mastermind Khalid Sheikh Mohammed operating in Lahore was the essential nexus between the London cell and al Qaeda commanders operating out of Waziristan.

And, a parallel plot disrupted only months before, in April 2004, likewise involved a group of British Muslims of Pakistani ancestry. Their plan was to bomb a shopping mall or London nightclub using 1,300 pounds of ammonium nitrate fertilizer they had stockpiled with which to fabricate their explosives. Members of this cell had also traveled to Pakistan for terrorist training in jihadi camps along the Afghan border. Their leader, Omar Khyam, admitted that while in Pakistan he had met with al Qaeda commanders and that his al Qaeda controller for the operation was Abdul Hadi al-Iraqi: the reputed new "number three" figure in the movement and a key liaison officer with the al Qaeda organization in Iraq. Khyam's claims were corroborated by another cell member, Mohammed Junaid Babar, who became a witness for the prosecution. Babar, a naturalized U.S. citizen who had emigrated from Pakistan as a young child, himself confessed to having attended an al Qaeda "summit" meeting held in Pakistan in March 2004 that was devoted to planning international terrorist operations.

Finally, this past summer's plot to simultaneously bomb ten U.S. airliners and crash them into targets over American cities was foiled after arrests in Pakistan once more led UK and U.S. officials to yet another terrorist cell of British Muslims of Pakistani heritage....And so it is with [another] case. Spanish authorities now intimate that evidence is accumulating that al Qaeda is behind the March 2004 Madrid bombings....

Thus, the portions of the National Intelligence Estimate released publicly last September are right. We're just as vulnerable as ever—not only because of Iraq, but also because of a revitalized and resurgent al Qaeda that continues to plot and plan terrorist attacks. Senior British intelligence and security officials publicly stated that they had reached this same conclusion the following month. And, in a speech delivered in November 2006 Dame Eliza Manningham-Buller, the Director-General of the Security Service (MI-5), was unequivocal in her assessment of the threat posed by a resplendent al Qaeda. "We are aware of numerous plots to kill people and to damage our economy," Dame Eliza stated. "What do I mean by numerous? Five? Ten? No, nearer 30 that we currently know of," she continued. "These plots often have linked back to al Qaeda in Pakistan and through those links al Qaeda gives guidance and training to its largely British foot soldiers here on an extensive and growing scale." Rather than al Qaeda R.I.P. then, we face an Al Qaeda that has risen from the grave....

In retrospect, it thus appears that Iraq has further blinded us to the possibility of an al Qaeda renaissance. America and Britain's entanglement in that country the past four years and our overwhelming preoccupation first with an escalating insurgency and now with an incipient civil war, consumed the attention and resources of our respective countries' military and intelligence communities—at precisely the time that bin Laden, al Zawahiri and other senior al Qaeda commanders were in their most desperate straits and stood to benefit most from this distraction. Iraq has thus had a pernicious effect on both our counterterrorism policies and perceptions of national security. As the situation in that country deteriorated, one could take solace in the President's argument that we were "fighting terrorists over there, so that we don't have to fight them here." The plots and attack plans against the U.S. previously described along with the Madrid and London attacks effectively challenge that once comforting, but now patently discredited, argument.

PLAYING RIGHT INTO AL QAEDA'S HANDS: IRAQ AND THE SURGE STRATEGY....

The clearest explication of al Qaeda's strategy in Iraq was provided by the group's second-in-command, Ayman al Zawahiri, on the occasion of the second and third anniversary of the 9/11 attacks. "We thank God," he declared in September 2003, "for appeasing us with the dilemmas in Iraq and Afghanistan. The Americans are facing a delicate situation in both countries. If they withdraw they will lose everything and if they stay, they will continue to bleed to death." Indeed, what U.S. military commanders had once optimistically described more than three years ago as the jihadi "magnet" or terrorist "flytrap" orchestrated by the U.S. invasion of Iraq has thus always been viewed very differently by al Qaeda. "Two years after Tora Bora," Zawahiri observed in December 2003, "the American bloodshed [has] started to increase in Iraq and the Americans are unable to defend themselves."

In other words, with America trapped in Iraq, al Qaeda has had us exactly where they want us. Iraq, for them, has been an effective means to preoccupy American military forces and distract U.S. attention while al Qaeda has regrouped and reorganized since the invasion of Afghanistan in 2001....

Iraq has also figured prominently in al Qaeda plans and propaganda as a means to reinvigorate the jihadi cause and recapture its momentum. By enmeshing U.S. forces in battle and thereby portraying America's efforts in Iraq as an oppressive occupation, al Qaeda has been able to propagate an image of Islam cast perpetually on the defensive with no alternative but to take up arms against American aggression. Finally, the ongoing violence in Iraq—coupled with the continued painful memories of the Abu Ghraib revelations—have all contributed to America's indisputable decline and increasingly poor standing in the Muslim world.

In sum, America's stubborn refusal to change its policy for Iraq has arguably played right into al Qaeda's hands. And Zawahiri's prophecy about "bleeding us to death" has proven depressingly prescient. Iraq not only daily consumes American lives and treasure but has arguably enervated our military: preoccupying U.S. attention and sapping America's strength precisely at a time when the threat posed by al Qaeda, the 2007 Annual Threat Assessment warns is increasing—and other even more portentous security challenges, like Iran and North Korea, grow more worrisome.

But, even if one dimension of Zawahiri's analysis has already been validated, it is still within America's power to prevent the other—even more consequential—dimension of Zawahiri's prediction from being realized—our "losing everything." But this requires nothing less than a dramatic reversal of the Administration's current strategy for Iraq—and accepting that even if it is beyond our capacity to solve the Iraq problem, we should be moving without further delay to contain it from spreading and de-stabilizing the entire region.

Redeploying the American military from Iraq to strengthen and build capacity among our key allies throughout the region could serve to affirm, not undermine, U.S. commitments there. It would also enable us to refocus our efforts more productively on countering the greater systemic threat to the region posed by al Qaeda's clarion call to radicalization and violence— than to remain in Iraq as America's power is expended and confidence in U.S. leadership continues to erode worldwide.

Finally, ending our military and intelligence preoccupation with Iraq would permit the U.S. to devote its full attention to thwarting al Qaeda's current resurgence. Al Qaeda's efforts to regain its foothold in Afghanistan and its growing strength across the border in Pakistan could be decisively negated. More critical, our efforts to kill or capture bin Laden, Zawahiri and the movement's other leading figures could be revitalized and redoubled. The benefits of making good on President Bush's now five-plus-year-old pledge to bring these murderers in "dead or alive" would potentially deliver a more crushing blow to al Qaeda's morale than continuing to pursue our quixotic ambitions in Iraq—which, after all, is precisely what al Qaeda wants.

CONCLUDING REMARKS: A WAY AHEAD?

Defeating al Qaeda suggests first and foremost that our assessments and analyses are anchored firmly to sound, empirical judgment and not blinded by conjecture, mirror-imaging, politically partisan prisms and wishful thinking. Second, is the need to refocus our attention and efforts back to South Asia—to Pakistan and Afghanistan, specifically—where it was following 9/11 and when al Qaeda was indeed on the run. Third, is the recognition that al Qaeda cannot be defeated with military means alone. As one U.S. intelligence officer with vast experience in this realm told to me over two years ago: "We just don't have enough bullets to kill them all." Accordingly, a new strategy and new approach is needed given a resuscitated al Qaeda organization that relies as much upon clandestine subversion of targeted communities as it does upon propaganda and radicalization. Its success will depend on effectively combining the tactical elements of systematically destroying and weakening enemy capabilities alongside the equally critical, broader strategic imperatives of countering the continued resonance of the radical's message and breaking the cycle of terrorist recruitment and replenishment that has both sustained and replenished al Qaeda.

The war on terrorism has now lasted longer than America's involvement in World War II: yet, even today we cannot claim with any credibility, much less, acuity to have fulfilled Sun Tzu's timeless admonition. Indeed, what remains missing five and a half years since this war began is a thorough, systematic understanding of our enemy: encompassing motivation as well as mindset, decision-making processes as well as command and control relationships; and ideological constructs as well as organizational dynamics....

...[T]he attention of the U.S. military and intelligence community is directed almost uniformly towards hunting down militant leaders or protecting U.S. forces—not toward understanding the enemy we now face. This is a monumental failing not only because decapitation strategies have rarely worked in countering mass mobilization terrorist or insurgent campaigns, but also because al Qaeda's ability to continue this struggle is ineluctably predicated on its capacity to attract new recruits and replenish its resources.

The success of U.S. strategy will therefore ultimately depend on Washington's ability to counter al Qaeda's ideological appeal—and thus effectively address the three key elements of al Qaeda's strategy:

- the continued resonance of their message,
- their continued ability to attract recruits[to]replenish their ranks; and,
- their capacity for continual regeneration and renewal.

To do so, we first need to better understand the mindset and minutia of the al Qaeda movement, the animosity and arguments that underpin it and indeed the regions of the world from which its struggle emanated and upon which its hungry gaze still rests. Without knowing our enemy we cannot successfully penetrate their cells; we cannot knowledgeably sow discord and dissension in their ranks and thus weaken them from within; and, we cannot fulfill the most basic requirements of an effective counterterrorist strategy—preempting and preventing terrorist operations and deterring their attacks. Until we recognize the importance of this vital prerequisite, America will remain perennially on the defensive: inherently reactive rather than proactive—deprived of the capacity to recognize, much less anticipate, important changes in our enemy's modus operandi, recruitment and targeting.

NOTES

1. Marc Sageman, *Leaderless Jihad: Terror Networks in the Twenty-First Century* (Philadelphia PA: University of Pennsylvania Press, 2008).
2. See his review of Sageman "The Myth of Grass-Roots Terrorism: Why Osama bin Laden Still Matters," *Foreign Affairs*, Vol. 87, No. 3 (May/June 2008), pp. 133–138.
3. Khalid Sheikh Mohammad, a leading associate al Qaeda, who was characterized by the 9/11 Commission as the "principal architect of the 9/11 attacks." He has also been implicated and claimed credit for many other terrorist acts. Captured in Pakistan in 2003, KSM was transferred to American custody, where he remains.

4

"Right Islam vs. Wrong Islam: Muslims and Non-Muslims Must Unite to Defeat the Wahhabi Ideology"

Abdurrahman Wahid

Abdurrahman Wahid, the former president of Indonesia, is co-founder and patron of the LibForAll Foundation, a nonprofit organization that is dedicated to reducing religious extremism and discrediting the use of terror worldwide. In the following article, which appeared in the *Wall Street Journal* on December 30, 2005, President Wahid, analyzes the strength and wide appeal of a virulent Wahhabi/Salafi fundamentalism that supports Islamist terrorism. He summons both Muslims and the non-Muslims to unite in a campaign against religious extremism, "a global struggle for the soul of Islam." Such a campaign should develop strategies based on an understanding of our own strengths and weaknesses. Among our strengths, we should recognize that the large majority of Muslims and Muslim religious leaders have not been radicalized, that we can work with individuals and organizations that represent moderate religious views, that we dispose of considerable resources to spread our message, that "the power of the feminine spirit" can play an important role because women have a vital stake in the outcome of this struggle, and that the "desire for freedom, justice, and a better life" is universal.

* * *

Jakarta—News organizations report that Osama bin Laden has obtained a religious edict from a misguided Saudi cleric, justifying the use of nuclear weapons against America and the infliction of mass casualties. It requires great emotional strength to confront the potential ramifications of this fact. Yet can anyone doubt that those who joyfully incinerate the occupants of office buildings, commuter trains, hotels and nightclubs would leap at the chance to magnify their damage a thousandfold?

Imagine the impact of a single nuclear bomb detonated in New York, London, Paris, Sydney or LA! What about two or three? The entire edifice of modern civilization is built on economic and technological foundations that terrorists hope to collapse with nuclear attacks like so many fishing huts in the wake of a tsunami. Just two small, well-placed bombs devastated Bali's tourist economy in 2002 and sent much of its population back to the rice fields and out to sea, to fill their empty bellies. What would be the effect of a global economic crisis in the wake of attacks far more devastating than those of Bali or 9/11?

It is time for people of good will from every faith and nation to recognize that a terrible danger threatens humanity. We cannot afford to continue "business as usual" in the face of this existential threat. Rather, we must set aside our international and partisan bickering, and join to confront the danger that lies before us.

An extreme and perverse ideology in the minds of fanatics is what directly threatens us (specifically, Wahhabi/Salafi ideology—a minority fundamentalist religious cult fueled by petrodollars). Yet underlying, enabling, and exacerbating this threat of religious extremism is a global crisis of misunderstanding.

All too many Muslims fail to grasp Islam, which teaches one to be lenient toward others and to understand their value systems, knowing that these are tolerated by Islam as a religion. The essence of Islam is encapsulated in the words of the Qur'an, "For you, your religion; for me, my religion." That is the essence of tolerance. Religious fanatics—either purposely or out of ignorance—pervert Islam into a dogma of intolerance, hatred and bloodshed. They justify their brutality with slogans such as "Islam is above everything else." They seek to intimidate and subdue anyone who does not share their extremist views, regardless of nationality or religion. While a few are quick to shed blood themselves, countless millions of others sympathize with their violent actions, or join in the complicity of silence.

This crisis of misunderstanding—of Islam by Muslims themselves—is compounded by the failure of governments, people of other faiths, and the majority of well-intentioned Muslims to resist, isolate and discredit this dangerous ideology. The crisis thus afflicts Muslims and non-Muslims alike, with tragic consequences. Failure to understand the true nature of Islam permits the continued radicalization of Muslims worldwide, while blinding the rest of humanity to a solution which hides in plain sight.

The most effective way to overcome Islamist extremism is to explain what Islam truly is to Muslims and non-Muslims alike. Without that explanation, people will tend to accept the unrefuted extremist view—further radicalizing Muslims, and turning the rest of the world against Islam itself.

Accomplishing this task will be neither quick nor easy. In recent decades, Wahhabi/Salafi ideology has made substantial inroads throughout the Muslim world. Islamic fundamentalism has become a well-financed, multifaceted global movement that operates like a juggernaut in much of the developing world, and even among immigrant Muslim communities in the

West. To neutralize the virulent ideology that underlies fundamentalist terrorism and threatens the very foundations of modern civilization, we must identify its advocates, understand their goals and strategies, evaluate their strengths and weaknesses, and effectively counter their every move. What we are talking about is nothing less than a global struggle for the soul of Islam.

The Sunni (as opposed to Shiite) fundamentalists' goals generally include: claiming to restore the perfection of the early Islam practiced by Muhammad and his companions, who are known in Arabic as al-Salaf al-Salih, "the Righteous Ancestors"; establishing a utopian society based on these Salafi principles, by imposing their interpretation of Islamic law on all members of society; annihilating local variants of Islam in the name of authenticity and purity; transforming Islam from a personal faith into an authoritarian political system; establishing a pan-Islamic caliphate governed according to the strict tenets of Salafi Islam, and often conceived as stretching from Morocco to Indonesia and the Philippines; and, ultimately, bringing the entire world under the sway of their extremist ideology.

Fundamentalist strategy is often simple as well as brilliant. Extremists are quick to drape themselves in the mantle of Islam and declare their opponents kafir, or infidels, and thus smooth the way for slaughtering nonfundamentalist Muslims. Their theology rests upon a simplistic, literal and highly selective reading of the Quran and Sunnah (prophetic traditions), through which they seek to entrap the worldwide Muslim community in the confines of their narrow ideological grasp. Expansionist by nature, most fundamentalist groups constantly probe for weakness and an opportunity to strike, at any time or place, to further their authoritarian goals.

The armed ghazis (Islamic warriors) raiding from New York to Jakarta, Istanbul, Baghdad, London, and Madrid are only the tip of the iceberg, forerunners of a vast and growing population that shares their radical views and ultimate objectives. The formidable strengths of this worldwide fundamentalist movement include:

(1) An aggressive program with clear ideological and political goals; (2) immense funding from oil-rich Wahhabi sponsors; (3) the ability to distribute funds in impoverished areas to buy loyalty and power; (4) a claim to and aura of religious authenticity and Arab prestige; (5) an appeal to Islamic identity, pride, and history; (6) an ability to blend into the much larger traditionalist masses and blur the distinction between moderate Islam and their brand of religious extremism; (7) full-time commitment by its agents/ leadership; (8) networks of Islamic schools that propagate extremism; (9) the absence of organized opposition in the Islamic world; (10) a global network of fundamentalist imams who guide their flocks to extremism; (11) a well-oiled "machine" established to translate, publish and distribute Wahhabi/ Salafi propaganda and disseminate its ideology throughout the world; (12) scholarships for locals to study in Saudi Arabia and return with degrees and indoctrination, to serve as future leaders; (13) the ability to cross national and cultural borders in the name of religion; (14) Internet

communication; and (15) the reluctance of many national governments to supervise or control this entire process.

We must employ effective strategies to counter each of these fundamentalist strengths. This can be accomplished only by bringing the combined weight of the vast majority of peace-loving Muslims, and the non-Muslim world, to bear in a coordinated global campaign whose goal is to resolve the crisis of misunderstanding that threatens to engulf our entire world.

An effective counterstrategy must be based upon a realistic assessment of our own strengths and weaknesses in the face of religious extremism and terror. Disunity, of course, has proved fatal to countless human societies faced with a similar existential threat. A lack of seriousness in confronting the imminent danger is likewise often fatal. Those who seek to promote a peaceful and tolerant understanding of Islam must overcome the paralyzing effects of inertia, and harness a number of actual or potential strengths, which can play a key role in neutralizing fundamentalist ideology. These strengths not only are assets in the struggle with religious extremism, but in their mirror form they point to the weakness at the heart of fundamentalist ideology. They are

(1) Human dignity, which demands freedom of conscience and rejects the forced imposition of religious views; (2) the ability to mobilize immense resources to bring to bear on this problem, once it is identified and a global commitment is made to solve it; (3) the ability to leverage resources by supporting individuals and organizations that truly embrace a peaceful and tolerant Islam; (4) nearly 1,400 years of Islamic traditions and spirituality, which are inimical to fundamentalist ideology; (5) appeals to local and national—as well as Islamic—culture/traditions/pride; (6) the power of the feminine spirit, and the fact that half of humanity consists of women, who have an inherent stake in the outcome of this struggle; (7) traditional and Sufi leadership and masses, who are not yet radicalized (strong numeric advantage: 85% to 90% of the world's 1.3 billion Muslims); (8) the ability to harness networks of Islamic schools to propagate a peaceful and tolerant Islam; (9) the natural tendency of like-minded people to work together when alerted to a common danger; (10) the ability to form a global network of like-minded individuals, organizations and opinion leaders to promote moderate and progressive ideas throughout the Muslim world; (11) the existence of a counterideology, in the form of traditional, Sufi and modern Islamic teachings, and the ability to translate such works into key languages; (12) the benefits of modernity, for all its flaws, and the widespread appeal of popular culture; (13) the ability to cross national and cultural borders in the name of religion; (14) Internet communications, to disseminate progressive views— linking and inspiring like-minded individuals and organizations throughout the world; (15) the nation-state; and (16) the universal human desire for freedom, justice, and a better life for oneself and loved ones.

Though potentially decisive, most of these advantages remain latent or diffuse, and require mobilization to be effective in confronting fundamentalist ideology. In addition, no effort to defeat religious extremism can succeed without ultimately cutting off the flow of petrodollars used to finance that extremism, from Leeds to Jakarta.

Only by recognizing the problem, putting an end to the bickering within and between nation-states, and adopting a coherent long-term plan (executed with international leadership and commitment) can we begin to apply the brakes to the rampant spread of extremist ideas and hope to resolve the world's crisis of misunderstanding before the global economy and modern civilization itself begin to crumble in the face of truly devastating attacks.

Muslims themselves can and must propagate an understanding of the "right" Islam, and thereby discredit extremist ideology. Yet to accomplish this task requires the understanding and support of like-minded individuals, organizations and governments throughout the world. Our goal must be to illuminate the hearts and minds of humanity, and offer a compelling alternate vision of Islam, one that banishes the fanatical ideology of hatred to the darkness from which it emerged.

Part 4

SUICIDE BOMBERS:
MOTIVATION, RECRUITMENT,
INDOCTRINATION, AND
EFFECTIVENESS

Terrorist attacks against Western targets, particularly the events of 9/11, have compelled analysts to investigate what impels some Muslims to embrace jihadism even to the point of becoming suicide bombers. Jihadists often feel that the West has oppressed and humiliated Muslims. Did not Europeans rule Muslims in the era of imperialism and do they not continue to victimize Muslims today? Did not Westerners establish a hated Zionist state on Arab land? And does not the United States, the principal supporter of Israel, supply the Zionists with weapons that are used against helpless Palestinians? Does not the American and European occupation of Iraq and Afghanistan show that a crusader mentality still governs the West's attitude toward Muslims? Do not Westerners exploit Muslim lands for their oil? Do they not denigrate Muhammad and his teachings? By supporting al Qaeda and its sacred mission of recreating an Islamic world-state and enforcing Muslim law, jihadists believe they are doing something noble for their people and their faith.

The contemporary wave of suicide bombings was initiated by Hezbollah (Party of God), a Shi'ite organization in Lebanon. On October 23, 1983, it launched synchronized attacks in Beirut on U.S. Marine barracks that took the lives of 241 American marines and on an apartment building housing French soldiers, which killed fifty-eight more. Both American and French troops had been sent to Lebanon as a peacekeeping force in that country's vicious sectarian civil war. The practice was continued against Israelis who had invaded Lebanon to crush the leadership of the Palestine Liberation Organization (PLO) that was ordering frequent attacks against northern Israel. The fierce dedication of Hezbollah suicide bombers inspired imitators in Lebanon and other Muslim lands.

Jihadists and their clerical supporters extol the "honor of martyrdom" as a most solemn declaration of faith, the noblest deed a Muslim can perform. These true believers, products of a culture that values death more than life, are convinced that it brings not only victory but the assurance of eternal life in Paradise with all its rewards as the following statement prepared by Hamas (see part 6, chapter 4) reveals:

> Allah builds good and pleasant dwellings in heaven. The inhabitants receive rooms, under which flow rivers. There are also tents in heaven, each one made of pearl sixty miles high and sixty miles wide. Each mile contains a special corner for family members of the believer, hidden from the others....In paradise Allah provides the inhabitants...with rivers of water, milk, honey, and wine..... The shahid [martyr] for Allah receives immediate atonement of all his sins with the first drop of his blood being shed...and he weds seventy-two virgins. The shahid receives the potency of seventy men.[1]

Regarding the suicide bomber as a hero and martyr who has brought honor to the family, parents and relatives often take great pride in the bomber's deed and death. On June 1, 2001, Saeed Hotari, a twenty-two-year-old Palestinian carried out an attack outside a disco in Tel Aviv, that killed twenty-one young Israelis and injured nearly 100. Hotari's relatives and neighbors hung pictures of him holding dynamite sticks on trees and displayed on their doors flowers arranged like a heart or a bomb. "I am very happy and proud of what my son did," commented the suicide bomber's father. "My son has fulfilled the Prophet's wishes. He has become a hero! Tell me, what more could a father ask?"[2] Relatives are also comforted by the belief that the holy warrior will become their heavenly advocate, helping them to gain entrance into Paradise.

To be sure, the Qur'an and traditional Islamic teachings unequivocally condemn taking one's own life and confine the suicide to Hell. Islamic teachings also caution against the killing of civilians. For these reasons, some contemporary religious authorities have denounced suicide bombings, which kill and maim civilians indiscriminately, as violations of the word and spirit of Islam. Other Muslim religious authorities, however, have blessed the suicide bombers, arguing that their deeds are acts of heroic sacrifice and martyrdom for their faith and their people—the highest form of jihad—that have Allah's approval.

Although religious motives often predominate, suicide bombers are also moved by other considerations often derived from feelings of victimhood: revenge for the loss of a loved one killed in conflicts with Israelis or Americans; an altruistic desire, a solemn duty, to aid their family and the society to which they belong by retaliating against enemies, particularly hated foreign occupiers; a yearning for adventure; and a way of gaining the respect of their peers, bringing credit to their families, and giving meaning and purpose to their lives. They see themselves as soldiers fulfilling an important mission to inflict heavy casualties on the enemy in defense of their homes and families. And if on the appointed day they have second thoughts, fear of losing face among their peers makes it difficult to back out, particularly in a culture that honors martyrdom. Also entering the equation are the skillful recruitment and indoctrination methods employed by al Qaeda and other Islamic terrorist organizations.

Leaders of terrorist organizations make a rational decision when they launch suicide missions, for they understand the strategic advantages of such operations. Since they can get close to the target, human missiles in crowded urban areas and facilities are extremely deadly weapons. They are also inexpensive, readily available and difficult to defend against, as the frequent suicide attacks in Iraq testify. Moreover, these attacks send an effective message to both friend and foe alike. Terrorist leaders see them as an effective way to radicalize the Muslim masses. Publicizing and celebrating the self-sacrifice of their heroic martyrs, they believe, will gain them more adherents, more recruits, and more volunteers for future suicide missions, which figure large in their strategic planning. They also hope that by demonstrating the inability of the government to protect its citizens, and by robbing it of the satisfaction of capturing and punishing the perpetrators, suicide terrorism will create a climate of fear that will undermine the enemy's morale.

NOTES

1. From material captured by Israel from the Hamas Student Association at al-Najah University in Nablus, quoted in Samuel M. Katz, *Jihad in Brooklyn: The NYPD Raid That Stopped America's First Suicide Bomber* (New York: New American Library, 2005), pp. 123–124.
2. *USA Today*, June 26, 2001, p. A01.

1

"Indoctrination Is the Central Factor"

Walter Laqueur

In *No End to War: Terrorism in the Twenty-First Century* (2004), Walter Laqueur, an American historian specializing in modern European history, analyzes contemporary terrorist movements. In his discussion of suicide bombers, excerpted below, Laqueur stresses the importance of indoctrination, particularly in the bomber's formative years

*   *   *

The suicide terrorist is only the last link in a chain. There is no spontaneous suicide terrorism. The candidates are chosen by those in charge in the organization. The suicide terrorists are indoctrinated and trained—receiving intelligence information to guide them—and eventually are given the arms and explosives to carry out their mission. The people who guide the suicide terrorists have their political agenda. They organize the missions not as a purposeless manifestation of despair but to attain a certain political aim. While the suicide terrorist may be unstoppable, those behind him are certainly not; they can be deterred by inflicting unacceptable damage on them. Thus the leadership of the Lebanese Hizbullah after years of suicide terrorism discontinued these operations realizing that they were no longer very effective. Among Palestinians too, support for suicide terrorism vacillated. During Intifada Two, such support was high, but it declined following Israeli military counterblows. Enthusiasm for suicide terrorism seems to be confined to members of a certain generation. Once it is realized that the martyrdom of these young people does not bring the desired goal any nearer, the readiness to sacrifice one's life is bound to wane.

The motivation of the religious suicide terrorists is in many ways easier to explain than the secular. The radical Muslim has been promised various rewards such as life in paradise, his family will be taken care of, he knows he will not really be dead but continue another and much richer existence in the future. Support for the families of martyrs is an important consideration, as is the religious obligation to repay one's debts prior to the suicide mission—hence the financial help (amounting to about twenty-five thousand dollars) given to the families of suicide bombers by Iran and Iraq, as well as other Arab countries and Muslim foundations. In comparison, the families of those killed in open combat with the Israelis were paid merely two thousand dollars. Saudi Arabia provides a trip to Mecca for the members of the family of the suicide bomber, as well as other fringe benefits, such as housing. If in Sri Lanka the candidates for suicide had their last supper with the leader, there has been a thorough ritual in Lebanon and Palestine for the suicide terrorist to be photographed on the eve of his scheduled mission, to give his mission a solemn, quasi-religious character.

The secular suicide terrorist cannot have such expectations. But the differences between religious and secular motivation could be less wide than often assumed, for the underlying motives might be quite similar. There is the feeling of doing one's duty (religious, patriotic, or a mixture of the two) and of hate of the enemy, the infidel, the occupant. There are social and psychological pressures to engage in suicide missions. The readiness to sacrifice one's life is generated through a process of indoctrination—in orthodox religious schools or conspirational circles. Religious or ideological indoctrination needs some rootedness in an objective situation; the rage and the hate of the enemy have to be perceived as obvious. But in some cases the personality of the leader is sufficient to play the decisive role in committing acts that otherwise are incomprehensible. . . .

A variety of psychological explanations, analytical and from the field of orthodox psychiatry, have been adduced to explain suicide terrorism, including the concept of "overvalued ideas"—that is to say, the obsessive belief in an idea, or ideology or set of values. This might account for a fanaticism which includes the willingness to sacrifice one's own life but also for those who are sending the suicide bombers on their mission. But it is doubtful whether complex explanations are apposite; the motives are almost always rooted in the general historical, cultural, and social context, in the society in which the future suicide bombers are growing up.

This is a closed society with the emphasis on obeisance; a critical attitude, so dear to the West in modern times, is wholly absent. Into this society the suicide terrorist is born—or he opts for it in his search for spiritual certainties; converts become more easily fanatics than others. It is doubtful whether the content of the indoctrination is of decisive importance. It could be a firm religious belief, or extreme nationalism or another ideology appealing to deep-seated urges. Dr. Eyad Serraj, a Gaza psychiatrist, has argued that in every case of suicide bombing there has been a personal trauma or tragedy, such as the killing of a friend or close relation by the Israeli occupants. But this explanation does not apply to the Saudi suicide bombers of September 11, none of whom lived under Israeli occupation, nor, if true, is it of any relevance to suicide bombers in Lebanon, Kashmir, or other parts of the world. Algerian psychiatrists have pointed to the central importance of the appeal to *khulud* (immortality), *shahid* (martyr), and *al adhiya* (sacrifice), as well as the cult of death in the indoctrination of the Algerian radical preachers...of youth. But Algeria has been free for decades. The occupation of the country by foreigners cannot have been an issue....

How does one account for the fact that, as in the cases of the Manhattan and Pentagon bombers, the indoctrination survived years of exposure to the temptations of Western civilization? We are dealing with a relatively small group, and it is not at all certain that, in the long run, the majority of those exposed to the temptations are not bound to be corrupted. As for the minority who will remain impervious, they physically live in Western society but their hearts and minds are still at home with the gurus of their formative years. In a very few cases, al Qa'ida members (such as the shoe bomber from London or a young Arab of Swedish nationality with a Finnish mother) were actually born in Europe; for them, the excitement of belonging to a conspiracy may have been the single most powerful motive.

The great majority has, however, come from the Middle East. They lived together even in London, Paris, and Hamburg; they prayed and spent most of their free time in a small circle of like-minded people. Far from being absorbed by the customs and manners of this civilization, they may feel pushed into the defensive, alienated by what is (or what they consider to be) the sinful way of life to which they are exposed....

The psychology of the closed mind has not been studied so far very thoroughly. The fact that the suicide terrorist may have acquired a technical education in the West does not mean that he has understood (let alone shares) Western values. The indoctrination begins at a very early age; signs on the walls of Hamas kindergartens in the occupied territories in Palestine read "the children are the holy martyrs of tomorrow." According to Dr. Huda Zakaria, an Egyptian sociologist who has studied the suicide terrorist phenomenon, the terrorist group is different from the previous group (such as the family); it does not plant its values gradually through childhood and youth toward a constructive aim but prepares him for destruction and death: "The person who plants such ideas in the mind of a youngster turns him into a loose cannon after his personality has been reshaped in the interests of the new group.... It activates rapid indoctrination by the most sacred means for the soul such as religious belief." In the words of the Egyptian sociologist, the candidate for suicide terrorism is activated by remote control and can explode at any moment. In at least one case in Palestinian suicide terrorism, the detonation was effected not by the bomber but by remote control—a phone call.

Indoctrination is the central factor....The suicide terrorist no longer thinks; he finds his inspiration and refuge in prayer, as outlined in Mohammed Atta's letter to his comrades before the attack of September 11, 2001. There should be a ritual washing and shaving, and the night is to be spent in prayer trying to forget the world. Then there should be further prayers, and after this Atta advises the others, "Smile and feel secure. For God is with the believers and the angels are guarding him without him feeling it." We do not know, however, whether all or any of the suicide bombers did indeed spend the last night praying; some reportedly spent it in a bar or a night club.

Once the terrorist is seated in the plane, there is more prayer. He is to keep busy with repeated invocations of God and the travel prayer should be recited, because the terrorist is traveling straight to God. His heart is now purified and he is entitled to slaughter like cattle anyone resisting him and also hostages who do not resist. Slaughtering is an offering on behalf of God, as well as his parents; it is an act of grace conferred on the terrorist by Allah.

These, in brief outline, are some of the features of the psychology of the suicide terrorist motivated by religion or quasi-religious creeds. The subject is exceedingly difficult to investigate. Just as there are various terrorisms, the character and the motivation of suicide terrorists differ from country to country. Only very few of those who feel intensely motivated about politics or religion are willing to sacrifice their lives. In other words, while indoctrination is crucial, a psychological predisposition ought to exist too....

Muslim terrorist groups, but also others engaging in suicide terrorism, have argued that indoctrination is of no importance, that jihad is a religious obligation, and that more volunteers apply for action than they can use for such missions. But the evidence shows that wherever suicide terrorism occurs, preachers (or nationalist propagandists) play a crucial role in creating a climate conducive to such action. As for the psychological disposition, it has emerged from interviews with suicide bombers who were caught or failed in their missions that, when asked for their motives, they repeated, usually verbatim, what they had been told by their spiritual teachers. Obviously, one would look in vain for critical spirits or independent thinkers among them.

Suicide terrorism has appeared incomprehensible to people living in secular societies in which, by and large, ideological passion was a spent force and fanaticism had become a phenomenon restricted to marginal groups. It seemed not only mysterious but also invincible, for how could anyone resist enemies willing to sacrifice their lives? Suicide terrorism can spread panic, at least momentarily, among the "enemy"; it can cause substantial financial damage to the enemy, as in the case of Israel.

It is also a useful tool in the battle for public opinion outside the country directly involved. With all this there has been a tendency to overrate the importance of suicide terrorism. It has been tried in a dozen countries and it has been discontinued in most....The economic damage caused has not been fatal; a handful of dishonest heads of corporations in the United States have caused more damage to the stock markets and the reputation of the capitalist system than all terrorists taken together....

Suicide terrorism is asymmetric warfare par excellence: It knows no rules. The martyrs are permitted to use even the most devastating weapons, concentrating attacks against civilians, for they seem people driven to despair by lack of hope. The state, in contrast, is not permitted to retaliate effectively; it has to stick to rules and conventions. It is curious that there has been so much emphasis on the elements of despair and lack of hope among Western commentators; they probably played a role in some cases but not in many others. The young Saudis who hijacked the planes on September 11, to give but one example, were certainly not driven by lack of hope, and in any case those motivated by religious belief are certain to enter paradise upon blowing themselves up. In other words, they are full of hope, rather than despair....

Suicide terrorism is not a sporadic phenomenon. It needs not only people willing to become martyrs but also organizers and coordinators. This is where suicide terrorism is most vulnerable, and it is doubtful whether there is an unlimited reservoir of candidates for such missions. Suicide terrorism has been a more effective weapon than other terrorist strategies, but only when those targeted have adopted the wrong political and military countermeasures.

2

DYING TO WIN: THE STRATEGIC LOGIC OF SUICIDE TERRORISM

Robert A. Pape

The commonly accepted interpretation is that a religious motive—the desire to please God—is the principal reason why people volunteer for suicide missions. American political scientist Robert A. Pape rejects this view. For him the common thread linking suicide bombers is a political objective—driving out an occupier from one's homeland, which they see as furthering the common good of their society. In arriving at this theory, Pape relied on the concept of "altruistic suicide," developed by French sociologist Emile Durkheim in his pioneering work *Suicide* (1897). These ideas are discussed in *Dying to Win: The Strategic Logic of Suicide Terrorism* (2005), from which the passage below is taken.

* * *

Suicide can take multiple forms. The most common, "egoistic suicide," occurs when an individual is excessively isolated from society, cannot cope with intense psychological trauma, and chooses voluntary death as a means to escape this painful existence. The less common and fundamentally different "altruistic suicide" occurs when high levels of social integration and respect for community values cause otherwise normal individuals to commit suicide out of a sense of duty. The extremely rare "fatalistic suicide" happens when individuals are confined under conditions of such excessive regulation, oppressive discipline, and seclusion from society that they can be made to carry out extreme acts through what lay people call brainwashing.

This new conceptual lens helps us to see the distinctive qualities of suicide terrorism. Many suicide terrorists are acting out of altruistic motives, not the egoistic motives that are typical of almost all other suicides. Numerous suicide terrorists are acting at least partly to serve their community's interest in fighting the national enemy. These individuals are rarely brainwashed into accepting such missions through the heavy indoctrination associated with the recent mass suicides by religious cults, but accept the task much like a soldier who accepts a "suicide mission" in an ordinary war....

Many acts of suicide terrorism are a murderous form of what Durkheim called altruistic suicide. Although one might object to using the term "altruistic" to describe a behavior clearly intended to kill others, it is important to remember that our purpose is to explain what causes a suicide attacker to willingly kill himself in order to complete the mission. The murder of innocents is surely evil. Explaining it hardly justifies it. However, the homicidal dimension of the act should not cause us to overlook an important cause leading to it—that many suicide terrorists are killing themselves to advance what they see as the common good.

The circumstances of numerous suicide attackers support this finding. In contrast to persons who commit egoistic suicide, numerous suicide attackers are integrated into society, espouse collective goals for their missions in highly public ceremonies, and raise their social status and their families' by executing the act. Further, suicide terrorist groups exhibit few of the defining features of the religious cults whose members have committed recent mass suicides. Far from creating hard boundaries between the groups and surrounding society, the groups generally make strenuous efforts to integrate into the community, and the surrounding society often approves of the group's behavior. This is not to say that there are no instances of egoistic suicide among suicide terrorists. Some do exist and more may not yet have been detected. However, the data we have show that suicide terrorism is (1) surely not predominantly egoistic; (2) not likely fatalistic; and (3) probably mostly committed by people who are anchored to community or friendship networks....

The analysis below follows this comparative method. It identifies four patterns that, together, demonstrate that altruistic motives likely account for a substantial portion of suicide terrorism. First, the rate of ordinary suicide is not normally high in countries most associated with suicide terrorism; this undermines the notion that a cultural predisposition for egoistic suicide accounts for this phenomenon. Second, although ordinary suicide sometimes increases abruptly during violent nationalist rebellions associated with suicide terrorism, an important counterexample—Palestinian suicide terrorism since 2000, which has not been accompanied by a rise in ordinary suicide—indicates that even the anomic variant of egoistic suicide does not account overwhelmingly for suicide terrorism. Third, there is a particular method of suicide terrorism—the team attack—that is more likely associated with altruistic than with egoistic motives. Fourth, the social construction of the "altruistic motive" in suicide terrorism is not mainly a product of the separation of the group from society, as is common in recent mass suicides by religious cults, but is typically the result of a close integration of suicide terrorist groups with the surrounding society....

THE SOCIAL CONSTRUCTION OF
ALTRUISTIC MARTYRDOM

Altruistic motives are, heavily influenced by social approval. Although one could believe that an action would benefit others even if those others did not agree with the judgment, an individual is more likely to conclude that an act is beneficial if society actually supports and honors it. In fact, social approval is central to the logic of altruistic suicide as Durkheim conceived it. Whereas an egoistic suicide seeks to escape pain that society would normally expect a person to endure, the altruistic suicide willingly accepts a voluntary death precisely because society supports and honors the act.

The altruistic motive in suicide terrorism also depends on social approval. Suicide terrorist organizations are commonly thought of as "religious cults," as if they consisted of individuals separated from their surrounding communities and with aspirations fundamentally different from those of society, at large. This is a mistake. A suicide terrorist organization is generally an integral part of society rather than a separate entity. Indeed, members of the group typically go to great lengths to deepen their social ties, to participate actively in social institutions, and to adopt customs that display communal devotion. For its part, the local society commonly honors individuals who carry out suicide terrorist attacks. As result, it is impossible to understand the conduct, motivation, and self-perception of individual suicide attackers without considering the importance of the intimate ties that generally exist between suicide terrorist organizations and their communities.

Suicide terrorist organizations are bound to their societies by virtue of pursuing political goals viewed as legitimate by the society at large, by their participation in local charities and other institutions that benefit society, and by the use of elaborate ceremonies and other rituals that identify the death of a suicide attacker with the good of the community. These close social bonds do not create altruistic individuals. However, they do create the conditions under which individuals who wish to sacrifice for their community can be confident that their self-sacrifice will be viewed as altruistic....

CONCLUSION

Altruistic motives are significant in the individual logic of suicide terrorism. Many suicide attackers may also wish to escape personal problems, but the egoistic motives that account for ordinary suicides are insufficient, on their own, to explain why many individuals voluntarily carry out suicide terrorist attacks. This is especially true for one category of suicide terrorism—the team suicide attack—that by its nature involves multiple individuals working together for a collective purpose. Moreover, suicide terrorist organizations are not socially isolated groups with socially unacceptable goals, but go to great lengths to embed themselves in their surrounding communities and to pursue socially acceptable political objectives. Although this social construction of altruistic martyrdom does not create altruistic individuals, it does produce the circumstances under which an individual who wishes to sacrifice for the community can be confident that the act is understood in this way. As a result, the altruistic motive is often a necessary if not sufficient condition for suicide terrorism. Absent the altruistic motive, many suicide attacks would probably not occur and many suicide attackers might well seek other opportunities to contribute to their community.

This finding has important implications. First, it suggests that the number of people who would engage in suicide terrorism is potentially much greater than the number of those who are suicidal in the ordinary sense. Far from the common stereotype of a poor, socially isolated, uneducated religious fanatic, we should expect that suicide attackers are likely to come from a broad cross section of society. As the next chapter shows, a remarkable portion of suicide attackers are indeed secular, employed, reasonably well-educated, and otherwise contributing members of their societies. Although many of us would like to believe that suicide terrorism is limited to a tiny fringe, the fact is that there may be no upper bound on the potential number of suicide terrorists. Second, the role of altruism in suicide terrorism suggests that there may be a geometric multiplier built into the process of suicide terrorism. Unlike suicides following a stock market crash or mass suicides of a religious cult, the trajectory of suicide terrorism is often an upward slope. From Lebanon in the 1980s to the Palestinians in the second Intafida in 2000–2003 to al Qaeda's attacks in 2002–2003, suicide terrorist campaigns tend to gather pace—and attract more walk-in volunteers—over time. Given the dynamics of altruism, this trajectory is something we should expect in future suicide campaigns.

Finally, the role of altruism means that any attempt to profile suicide terrorists that is based on the known profiles of ordinary suicides is likely to miss a substantial portion. Indeed, since the pool of individuals potentially available in suicide terrorist campaigns is probably not limited to those who would commit suicide anyway, nations under fire may have little choice but to deal with the root causes of suicide terrorism.

3

" 'ORDINARY PEOPLE' AND 'DEATH WORK': PALESTINIAN SUICIDE BOMBERS AS VICTIMIZERS AND VICTIMS"

Anat Berko and Edna Erez

Suicide bombings require motivated individuals, organizations that foster and channel this motivation, and a cultural milieu that lauds the perpetrator as a hero or martyr. Anat Berko, International Policy Institute for Counterterrorism, Hertzliya, Israel, and Edna Erez, Kent State University, Ohio, interviewed seven Palestinian security prisoners serving time in Israel for attempting suicide bombings. Their research, excerpted below, provides valuable insights into the motivation of suicide bombers and the methods of organizations that recruit them.

* * *

FINDINGS

Sample Description

The participants were Muslim Palestinians who resided in cities, villages, or refugee camps in the Palestinian territories of the West Bank or Gaza. Their age ranged between 16 and 28 years old, and all came from large families (the average number of children in the family was ten). During most of the interviewing sessions, the female participants except for one were dressed in traditional Muslim dark garments.

The educational level of the sample extended from third grade to second year of university studies. The women had higher educational level than the men. At the time of their arrest, two of the interviewees were in high school, two were university students, and the rest worked in skilled or unskilled labor or in providing services. None of the participants were married at the time of their arrest. One man was married (and had one child) but got

divorced prior to his involvement in suicide bombing; his wife's family
pressured him to divorce her due to marital problems.

Social Background of the Suicide Bombers

The interviewees grew up in families where the mother was a homemaker
and the father was the breadwinner. The economic situation of the
interviewees mirrored that of the rest of the Palestinian society, and in some
cases was comparatively better than the norm. The families owned a home,
and there was a steady income from a shop, from the father's employment in
some Palestinian agency or from unskilled labor.

Most of the interviewees described a relatively normal family life, with a
dedicated loving mother and strict disciplinary regimen exercised by the
father. In two cases the father married a second wife, and both wives bore
children. The individuals whose father married a second wife younger than
their mother discussed some of the problems related to the second marriage.
It created tension between the two families, and generated conflict and
competition between the wives and their respective offspring for the father's
attention and family resources. The two interviewees whose father married a
second wife empathized with their mother and shared her feelings of rejection
and humiliation. They consequently felt distant from the father, experiencing
ambivalence toward him.

Two of the women lost their fathers in early childhood, one died in a
traffic accident and the other from serious illness. In one case the mother,
who lived with her child in a neighboring Arab country, decided to remarry
and the daughter had to move to the Palestinian territories where the father's
family lived. This woman, as the child of another man, could not live with the
mother and her new husband, whom the interviewee referred to as "a strange
man that my mother favored over me." She moved to her paternal grandmother
and her unmarried aunts who raised her from the age of 10.

The interviewees described the father as the only authority in the household,
whom they treated with respect and fear. The father was often perceived as
distant, one who could not be approached easily. Sometime to reach him, the
children had to go through the mother. All participants described their mothers
as "a warm and simple woman" who dedicated her life to the family. The interviewees expressed deep love and affection for their mother, whom they always
wanted to please. One of the women who decided to become a martyr (shahida)
noted that hurting her mother by committing suicide was the most difficult
thing for her to bear. One man commented that it was extremely difficult for
him to go to the court, see his mother there, and not be able to communicate
with her. Another man responded to a question about what would have made
him stop from perpetrating his suicide mission, "only my mother."

The participants' social identity as Palestinians, who are dispossessed,
oppressed, and humiliated, was a recurrent theme in discussing their lives.
Whether they resided in cities, villages or refugee camps in the West Bank or
Gaza strip, they were raised in Palestinian homes, which continuously

exposed them to their version of the Israeli-Palestinian conflict and its history. Growing up they heard their parents' stories about houses that were left behind, or about land that was lost when Israel was established and the Independence War (1948) erupted. The anger was exacerbated and the hatred deepened during the Israeli military control of the Palestinian territories following the Six Days War in 1967. As one of the men said:

> For me, a Jew is not a problem. But he sits in my country, doing things that are not acceptable. I grew up with it.

These issues were also topics of discussion in school, social activities, cultural events, and religious gatherings. The private stories, coupled with indoctrination in mosques or over the media, and reinforced through condemnations by Palestinian public figures, led to the interviewees' forming hostility and resentment toward Israeli Jews from an early age.

The one participant who had personal experiences with Israeli Jews through working in Israel explained that he did not have anything personal against Jews but the determination to engage in the struggle revolved around the feelings of loss of land and/or the occupation. The rest of the participants talked about the fact that they never had any contact with Israeli Jews prior to their imprisonment. One woman commented,

> Before I came to this prison I thought that all Israelis are soldiers shouting and yelling at Palestinians in checkpoints. Meeting here other (Israeli) prisoners and staff, I see we have a lot in common; we have the same life problems.

Those who have had direct or indirect contact with Israelis (or the West) prior to imprisonment talked about cultural, social and behavioral differences between Arabs and Jews or westerners in general. The participants took much pride in the closeness, warmth, and loyalty of the Arab nuclear and extended family, the friendly relationship with neighbors, and the collective efforts of their community in helping its members. They particularly elaborated on gender differences between Arabs and Israelis, and the barriers that Arab culture poses for interactions between Arab men and women. Quite often the interviewees restated the fact that they live in Arab society or are part of a culture that dictates various restrictions, and monitors gender-appropriate behavior. They mentioned that they cannot date or socialize unless the contact is for engagement or marriage purposes, is approved by the family and under its supervision. As the next section suggests, the social background of the interviewees and the cultural gender scripts that Arab society provides for men and women were reflected in the paths the participants took in becoming suicide bombers.

Decision to Become a Martyr (Shahid)

Of the seven interviewees, four initiated contact with an organization that produces suicide bombing; the other three were approached by activists looking to recruit candidates. The motivation that led the ones who initiated the contact to volunteer was varied. One of the male interviewees was a veteran of terrorism who has engaged in the past in various activities ranging from stone throwing to shooting and other subversive acts. Following problems he had with his wife's family [who forced him to divorce his wife], he decided to volunteer to become a martyr. He was well connected with a fundamentalist Muslim organization known to produce suicide bombing and he offered himself as a martyr (shahid). He suggested blowing himself up in a bus of Israelis in Jerusalem, where he used to work. His offer was accepted and he went on this mission but the explosives failed to detonate.

One woman explained that she decided to become a *shahida* in order to get back at her father, who did not allow her to marry the man of her choice. She described how one day on the street she saw a man, whose body was deformed, getting off a taxi. She stated: "We looked at each other's eyes and we fell in love with each other. I was 25 years old and it was my last chance to get married." Because the man's family was unable to meet her father's dowry demands, they could not get married. The woman was very angry with her father that he would not compromise about the amount of money he wanted and she decided to volunteer, "to take revenge on my father." She then went to a town near her village, where she happened to meet a military activist. She told this activist that she wanted to be a suicide bomber, and he started to roll the operation. She went on to explain,

> My life was useless, my life had no use to anyone . . . there are many people who want to do that, to be shahids and no one could prevent them from doing it.

She described what she thought was awaiting her if she was to become a martyr (shahida):

> The *shahida* is one of the 72 virgins. Life in the Garden of Eden is more than life in this reality. We do not live real life. We are just by-passers. The real life is in the Garden of Eden. Everything is there. Everything! All what we think about is in the Garden of Eden. There is food, excellent cooked food. . . . This is what was said in the (Qur'an's) chapter of The Cow (Surah Al-Baqarah) "do not refer to those who are killed for Allah as dead because they are alive."

A young woman from a refugee camp, a high school student at the time of her arrest relayed how she and her girlfriend who was a classmate were preparing homework assignments at her home. They both were bored and felt that "there was nothing to do" and looked for some excitement. Living in a militant town that produced dozens of suicide bombers, they felt they "wanted to do something" and decided that they would volunteer to become shahidas. This young woman contacted a man in the camp who was involved in military endeavors. She described the interactions that followed:

> At first, he (the military activist) refused my request to become a shahida, and he said "you are a minor and you should go to school." Later he offered me

another type of military work, not suicide bombing. But I did not give up. I told him I want to be a shahida.

She described how she went to a girls' school, and enjoyed studying there. But the idea of volunteering to be a shahida was something that she and her girlfriend got excited about and it became their shared secret. After few more appeals to the military activist, the man agreed to send her on a suicide mission, and they started to plan the attack. She was caught in her home just a few days before the mission was scheduled to take place.

One of the participants was a university student at the time of her arrest. When she was a young child, she stated, one of her brothers, whom she referred to as a shahid, was killed by the IDF (Israel Defense Forces) as a result of his involvement in terrorism, and three of her brothers were in Israeli jails for similar activities. She described how during her university years she was exposed to religious material and was engaged in bringing women back to religious lifestyle. As part of the experience of becoming a reborn Muslim, she visited families of shahids and eventually decided to become a shahida to avenge the death of Palestinians. She explained her reasons and the way she had to conceal the decision from her mother:

> I wanted to become a *shahida* for revenge [against] the Jews, [for] my religion and the love of the Garden of Eden. It was my own decision...If I were to tell someone that I was going to be a *shahida* they would prevent me [from doing it]. Thus I preferred to keep it to myself.

This woman contacted a military activist whom she knew was involved in dispatching suicide bombers and her preparation for the mission began shortly thereafter.

The interviewees who did not initiate the contact with the recruiting organization relayed the circumstances that led to their involvement in suicide bombing. One woman explained that she wanted "to get out of the house" so she decided to pursue military training. A girlfriend, who knew activists through her own experience with training, made the contact with the organization. The interviewee went on to explain:

> There are women who come and offer themselves. I did not volunteer. I did not want to die. I just wanted to get trained with weapon....I had a friend who introduced me to the guys (*shabab*). They told me. to sign a document that I have willingly chosen to train, so that no one says that they (the guys) forced me to do it. I do not know if they also make men sign such a document...

Before allowing her to get trained, the organization wanted to verify her social background and motivation to be involved:

> The guys would ask what made me work with them...they wanted to know if there was something in the home or whether I was forced to get married...they did not want someone who has something social but someone who is regular...

Once she passed the initial screening her training began:

> Three months before the mission I started to get trained...when I asked them
> to get trained they offered me an explosive belt and things like that...I said I
> only came for training, I do not want to die.

To include women in operations, which require contact with men, and for
women to be able to avoid the watching eyes of the family as they venture
out, cover up is always necessary. One woman explained:

> We do not live in the West. When I went to training, I told my father that I
> was going to a girlfriend. My father did not prevent me from going to girl-
> friends. I had freedom, even though our family is religious. It is natural to go
> and see girlfriends. They did not ask too many questions.

The woman explained how she managed to avoid suspicion, overcoming the
community restrictions of social interaction between men and women:

> ...Thus for 3 months I went to training. I would go in a car that collected me
> in the refugee camp...There was always a woman in the car so that I will not
> be with a guy alone...

In addition to having a woman accompany another woman to the training
sites, the organization also took measures to protect its own operations:

> There were times when they will cover my eyes until we came to the training
> place of the Al Aksa Brigades (a militant Palestinian organization). I was not
> alone; there were other women who got trained...

The woman, who merely wanted the excitement and adventures of secret
contact with men, soon realized that she got herself in a difficult situation.
She explained:

> ...I did not think it was going to be like that. I did not think I will die and I did
> not want to die. They (the recruiters and dispatchers) planned that I will be a
> suicide bomber. I did not ask for that. They offered me the explosive belt and
> other things. But I did not agree. At first they did not force me. But things
> developed and the situation got to where it got. I was a spoiled child and did not
> plan to die....The dispatcher told me that I would be going on a suicide mission
> "*istishhad*" (self-sacrifice) on Monday. He said to me, "Get yourself ready, and
> be prepared"...I was very surprised that he was ordering me to be a "*shahida*"
> (a female martyr). I hadn't planned to die in this way. At first I thought he was
> joking, but now, he wasn't joking. He said—"you prepared, you practiced, you
> know us, you're active in the organization and you have to do this."

In a panic, she tried to get out of this situation, explaining why she is not
suitable for the task:

> I told him that I had only come for the training, not to go on a suicide mission
> like this...then we argued. I told him that I don't practice all the religious

rules like traditional dress and covered hair, nor do I observe prayer times; sometimes I do pray and sometimes I don't...then I told him that someone who wants to be a "*shahida*" has to observe the rules of dress and prayer....I added that I watch television and listen to songs, things that observant Muslims don't do, and that I hadn't planned to undertake such an operation and become a "*shahida*." If I had, I would have been more religious.

Her demands and requests to get out of this entanglement, however, fell on deaf ears:

> I reached the point where, without realizing it, I found myself yelling at him. "I thought this was a prank," I said, but my girlfriend said it was for real. I asked the man to call the whole thing off, to forget the association between us, that I would forget them and they would forget me. They refused and told me—"You know everything about us, and we're not sure what will happen when you leave this room, perhaps you will make a mistake and tell on us."..."I swore on the Quran that I would not reveal anything. They said—'We're an "organization," not regular people, and that (oath) doesn't work with us.'" They feared for me and for themselves, that I might reveal their identity and training site.

In explaining his decision to become a suicide bomber, one of the male interviewees, a high school student, described being at a friend's home with some friends. In the presence of other youth, a classmate named Hassan approached him, offering him 100 shekels (about $22) and asking whether he wanted to become a shahid. The interviewee replied, "Why not?" He noted that the classmate who recruited him, and according to the interviewee received much more money for it than he did, admitted that he himself was scared to do it. The interviewee then added "I'm more of a man than Hassan, so I will do it." He then explained some of the other reasons for agreeing:

> *Shahids* are for God, I wanted to kill many Jews and take revenge....I would have sold my parents and the whole world for the Garden of Eden.

In responding to why he needed the 100 shekels he received for agreeing to be a suicide bomber, the interviewee stated that if he were to feel hunger on his way to the suicide mission, he could go to a restaurant and eat. He also said that he used the money to buy a cooking pot for his mother. He then went on to explain:

> All that is forbidden in this world is permitted in the Garden of Eden. The Garden of Eden has everything—God, freedom, the Prophet Mohammed and my friends, the "*shahids*".... There are 72 virgins. There are lots of things I can't even describe....I'll find everything in the Garden of Eden, a river of honey, a river of beer and alcohol...

A young woman described a combination of reasons and life events that led her to agree to become a suicide bomber. She was fond of a young man who was killed by the IDF while being involved in terrorist activities. In a social gathering she was approached by an activist who knew about her affection for the young deceased man. This activist asked her whether she wanted to avenge his death. She thought about the idea and eventually decided to accept the offer, as she believed she would meet the deceased man in heaven. At the time she started wearing traditional Muslim clothes. Her uncle, who was concerned about some of the changes he noticed in her behavior and appearance, inquired about what had transpired. She responded, allaying his worries:

> Do not worry about me. People who commit suicide do not think about their own families, only about themselves and their lives. I am not going to do it as I care about you.

Her family believed her and did not approach her any more about this issue. Two days after the activist approached her, she began to prepare for the mission.

Most of the interviewees reported feeling spiritually uplifted when they decided to become shahids. One man expressed it as "I felt like a groom." Another interviewee described it as "the happiest day of my life." One of the women described how she felt once she arrived at her decision to be a martyr:

> It took me a long time to make this decision.... It was wonderful to say good-bye to life, I felt I was in the clouds from the moment I knew I was going to be a *shahida*.

Preparing for the Suicide Bombing and on the Way to the Target

The interviewees described the last days before their scheduled departure for the mission as days of reflection and self-imposed isolation. They were withdrawn, avoided any conversation with household members, and would not divulge to concerned parents, siblings or relatives what was on their mind. They did not share their plan with anyone, and made up various excuses for their withdrawal or unusual behavior. They also avoided questions about their well being, or provided elusive answers to such inquiries.

The interviewees explained that they did not want to hurt their loved ones by revealing to them their imminent suicide. One woman who was supposed to participate in a double suicide mission described her feelings about the young person who was to be her partner in the mission:

> They prepared us separately. We met just 2 hours before the mission. I did not know the youngster before. When I saw him, he looked much younger than his age, just like a child. I could not stop thinking about his young age, that he had no time as yet to live, and that he may not understand what he is doing to himself and his family...

The female interviewees had also to conceal the suicide plan for additional reasons. As one of the women explained:

> I was scared to go and tell my father, to ask for help, because then he would know that I had been to military training with the guys, without permission...

This woman went on to describe what transpired in the days before the mission:

> I began counting the days till my death, because they forced me to. I hate death. I love life. I was very spoiled....When they told me that I was to go on the "mission," I cried so much, I almost fainted, everything looked black. I begged the "adult" who was in charge of the military trainees, to release me from it. He told me "*Halas ya-binti*" [enough, my daughter]. I repeated my claim that I am not religious, that I don't pray, and he replied, "when you die, you will be closer to God. God will forgive you and allow you into the Garden of Eden, in spite of not praying." That was that. He refused to release me....

Most of the interviewees went to the mission from their homes. On the day of the mission or at some point near the scheduled day a representative of the organization picked them up. They were taken to an apartment, which contained a decorated room, where they were videotaped reciting what they described as their farewell, their commitment to follow through with their mission and their final will. The will often was a letter to the family containing requests such as pay a debt the person making the will owes or rejoice [in] his or her becoming a shahid.

One of the interviewees described how on the morning scheduled for the mission he got up and kissed his sleeping mother's hand, recited prayers, and went on his way. In an apartment in his Palestinian town, the interviewee was videotaped with the Quran, two rifles, hand grenades and a green bandanna marked with Quranic quotations. During the interview, this man relayed this experience with enthusiasm and demonstrated with much pride the courageous posture he assumed for the videotaping.

After the videotaping the interviewees received the equipment necessary for the suicide mission. In some cases the explosive belt was placed on their body while they traveled to the target. An organization member, who was familiar with the area and knew how to reach the target, escorted the interviewees to the designated site, bypassing checkpoints and other security measures.

The interviewees described their feelings and conduct on the way to the target. They spoke of "robotic behavior" and of being emotionally detached....

During the travel to the target, some of the interviewees reported being told by those who escorted them how the community cherishes their actions, and how they will bring honor to themselves and their families. Several interviewees noted that they were asked to think only about the operation and were continuously encouraged to execute the mission, being reminded of the rewards that await them and their families after their death....

The woman who reached the target with the explosive belt on her body but changed her mind before detonating it explained her reasons for changing her mind:

> I thought about many things that time. I saw a woman with a little boy in the carriage, I thought, why do I have to do it to this woman and her boy. The boy was cute and I thought about my nephews. I looked up to heaven and I thought about God. Something from inside told me—No, you should not do that....I thought about the people that love me and the innocent people in the street who did not do any crime. It was a difficult moment, and I had to make a decision. I did not want to die....I did not think in a deep way....I even thought I may go to hell....I decided to change my mind as I thought I would not get out of this hell as I may kill innocent (Israeli) people, and cause the death of regular people who just happen to walk in the street. I know that God prohibits this kind of action.

Following her change of heart, she wanted to return home. Her decision to withdraw at the last minute and not to follow through with the mission was not favorably received by the organization:

> I called those who sent me to come and take me back. In the meantime, there was a suicide bombing (perpetrated by the young man who was driven with her to the target for the planned double suicide mission). There was a lot of mess. They (the dispatchers) hung up the phone on me. They told me that a lot of people are waiting for me to blow myself up, so I better do it. I cried and begged them to come and take me back to my village. I was in the middle of an Israeli city, and the youngster that came with me already blew himself up. I did not know what to do. So I called them three times, until they finally picked me up. The one who dispatched me said, "perhaps God chose this for you, to live, and perhaps it is better than death." I went back home and experienced depression. After one week I was arrested....

SUMMARY AND CONCLUSION

Suicide bombing is a discrete act executed by pushing a button. Yet, the data presented, although based on a small sample and thus should be interpreted with caution, portray suicide bombing as a social process amenable to criminological/victimological analyses. The recruit's background and social context, including associations, motivation, membership in subcultures that endorse violent responses to perceived social problems or indignation, and available opportunity structures—all play a role in individuals embarking on a suicide bombing "career."

In many cases the process begins with a motivated individual approaching an organization's representative about his or her interest in becoming a shahid. In others, a person identified as a potential candidate—someone who can be persuaded to commit an attack—comes to the attention of an organization that produces suicide bombing. Recruitment commonly occurs through one's social network; it often involves friends, classmates, or neighborhood acquaintances.

Individual motivation to become suicide bombers varies; it ranges from ideological persuasion, through desire to avenge the death of a loved one or fellow Palestinians, to enhancement of one's social status or augmenting one's prospects of a gratifying afterlife. But whether the decision to commit suicide bombing emanates from an ideology of struggle, despair or hope for a better afterlife, it is often triggered by mundane reasons, such as proving one's manhood, retaliation at an uncompromising father, search for excitement or ways to relieve boredom.

In some cases, individuals who are identified as vulnerable, or disenchanted with their personal lives or family situation, are swayed to become shahids, thereby ending their difficulties. Cajoling and persuading hesitant candidates with what awaits them if they comply, or enumeration of the rewards they and their families will receive, ascertain that recruits do not change their mind or deviate from the plan.

Once a decision to volunteer is made, finding an organization that will implement one's wish to become a shahid is straightforward. In most areas where candidates reside, information on who is involved in military operations is common knowledge. Easy access to suicide-facilitating organizations, beliefs in impending rewards for martyrs, together with ever-present communal exaltation of shahids, creates an environment that produces a steady supply of candidates, emboldens hesitant recruits, and persuades initially reluctant individuals to join the suicide industry.

The contact with an organization embarks the recruit on a journey, which in the normal course of events cannot be aborted. The contact itself becomes a "non-sharable problem," which leads to the recruit's isolation and withdrawal from family and relatives, whom the candidate does not want to upset. This isolation, in turn, makes the recruit more susceptible to the organization's pressures to follow through, as he or she is further distanced from the only persons who can stop this journey—father, siblings, other significant others, and above all the mother.

Preparation for suicide bombing can extend over several weeks or even months but may also be as short as a few days or several hours. In making a suicide bomber, the organization that recruits and trains candidates employs various strategies to maintain the recruit's interest: it strengthens his or her resolve to go forward with the mission, as it alleviates any fear or anxiety that may arise. The candidate receives constant reminders of the reasons for which one has volunteered or has been recruited. The contact and interaction with the organization leads recruits to a point of "no return." For men, it is often associated with the wish not to lose face and "to be a man." For the female recruit, the association with male organizations tarnishes her reputation, blocking her return to her family. In a culture that restricts social interaction between the sexes, it seals her fate as "a loose woman," making the alternative—death as a shahida—more appealing, if not worthwhile.

The findings demonstrate that for Palestinian men and women recruits, the path to martyrdom through suicide is, by and large, a one-way street. Social structures, value systems, and the collective memory of a group combine to produce a steady supply of motivated candidates, exert pressures on hesitant candidates, and persuade reluctant recruits to go forward with the act. In designing ways to curb suicide bombing, policy makers should consider the social, cultural, and religious contexts that create "push and pull" forces and attempt to address or ameliorate them in order to bring about change.

Special attention should be paid to identifying and supporting those who have the power to inhibit motivation to commit suicide, or dissuade recruits from following through with their plan. The data indicate that family members, particularly mothers, can detect in their offspring or relatives behavioral precursors to suicide, such as changes in routines, unusual or out of character conduct, sudden absences, withdrawal, or increased religiosity. Although it has been argued that mothers of shahids are powerless in Palestinian society, in suicide bombing cases, mothers or other close relatives may hold the key to detecting suicide plans as well as the power to dissuade their loved ones from carrying them out. Concerned parents or relatives need to report behavioral changes to authorities. Officials, in turn, should take such reports seriously and investigate them promptly and thoroughly. Authorities should also facilitate open communication with parents or other concerned family members, making them willing to report suspicions or appeal for help.

Part 5

THE THREAT TO THE WEST:
TERRORISTS IN OUR MIDST

In the 1950s and 1960s Western Europe's booming economy created a demand for cheap labor that was met by an influx of millions of Muslim from Turkey, Pakistan, and North Africa. In succeeding decades additional millions of Muslim immigrants from the Middle East and sub-Saharan Africa, seeking to join relatives, find economic opportunities, or escape from oppressive regimes, and taking advantage of European countries' liberal admission policies, settled in various European lands. Many of these countries, including France, Germany, Britain, Belgium, Holland, and Spain, now have substantial Muslim populations. While many Muslims have integrated well into European society, a substantial number have not, many of them suffering from high unemployment, poverty, and discrimination. Alienated Muslims, particularly youth, frequently drift into criminal behavior. In France, for example, Muslims, about 10 percent of the nation, comprise more than 50 percent of country's prison population, where they are often recruited and indoctrinated by Islamic extremists. A similar situation exists in Britain where Muslims are 2 percent of the population but more than 8 percent of the prison population.

The appeal of radicalism is linked to a growing Islamic religious revival, particularly among young people, who increasingly are becoming more devout than their parents. Many young European Muslims, searching to give their lives a richer meaning and finding Western culture spiritually empty, are returning to their ancestral faith. Disaffected and spiritually awakened Muslims, a significant number of whom are seemingly assimilated and educated, often professionals, have been receptive to firebrand imams. Often imported from Arab countries and financed by the Saudi government, these imams despise Western values, demonize Jews, and preach the duty of jihad. And to listeners their message carries the imprimatur of authority, for always it is buttressed by selective quotes from the whole corpus of Islamic law, including the Qur'an and other religious texts. Because of these imams, a number of mosques in Europe have become terrorist recruitment centers.

As a result of the preaching of radical imams and the efforts of militant recruiters who spot likely candidates—usually susceptible young men, in mosques, discussion groups, Islamic book stores, and coffee shops in Muslim neighborhoods—terrorist cells have been established in various European cities. The Internet has become a powerful recruiting and networking tool for al Qaeda. Jihadist Web sites, numbering in the thousands, propagate extremism. They feature imams extolling Wahhabism, a puritanical, fundamentalist form of Islam; Islamists providing religious justification for holy war; images of dead Americans killed by "glorious" jihadists; suicide bombers giving their farewell speech; and instructions for making explosive devices.

Extremist Islamic cells in Europe have engaged in numerous acts of terror. Much of the planning for 9/11 took place in Hamburg, Germany. In 2004, Muslim terrorists of North African origin, who were linked to al Qaeda, blew up four crowded commuter trains in Madrid, Spain, killing 191 and wounding about 2,000. In July 2005, Muslim suicide bombers killed more than 50 people and injured 700 in a terrorist attack on London's transit system. In a second attack two weeks later the bombs failed to detonate and the suspected suicide bombers were arrested. The following year, British security foiled a terrorist plot to blow up several transatlantic flights departing Heathrow airport that would have killed more people than had perished on 9/11. That the planners and perpetrators of these attacks were not foreign jihadists, but British citizens raised and educated in Britain who were terrorizing their fellow citizens, was viewed by analysts as an ominous sign. They feared that the 15 to 20 million Muslims residing in Europe, many of them alienated from European culture, poorly integrated into European society, and believing that the West has exploited Muslims and mocked their faith, were potential recruits for extremist Islamic groups, including al Qaeda, and that European cities would become targets of fanatical jihadists. German authorities reported that in 2004 some 32,000 Muslims were affiliated with radical Islamist organizations operating on German soil. Frequently these recruits have been radicalized by the Arab imams trained in the Middle East who proclaim that Islam is engaged in a holy war against the West and that martyrdom will redeem Muslim honor and assure victory.

Nor are Western-educated Muslims immune from the lure of jihad. It was a recently radicalized Dutch-born, Dutch-speaking, and Dutch-educated Muslim of Moroccan extraction who in 2004 cruelly and gleefully ritually butchered Theo Van Gogh for making a film about the suppression of women in Muslim lands. One of the terrorists sentenced to death in Pakistan for the murder of *Wall Street Journal* reporter Daniel Pearl was born in London and educated at exclusive British schools, including the London School of Economics. Doctors and engineers, in particular, seem drawn to radical Islam; several of these professionals have been involved in terrorist attacks in Britain. These terrorists are filled with moral outrage; they see themselves as idealists striking back at the West, which they perceive as waging a war against Islam in which their fellow Muslims are being humiliated, oppressed, and killed. European jihadists continue to recruit young Muslims to fight in Kashmir, Chechnya, Afghanistan, and Iraq.

Islam is also attracting European Christian converts whose zeal for their new religion can be harnessed for terrorist purposes. At the end of 2001, an alert flight attendant prevented Richard Reid, a recent British convert who discovered Islam while serving a prison sentence, from igniting an explosive device hidden in his shoe that would have blown up the plane in mid-air. In September 2007, German authorities charged a native German and youthful convert to Islam with heading a terrorist cell planning attacks against American targets in Germany that could have killed hundreds of people.

For years Europeans were largely indifferent to the threat of Islamic terrorism, and London, Paris, Hamburg, and Milan became hubs of jihadist movements. A mounting sympathy with Palestinians and a revived anti-Semitism led them to overlook, minimize, or even to justify both terrorist violence against Israel, including the murder of civilians by suicide bombers, and Muslim attacks on individual Jews and Jewish property in Europe. Similarly, an intense anti-Americanism and an unwillingness to offend Arab countries with whom Europeans had strong commercial ties, inclined many Europeans to minimize the significance of Muslim terrorism against the United States. However, growing increasingly concerned about terrorist threats, particularly after the bombings in Madrid and London, the European Union is now instituting and coordinating counterterrorism measures: mosques have been placed under surveillance and radical imams jailed or deported, and police authorities in several lands have thwarted attacks against European targets and dismantled terrorist networks, some of them engaged in smuggling fighters into Iraq. But many knowledgeable observers argue that European countries are still not fully committed to combating the jihadists. Moreover, they maintain that a growing disaffection with European values, the powerful draw of fundamentalism and jihadist culture promoted by radical imams, continued Muslim immigration, and an extremely high European Muslim birthrate will further undermine social cohesion and broaden the base of potential jihadists. And there is little doubt that the war in Iraq, by deepening resentment for the United States, has increased the number of Muslims in Europe eager to become foot soldiers for al Qaeda. There is also mounting evidence of a growing flow of militants from Europe receiving training in explosives in the tribal regions of Pakistan where al Qaeda operates freely. Continued radicalization of European Muslims represents a grave danger to the United States, as terrorist expert Michael Jacobson notes:

September 11 was proof positive that terrorist activity in Europe can have an immediate and catastrophic impact on the United States. The four core members of the September 11 conspiracy's "Hamburg cell." . . . spent years in the German city. They were part of a group of radical Muslims who met often to discuss and share anti-American sentiments. While September 11 is the most extreme example of how events in Europe can impact the United States, it is far from the only one. In fact, as one al-Qaeda expert testified, "Every single attack carried out or attempted by al-Qaeda throughout the world has some link to Europe, even prior to September 11. . . . There are numerous examples since September 11 of suspected terrorists arrested in Europe on suspicion of plotting to attack U.S. interests—both in Europe and elsewhere."[1]

NOTE

1. Michael Jacobson, *The West at War: U.S. and European Counterterrorism Efforts, Post-September 11* (Washington, DC: Washington Institute for Near East Policy, 2006), pp. 11–12.

1

"The Threat . . . Will Remain at a Very High Level for the Foreseeable Future"

Claude Moniquet

On April 27, 2005, Claude Moniquet, director-general of the European Strategic Intelligence and Security Center, testified at a House of Representatives Hearing of the Committee on International Relations' Subcommittee on Europe and Emerging Threats. His testimony, presented less than three months before the terrorist attacks on London's transit system, provides a brief but comprehensive overview of Islamic extremism in Europe. In his prepared statement to the subcommittee, which follows, Moniquet explained that English was not his native language.

* * *

An Overview of the Problem

For various reasons, it is quite difficult to draw a general view of Islamic extremism in Europe. This question has not yet been really addressed by academics, and we lack scientific data. Even the real number of Muslims living in Europe is open to question. For instance in France, various figures are circulating: 4 million, 5 million, 6 million, or more. But we could reasonably say that, without any doubt, the problem is real. Some concrete signs underline this reality:

- Before 2000, it was extremely rare to see a public demonstration by Islamists in the streets of Europe. Since September 11, we have seen this kind of street demonstration in countries like France and Belgium. Thousands of people took part in those demonstrations, for instance one at the beginning of 2004 in Paris, to protest the law banning the Islamic veil from public schools;
- Ten years ago, the Islamic veil was mainly worn by older women. Now at least half of the female Muslim population wear the veil. In some

municipalities in France, the figure is about 80%. From field investigation
we know that in most cases those girls and women didn't really choose
to wear the veil but were "forced" to do so by family or community
pressure. In some European cities, a Muslim girl who refuses to wear
the veil leaves herself open to insults, physical aggression, sexual harass-
ment, and even collective rape. In France, those aggressions happen
regularly;
- Before the end of the nineties, Islamist political parties didn't exist in
  Europe. Now you can find them in France or Belgium. Of course,
  they're still small parties, with no representation in Parliament. But, to
  take the case of Belgium, in May 2003 the "Parti de la Citoyenneté et
  Prospérité" (PCP, "Party of Citizenship and Prosperity") which advocates a radical Islam, won more than 8,000 votes in Brussels. If we
  reckon that approximately 200,000 Muslims live in Brussels, that means
  that approximately 4% of those people gave their vote to the PCP. Now,
  if we consider only old enough to vote, the figure is more than 4%. Last
  but not least, if we consider that most of the votes were registered in the
  same municipality, where approximately 50,000 Muslims live, that
  means that between 10 and 16% of those people gave their vote to a
  party advocating radical Islam;
- Police and intelligence services know that fundamentalist and hate
  preaching are common in many mosques;
- Youth associations acting as front organizations for the Muslim Brothers
  are extremely popular;
- Since 2000 the number of anti-Semitic aggressions has dramatically
  increased; these acts—hundreds of which have been recorded over the past
  four years—are mainly the work of young Muslims;
- In schools attended by young Muslims, some kinds of teaching are becoming more and more difficult. For instance it's quite impossible to teach the
  history of the Shoah [Holocaust]; in biology, young men and girls openly
  question the theory of the origin of life and the evolution of species and
  humanity;
- In the same schools there is frequently a de facto sexual segregation. For
  instance, in a class room it is common to see the boys grouping themselves in one part of the room and girls in the other;
- In hospitals, the refusal of treatment by a man on a woman or by a woman
  on a man is becoming more and more common;
- The Islamic presence in European prisons, where the Muslim population
  is frequently in the majority, is a reality observed in various countries;
- Since September 11, hundreds of suspected terrorists have been arrested in
  Europe (in France, Belgium, Germany, Great Britain, Italy, Spain, The
  Netherlands, etc). But each week police arrest new suspects. This demon-
  strates that the number of people willing to go from ideas to action is
  growing;
- Last but not least, dozens if not hundreds of young people—some very
  young—have been recruited since the summer of 2003 and sent to Iraq.

But the exact scale of the threat is still difficult to determine. The French domestic intelligence service, *les Renseignements Généraux,* has tried to establish a formula to calculate the number of fundamentalists in a given population. Based on an extensive screening of the French scene, the formula is as follows: normally, in a given Muslim population, we'd find an average of 5% of fundamentalists. And, of those 5%, 3% could be considered as dangerous. That means, if we take France and a Muslim population of 6 million people, we'd have 300,000 fundamentalists. And, of those fundamentalists, 9000 are potentially dangerous.

The most exposed countries are France, Belgium, the Netherlands, Italy, Spain, Great Britain, and Germany. Outside the European Union, Bosnia is at high risk.

Obviously, it is in those countries that we'll find the highest number of Muslims. That doesn't mean, of course, that the average Muslim population is fundamentalist or dangerous. Most Muslims, even if the trend of a return to the religion is clear and massive, want to live a normal and decent life. But of course, the presence of a large Muslim community offers both better statistical chances of recruitment and places to hide.

But countries that don't have a large Muslim community are still not immune. I was told very recently that in Slovakia—where there is virtually no Muslim community—a propaganda and financing cell of Hezbollah is in place at the University of Bratislava.

THE CAUSES OF ISLAMIC EXTREMISM IN EUROPE

The causes of Islamic extremism in Europe are many and various

First; Muslim communities vary from one country to the next. In France, for instance, most Muslims are of Algerian descent, and as you know Algeria was a French colony for more than 130 years. In 1962, Algerian communities were established in France, and the number of Algerians grew as more came to Europe to find jobs and a better life. After a few years, in the seventies, the French government authorized the "*regroupement familial*" (the reunion of families) and so hundreds of thousands of new immigrants were transplanted into France. In Belgium, Germany, and Italy, Muslim immigration was not traditional, but was brought about for economic reasons: in the sixties, heavy industry and construction sites needed a work force that was extremely difficult to recruit locally. That was the beginning of immigration in those countries.

When we speak of immigration, we use the concepts of First, Second and Third generation. The First generation is made up of people who initially came to Europe to work. They are now aged 60 or more. The Second generation is made up of the children of those people. They were born outside Europe and came at a very young age, or they were born in Europe. They are aged between 30 and 50. The Third generation is made up of the children of the Second generation. They were born in Europe and they are less than 30 years old.

Sadly we must observe that, historical or not, Muslim immigration was not welcomed in Europe. Racism and exclusion were a reality, and with the beginning of economic decline in the seventies, and the slowing of European economy, problems increased.

So today, parts of the Second and Third generations make no effort to integrate into European society and adopt European humanist values. But it has to be pointed out that, until very recently (in fact in the nineties) absolutely nothing was done to help them integrate. This is the European reality and the European shame. We must live with it and we are paying for it.

To be brief, we had no problems with the First generation. Most of the problems until the very recent past were concentrated in the Second generation, and we had no real intelligence on what was going on with the Third generation. But over the past three to five years, we have been receiving a lot of very negative signals from the Third generation. For instance: violence at school, the rejection of "European values" such as sexual equality, etc.

There is not, obviously, a single explanation for the appearance of Islamic extremism in Europe. We could, nevertheless, try to work towards an explanation:

- The lack of integration and racism lead to some Muslims feeling excluded from the society in which they live;
- Some "lifestyles" (for instance polygamy or the birth rate) reinforce the rejection of the Muslim community by European society;
- The economic and social crisis hit the Muslim communities very hard. If average unemployment in France or Belgium is around 10%, it is commonly 20% within Muslim communities and even 40% among Muslim youth— the famous "Third generation." This reinforces the feeling of exclusion;
- Democracy, globalisation and a communication culture give people in Europe direct access to information. Events in Bosnia, Somalia, Chechnya, or the Israeli-Palestinian conflict lead some young Muslims to create what the French sociologist Farid Khosrokhovar called "an identity of vicarious humiliations." Feeling excluded in the country they're living in, they develop a kind of empathy with all the "Muslim victims in the world" and convince themselves that their own exclusion and the "persecution" of their brothers have the same roots: the rejection of Islam by the Western world;
- Most Muslim clerics, even those who are not radicals, come from abroad and are frequently trained in Saudi Arabia or by Saudi clerics. They have no real knowledge of the societies in which their followers live and, often, as shown by investigations in France and the Netherlands, they don't speak the local language. So they cannot take a role in easing tensions or helping integration;
- Many European Muslims reject these clerics, accusing them of preaching an "Islam of the rich" and turn to non-official mosques. But this could be

a bad idea: in what we call the "Islam of cellars and garages" (after the places where these informal communities meet) clerics are for the most part self-proclaimed. Their knowledge of religion is extremely questionable;

- In all the countries concerned radical clerics took advantage of the above facts to advocate a radical Islam and to attack western values, or European and U.S. policy which they denounce as "anti-Muslim" or pro-Zionist;
- They are helped by the presence in Europe (in the universities and high schools) of refugees who fled their native country because of repression for their Islamist activities. In the universities we find cells of Islamist or terrorist movements such as the Muslim Brothers, Hezbollah or Hamas, Algerian, Moroccan, Tunisian or Turkish groups, etc;
- Some of the existing groups were created out of solidarity with "persecuted Muslims" in Afghanistan, Algeria, Bosnia, and so forth. In most cases, these movements were not spontaneous but were launched and manipulated by front organizations for the Muslims Brothers;
- The "last generation" of European Islamism was born with the war in Iraq in 2003. This very young generation is starting to show up in various judicial inquiries into terrorist activities.

THE REALITY OF THE THREAT

The threat is very real and is both political and terrorist

On the political level, Islamists are trying to subvert western society by contesting humanist values such as sexual equality, freedom of religion, freedom of speech, etc. They advocate the creation of religion-based political parties; they advocate the creation of Sharia tribunals to judge civil and personal matters, etc.

They know, of course, that they will not win those battles, but their hope is to create or deepen the cultural and social divide between Muslims and non-Muslims. The idea in doing so is to radicalise Muslim communities.

On the terrorist level, the Islamists organize logistical and operational cells.... The "need" for the Jihadists to attack Europe is not innate in them, but it is bound to the essence of the old continent. Even if differences exist between the United States and Europe, these two entities, with some other countries (Australia, Canada, Japan, Korea) belong to the same "camp"— that of a "western world" (this qualifier having no ethnocentric character, which is why we can include Asian countries) which shares the same essential democratic values. It is these values which make us the "enemies" of the Islamists. Besides, even if not present militarily in Iraq, many European nations are or were in Afghanistan, and the European Union gave a political undertaking to the new Iraq to help in its reconstruction and stabilization.

These past twelve months also saw a "qualitative" evolution of the threat: more than ever, Islamism is asserting itself as a "mutant virus." Where since 2001 (and even before) security services faced terrorist structures mostly made up of experienced Jihadists, often with Afghan experience in common, between 25 and 40 years old, more and more we now find very young people, who by definition have no "past" in Islamist circles: French Jihadists killed or arrested in Iraq are from 18 to 20 years old; Samir Azzouz, one of the members of the "cell HOFSTAD" was 18 years old at the time of his arrest and was tracked down after he tried to go to fight in Chechnya at the age of 16. What we are now awaiting is the emergence of a new generation of terrorists: kids who were 12 to 15 years old on September 11 2001, and who have taken a year or two to make the same ideological progress that leads to violence, and which took...their elders ten years or more.

These small groups are more and more often made up of people with strong local ties, able thus to count on the solidarity of local communities and families. These groups are also connected to society's marginal groups and crime circles, which increases the danger they represent: "new Jihadists" have no problem getting hideouts, weapons or explosives. They are, despite their youth, initiated into the "underground" and have been, used to thwart police traps. Occasionally, they manage even to infiltrate the law as organized crime does: one of the members of the HOFSTAD cell was employed as a translator by the AIVD, Dutch civil intelligence.

Finally; the "new" terrorist cells are even more [widely active] than before: the HOFSTAD cell based in the Netherlands prepared its attacks while it was also involved in the economic planning of other attacks in Portugal or Spain. A fall in the average age, links with crime, and internationalization are all causes for anxiety among experts.

The threat against the interests of the United States from European terrorists is also very real. Of course, American interests in Europe (embassies, consulates, military personnel, hotels, American companies) are natural targets for Islamists.

But there is more: most of the Second generation people and almost all of the Third generation now hold European passports. So these people can travel freely to the United States or anywhere else they want to. I don't need to remind you that the September 11 attacks were planned in Germany, Great Britain, and Spain. And I don't need to remind you of the case of Richard Reid, the so-called shoe-bomber.

LINKS BETWEEN EUROPEAN ISLAMISTS AND AL QAEDA

I think a common mistake is to try to link each and every terrorist attack or plot to Al Qaeda

Al Qaeda had an "historical role" to play: to build an international terrorist coalition uniting dozens of organizations. Now that this has been achieved, an "International Islamist Terror" exists. And it is very effective. Information, arms and funds are exchanged among groups; Moroccan, Algerian, Chechen, Pakistani, Saudi, Iraqi and other organizations. Often these organizations collaborate in very sophisticated projects. The only role of Al Qaeda is to set the general framework of the jihad, designate targets and give lawful authorization (Fatwa) to act. Of course all those organizations or most of them are or were linked to Al Qaeda at one time or another. They take part in the global Jihad "against the Jews and the Crusaders" but they concentrate also on their own local problems—just as Al Qaeda concentrates mainly for the moment on Afghanistan and Pakistan, Saudi Arabia, Iraq and, of course, the United States....

ABILITY TO CARRY OUT ATTACKS

All of these groups and cells must be considered able to carry out terrorist attacks. The fact that the majority of attacks in recent years failed means that police and intelligence services are working well, and not that the groups concerned are unable to carry out attacks—even though we can sometimes see a kind of amateurism in their modus operandi, at the level of the security of the operations they plan to carry out.

More worrying: some of the failed attacks in Europe (in France and in Great Britain) were WMD attacks intending to use chemical products to produce high casualties.

The intelligence we have—notably the fact that some suspected terrorists have shown great interest in recent years in nuclear facilities—suggests they are also thinking of using a "dirty bomb." ...

THE "NEW GENERATION" OF ISLAMIST TERRORISM IN EUROPE IS ONLY STARTING TO APPEAR

This "new generation" of terrorism which we hinted at above has hardly begun to appear on the terrorist scene. Recruits come from the "Third generation" of immigration, who we know has identity problems and feels itself the victim of imperfect integration. These problems can push many young people towards violence. We are then confronted with a new situation where diffuse and informal networks of young people who were born in Europe, who know it well and who have scores to settle, could serve as a relay to more structured international organizations, or even try to lead its own "jihad" to take revenge for the real or supposed humiliations felt by these young people.

Given the current situation I have tried to describe to you, it's hard to be optimistic. The threat both against Europe and from Europe to the United States will remain at a very high level for the foreseeable future. And I'm afraid that a tragedy will be necessary to force the European authorities to face the reality of the problem and to really address the problem posed by Islamism.

The question, in my view, is no longer "if" a tragedy will happen, but "when" it will happen.

2

The Rising Tide of
Islamic Radicalism

Lorenzo Vidino

Lorenzo Vidino is associated with a data-gathering center on Islamic terrorism in the United States and author of *Al Qaeda in Europe* (2006). On April 27, 2005, he addressed the House Committee on International Relations' Subcommittee on Europe and Emerging Threats. In his address, Vidino stated that "almost every single attack carried out or attempted by al Qaeda throughout the world has some link to Europe, even prior to 9/11." This and other important themes were treated in Vidino's written testimony that follows.

* * *

Good afternoon, Mr. Chairman and Mr. Vice-Chairman, and thank you for the opportunity today to discuss the threat posed to Europe by Islamist extremism.

The deadly train bombings that killed almost 200 commuters in Madrid on March 11, 2004, shocked most Europeans, as the attacks represented the first massive strike by Islamist terrorists on European soil. The Madrid bombings, nevertheless, did not surprise security officials on both sides of the ocean, as the intelligence community was well aware that it was just a matter of time before Europe, one of the terrorists' favorite bases of operations, could become a target.

Over the past ten years, in fact, Europe has seen a troubling escalation of Islamist terrorist and extremist activities on its soil. This disturbing phenomenon is due to a combination of several factors and chiefly to:

- lax immigration policies that have allowed known Islamic radicals to settle and remain in Europe;
- the radicalization of significant segments of the continent's burgeoning Muslim population; and

- the European law enforcement agencies' inability to effectively dismantle terrorist networks, due to poor attention to the problem and/or the lack of proper legal tools.

Given these premises, it should come as no surprise that almost every single attack carried out or attempted by al Qaeda throughout the world has some link to Europe, even prior to 9/11. A Dublin-based charity provided material support to some of the terrorists who attacked the U.S. embassies in Kenya and Tanzania in 1998. Part of the planning for the thwarted Millennium bombing that was supposed to target the Los Angeles International Airport was conceived in London. False documents provided by a cell operating between Belgium and France allowed two al Qaeda operatives to portray themselves as journalists and assassinate Ahmed Shah Massoud, the commander of the Afghan Northern Alliance, just two days before 9/11. And, as we well know, the attacks of 9/11 were partially planned in Hamburg, Germany, where three of the four pilots of the hijacked planes had lived and met, and from where they received extensive financial and logistical support until the day of the attacks.

After 9/11, as the al Qaeda network became less dependent on its leadership in Afghanistan and more decentralized, the cells operating in Europe gained even additional importance. Most of the planning for the April 2002 bombing of a synagogue in the Tunisian resort town of Djerba that killed 21 mostly European tourists was done in Germany and France. According to Moroccan authorities, the funds for the May 2003 Casablanca bombings came from Moroccan cells operating between Spain, France, Italy, and Belgium. And cells operating in Europe have also directly targeted the Old Continent. Only after 9/11, attacks have been either planned or executed in Madrid, Paris, London (in at least 4 different circumstances), Milan, Berlin, Porto, and Amsterdam.

However, while investigations in all these cases revealed that different cells operating throughout Europe were involved in the planning of the operation, the role of these cells extends beyond the simple planning or execution of attacks. European-based Islamists raise or launder money, supply false documents and weapons and recruit new operatives for a global network that spans from the United States to the Far East. Within the last decade, their role has become essential to the mechanics of the network. It is, therefore, not far-fetched to speak of Europe as "a new Afghanistan," a place that al Qaeda and others have chosen as its headquarters to direct operations.

ORIGINS AND DEVELOPMENTS OF ISLAMIST TERRORISM IN EUROPE

The foundations for this security disaster were laid in the 1980s, when many European countries either granted political asylum or allowed the entrance to hundreds of Islamic fundamentalists, many of them veterans of the war in

Afghanistan against the Soviets facing persecution in their home countries. Moved by humanitarian reasons, for decades countries like Britain, Sweden, Holland, and Germany have made it their official policy to welcome political refugees from all over the world. But blinded by their laudable intentions of providing protection to all individuals suffering political persecutions from autocratic regimes throughout the world, most European countries never really distinguished between opponents of dictatorships who wanted to spread democracy and Islamic fundamentalists who had bloodied their hands in their home countries with heinous terrorist acts. As a consequence, some of the world's most radical Islamists facing prosecutions in the Middle East found not only a safe haven but also a new convenient base of operation in Europe.

Many European governments thought that, once in Europe, these committed Islamists would have stopped their violent activities. Europeans also naively thought that, by giving the mujaheddin asylum, they would have been spared their murderous wrath. All these assumptions turned out to be completely wrong. In fact, as soon as they settled on European soil, most Islamic radicals exploited the continent's freedom and wealth to continue their efforts to overthrow Middle Eastern governments, raising money and providing weapons and false documents for their groups operating in their countries of origin.

And it was in Europe that Islamic radicals from different countries converged and forged strategic alliances. Originally intending only to fight the secular regimes of their own countries, top members of various Islamist terrorists groups, drawn to the radical mosques of Europe, joined forces with their colleagues who all adhered to the same Salafi/Wahhabi ideology and shared the common dream of a global Islamic state. It was between London and Milan, for example, that the strategic alliance between Algerian and Tunisian terrorist groups was conceived. Europe, along with al Qaeda's Afghan training camps, was the place where Bin Laden's project of "global jihad" came to realization, as various Islamist groups progressively abandoned their local goals and embraced al Qaeda's strategy of attacking America and its allies worldwide.

Moreover, the mosques and networks established by radicals who had been given asylum played a crucial role in what could be considered Europe's biggest social and security problem, the radicalization of its growing Muslim population. Europe is facing monumental problems in trying to integrate the children and grandchildren of Muslim immigrants who have come to the continent since the 1960s. Dangerously high percentages of second-and third-generation Muslim immigrants live at the margins of European societies, stuck between unemployment and crime. While they hold French, Dutch, or British passports, they do not have any attachment to their native land, feeling like foreigners in their home countries.

"After things didn't work out with work, I decided to devote myself to the Koran," explained an Islamic fundamentalist interviewed by the German magazine *Der Spiegel*. As they perceive themselves with no economic future,

trapped in. a country that does not accept them and without a real identity, many young European Muslims turn to their fathers' religion in their quest for direction. While some of them find solace in their rediscovered faith, others adopt the most belligerent interpretation of Islam, embarking on a holy war against their own country. According to a French intelligence report, radical Islam represents for some French Muslims "*a vehicle of protest against…problems of access to employment and housing, discrimination of various sorts, the very negative image of Islam in public opinion.*"

Whether this troubling situation is due to the European societies' reluctance to fully accept newcomers or [is based] on some Muslims' refusal to adapt to new customs is hard to say. Nevertheless, given the burgeoning numbers of Muslim immigrants living in Europe, currently estimated between 15 and 20 million, the social repercussions of these sentiments are potentially explosive.

While it is true that the situation in the immigrant suburbs of many European cities is dramatic and that it is difficult for the children of Muslim immigrants to emerge in mainstream European society, the popular paradigm that equates militancy with poverty is simplistic and refuted by the facts. An overview of the European-born Muslim extremists that have been involved with terrorism, in fact, shows that many of them came from backgrounds of intact families, with financial stability and complete immersion in mainstream European society. The example of Omar Sheikh—the British-born son of a wealthy Pakistani merchant who attended some of England's most prestigious private schools, led a Pakistani terrorist group and was jailed for his role in the beheading of *Wall Street Journal* reporter Daniel Pearl—shows that the causes of radicalization are deeper for many individuals.

Nevertheless, it is undeniable that young, disaffected Muslims living at the margins of European societies are the ideal recruits for terrorist organizations. The recruitment takes place everywhere, from mosques to cafes in Arab neighborhoods of European cities to the Internet. As in the US, European prisons are considered a particularly fertile breeding ground for radicalism, a place where young men already prone to violence can be easily turned into terrorists. In France, for example, where unofficial estimates indicate that more than 60% of the inmates are Muslims (while Muslims represent only 10% of the total French population), authorities closely monitor the activities of Islamic fundamentalists, aware of the dangers of the radicalization of their jail population. Officials, who estimate that 300 militants are active in the Paris prisons alone, have seen cases of radicals who seek to get arrested on purpose so that they can recruit new militants in jail.

Similarly, in Spain, where one in ten inmates is of Moroccan or Algerian descent, Islamic radicals have been actively recruiting in jail for the past ten years. In October of 2004, Spanish authorities dismantled a cell that had been planning a bloody sequel to the March 11 Madrid bombings, intending to attack the Audiencia Nacional, Spain's national criminal court. Most of the men, who called themselves "The Martyrs of Morocco," had been recruited in jail, where they had been detained for credit card fraud and other common crimes and had no prior involvement with Islamic fundamentalism.

CURRENT TRENDS OF TERRORISM FINANCING IN EUROPE

If the European criminal underworld provides an excellent recruiting pool, crime also constitutes a major source of financing for terrorist organizations. Islamic terrorist groups operating in Europe have resorted to all kinds of crimes to finance their operations, including robberies, document forging, fraud and the sale of counterfeited goods. But more alarming is the fact that Islamist groups have built strong operational alliances with criminal networks operating in Europe.

Over the past few years, Islamic terrorists have been actively involved in one of Europe's most profitable illegal activities, human smuggling. The GSPC, a radical Algerian Islamist group operating in the desert areas of North Africa, is actively involved in smuggling large groups of Sub-Saharan migrants across the desert and then to Europe, where the group can count on an extensive network of cells that provides the illegal immigrants with false documents and safe houses. In 2003, German authorities dismantled a network of Kurdish militants linked to Ansar al Islam, the terrorist group led by Abu Musab al-Zarqawi[1] that is battling U.S. forces in Iraq. The Kurdish cells had organized a sophisticated and profitable scheme to smuggle hundreds of illegal Kurdish immigrants into Europe, raising hundreds of thousands of dollars. Considering that, on average, a migrant pays about $4,000 to his smugglers and that around 500,000 illegal immigrants reach Europe every year, terrorist groups have all the reasons to get involved in the human smuggling business.

Likewise, the terrorists' use of drug trafficking is also considered a particularly serious problem by European authorities, which believe that terrorist organizations have infiltrated around two-thirds of the $12.5 billion-a-year Moroccan hashish trade. Evidence from recent terrorist operations reveals that profits from drug sales have directly financed terrorist attacks. According to Spanish authorities, Jamal Ahmidan, a known drug dealer and one of the operational masterminds of the Madrid train bombings, obtained the 220 pounds of dynamite that were used in the attacks in exchange for 66 pounds of hashish. And Ahmidan also flew to the island of Mallorca shortly before March 11 to arrange the sale of hashish and ecstasy, planning to use the profits for additional attacks. The scheme is not new to Moroccan groups, which have used profits from the drug sales to finance the thwarted attacks against American ships in Gibraltar in 2002 and the Casablanca bombings.

European authorities are confronting criminal activities with relative success, but are facing an uphill battle when they have to prove the links to terrorism. Severe evidentiary requirements and the secretive nature of terrorism financing have prevented Europeans from effectively tackling known networks that financed terrorist activities. The most commonly used legal tool, the designation as a "terrorism financier," has had only modest results. In fact, since the various terrorism financing resolutions allow authorities only to freeze the bank accounts of suspected terrorism financiers, businesses, residential and commercial properties belonging to the designated individual cannot be touched.

The case of Youssuf Nada and Ahmed Idris Nasreddine is illustrative. Nada and Nasreddine operated a bank, Bank Al Taqwa, and a network of companies between Italy, Switzerland, Liechtenstein, and the Bahamas. The U.S. Treasury Department, which designated Al Taqwa and both men as terrorism financiers in the aftermath of the 9/11 attacks, claims that, since its foundation in 1988, Al Taqwa financed groups such as the Palestinian Hamas and the Algerian GIA. Moreover, according to the Treasury Department, Al Taqwa provided funding to al Qaeda until September of 2001 and granted a clandestine line of credit to "a close associate of Usama Bin Laden." European authorities have also designated the bank and the two financiers, but with scant results. Both men, financial experts with decades of experience, have devised a system of front companies, figureheads and secret bank accounts in off-shore banking paradises that allowed them to circumvent resolutions and shelter their finances from the authorities' action. And while Nada still maintains business interests in Switzerland and Liechtenstein, Nasreddine still owns a luxurious hotel in downtown Milan.

LEGAL OBSTACLES

The problems faced by European authorities in tackling terrorism financing are the same that prevent them from successfully prosecuting and dismantling terrorist networks operating on the continent. In many European countries, laws prevent intelligence agencies from sharing information with prosecutors or law enforcement agencies unless they follow a lengthy and complicated procedure. With few exceptions, the monitoring of individuals has to be authorized by a judge based on extremely strong evidence of the suspect's guilt presented to secure the order. Severe evidentiary requirements often prevent prosecutors from using information obtained by intelligence agencies in their cases. And prosecutors also have to prove the specific intent of an accomplice in a terrorist act, showing that he knowingly provided support to the person who carried out a terrorist attack.

These provisions are the product of centuries of democratic legal tradition and are meant to defend the citizen from the creation of a police state. They epitomize Europe's success in creating a civil society where the government cannot unduly interfere with its citizens' lives. But, at the same time, they create an ideal shelter for the terrorists. European laws need to be adapted to the new threat that it is facing.

"There has to be a balance between individual liberty on one hand and the efficiency of the system to protect the public on the other. In an ideal world, I would choose the first, but this is not an ideal world, and when dealing with Islamic extremists we have to be brutal sometimes," is the view of

Alain Marsaud, a member of the French Parliament and an antiterrorism magistrate. Marsaud's views represent France's attitude towards terrorism, as the French legal system provides investigators and anti-terrorism magistrates with powers that have no equal in Europe and in the United States as well.

But France is an isolated case. The aftermath of 9/11 showed that most European legal systems are not prepared to efficiently face the new legal issues that have arisen with the war on Islamic terrorism. The excellent work done by European intelligence agencies and law enforcement has often been thwarted by the courts, which are forced to enforce laws that do not adequately punish individuals that associate themselves for terrorist purposes. The German trials of Abdelghani Mzoudi and Mounir El Motassadeq, two of the accomplices of Mohammed Atta and the other hijackers in Hamburg, revealed how Europe often finds itself legally impotent against terrorism.

Mzoudi and Motassadeq, the only two men to go on trial in Europe in connection with the 9/11 attacks, have been engaged in a complicated legal battle against German authorities for more than three years. According to prosecutors, Mzoudi's Hamburg apartment served as the meeting place for a group of Islamic radicals who, bound by a common hatred for the United States and Jews, planned an attack that would shock the world. After countless meetings at Mzoudi's apartment, some members of the Hamburg cell went to the United States to attend flight schools and carry out the lethal 9/11 plan; others remained in Hamburg providing logistical help and wiring them money. Prosecutors assert that while the men who worked from Germany may not have known every detail of the plot, they were well aware of the fatal intentions of their U.S.-based cohorts. For instance, Mounir Motassadeq allegedly told a friend, "[The 9/11 hijackers] want to do something big. The Jews will burn and we will dance on their graves."

Motassadeq and Mzoudi were charged in Hamburg with being accessories to the murder of more than 3,000 people and being members of a terrorist organization. Motassadeq was initially found guilty and sentenced to 15 years. Mzoudi's trial was more complicated, as, by the time it began, Ramzi Binalshibh, one of the key members of the Hamburg cell, had been arrested in Pakistan. Mzoudi's lawyers demanded that they could examine Binalshibh, whose testimony they alleged was essential to uncover Mzoudi's real role. Since the U.S. government, which has detained Binalshibh since his arrest, refused to even disclose Binalshibh's location, German judges reluctantly acquitted Mzoudi. "*Mr. Mzoudi, you are acquitted, but this is no reason to celebrate,*" said the presiding judge, adding that the court was not convinced he was innocent and that he had been acquitted only because the prosecution had failed to prove its case. A month after Mzoudi's acquittal, an appeal court ordered a retrial for Motassadeq, claiming that he had been denied a fair trial because the US had refused to allow the testimony of Binalshibh.

The difficulty faced by German prosecutors in the case of both Mzoudi and Motassadeq lies in the fact that the two were facilitators, sending money and providing apartments to terrorists but not actually carrying out terrorist acts themselves. Indeed, the lawyers for both men have argued that their clients believed they were simply helping fellow Muslims. When asked why he wired money to 9/11 pilot Marwan al-Shehhi, Motassadeq explained: *"I'm a nice person, that's the way I am."*

Great Britain, America's closest ally in Afghanistan and Iraq, has similarly tied its own hands. Radical imams openly preach hatred for the West and incite worshippers in the mosques of London to carry out attacks inside England. And recruiters have operated freely in Britain for more than a decade, as the story of Hassan Butt proves. With British forces still battling the Taliban in Afghanistan, the British public was shocked to read in the tabloids the interview with Hassan Butt, a British-born Muslim who bragged: *"I have helped to bring in [to Afghanistan] at least 600 young British men. These men are here to engage in jihad against America and its allies.... That there are so many should serve as a warning to the British government. All of them are prepared to die for the cause of Islam."* Despite his activities and his not-so-veiled threats to the British government, Butt was allowed to return to England undisturbed.

Upon his return to England, Butt was contacted by a reporter from The *Mirror* and agreed to be interviewed for the price of 100,000 Pounds. When The *Mirror*'s reporter informed British counterterrorism officials of the meeting and asked them if they wanted to interview Butt themselves, their response was shocking: *"I know this sounds ridiculous,"* said a detective from the Anti-Terrorist Squad, *"But we can't get involved. All our checks, all our intelligence, show that he is not wanted for any offences in the UK."* Since recruiting for a foreign terrorist organization operating overseas was not a crime in Britain, Butt could not be charged with any crime.

Another example of this frustrating situation and of its dangerous consequences is represented by the results of a 2003 Dutch intelligence investigation on a group of 40/50 young North African radicals. Dutch intelligence had collected important information on the men, revealing their ties to some of the masterminds of the May 2003 Casablanca bombings and other terrorists throughout Europe. Moreover, some of the men had expressed their desire to die as martyrs and to kill prominent members of the Netherlands' political and cultural establishment. In the fall of 2003, some of the men were arrested. Nevertheless, the men had committed no crime and the Dutch legal system forbade the use of information obtained by intelligence agencies in a trial. As a consequence, the men had to be released.

Predictably, after a few months, the group decided to go into action. Last November, one of its members, Mohammed Bouyeri, who had been under surveillance for months, gunned down and tried to ritualistically behead in the middle of one of Amsterdam's busiest streets Theo van Gogh, a popular Dutch filmmaker who, according to Islamists, had dared to offend Islam with a controversial movie about the treatment of Muslim women.

A similar situation occurred in Spain, as some of the key planners and perpetrators of the Madrid train bombings had been known to Spanish intelligence as radical Islamists with ties to terrorism since 1999. Some of them had had their phone conversations intercepted and their apartments searched, but no charge could be brought against them since, technically, they had committed no crime.

Unfortunately, the results in the cases in Britain, Holland, and Spain are not the exception, but the rule. The legal systems of most European countries do not have provisions that provide authorities with preemptive measures that can be taken against a known fundamentalist who is overheard saying he wants to "die as a martyr," unless evidence of a specific plan is also uncovered. Moreover, the laws of few European countries adequately punish activities that, while not directly harming people, are instrumental and necessary to the execution of a terrorist attack. Enabling a terrorist to enter the country by supplying him with a false document is equally important as providing him with the explosives, but few countries punish the two crimes with the same severity.

THE IRAQI CONFLICT AND OTHER REPERCUSSIONS FOR THE UNITED STATES

Before 9/11, recruiting individuals for a terrorist organization, as long as the group operated outside of the country, was not a crime in most European countries. While some countries have recently changed their laws to allow prosecution, the phenomenon of recruitment in Europe is taking place with even greater intensity than it did prior to 9/11, and its consequences are dire for both Europe and the United States. Shielded by the fact that recruitment for a terrorist organization is difficult to prosecute, and exploiting the widespread opposition to the Iraqi war within Muslim communities in Europe, recruiters have been sending hundreds of European Muslims to Iraq, joining the ranks of the insurgency that is fighting U.S. and Iraqi forces on the ground.

In 2003, an investigation launched by Italian authorities dismantled a network that recruited more than 200 young Muslims in Germany, France, Sweden, Holland and Italy to train and fight with Ansar al Islam, the al Qaeda–linked group led by Abu Musab al Zarqawi that has carried out dozens of attacks against American and Iraqi civilian targets. Reportedly, five young Muslims recruited in Milan have died in suicide operations in Iraq, including the attack against the Baghdad hotel where U.S. deputy secretary of defense Paul Wolfowitz was staying. The investigation revealed that the network that had sent the volunteers to Iraq was the same that had recruited hundreds of militants before 9/11 for the al Qaeda training camps in Afghanistan, showing the continuity and adaptability of terrorist networks that have been operating in Europe for more than a decade.

The Iraqi war is also presenting evidence of a different phenomenon, the involvement of extremely young European Muslims who do not belong to any organized network or terror group, but who, nevertheless, feel the sudden urge of fighting "the infidels." While the Italians dismantled a very sophisticated network that had close links to Zarqawi and al Qaeda's leadership, investigators throughout Europe have noticed that many of the volunteers who leave for Iraq are groups of teenagers, high school students, and petty criminals from the continent's poor immigrant neighborhoods with no connections to a terrorist group, who seemingly decide to act on their own.

This phenomenon is the direct consequence of the social crisis that is affecting Europe, as local governments are struggling to integrate the continent's soaring Muslim population. And while it is true that only a minority of the millions of Muslims living in Europe espouse radical views or support violent activities, the dangerous consequences of the actions of this minority cannot be overstated. Every act of violence or foiled terrorist plot increases the rift between Muslims and the native European population. The brutal killing of van Gogh, for example, brought turmoil to the Netherlands, traditionally one of Europe's most tolerant and peaceful societies. Mosques and Islamic schools were firebombed in the wake of the filmmaker's assassination and a poll conducted after the attacks revealed that 40% of Dutch hoped that Muslims "no longer felt at home" in Holland. In retaliation, groups of Dutch Muslims attacked churches, igniting a spiral of hatred.

The spread of Islamic radicalism and terrorism in Europe needs to be closely monitored by the United States and not only for the historical and cultural links between the US to Europe. Hundreds of Islamist terrorists have, either by birth or through naturalization, European passports and can, therefore, enter the United States without a visa and with just a summary scrutiny once they attempt to enter the U.S. borders. It is not a coincidence, for example, that the three men who have been charged just two weeks ago for their role in a plot to attack various financial institutions in the United States were all British citizens whom al Qaeda had dispatched on several surveillance missions to the States, counting on the fact that their British passports would have made their entrance into the US easier.

As the attacks of 9/11 have painfully shown, events that occur overseas can have a direct impact on the security of this country and its interests abroad. It is therefore crucial for the United States to follow carefully the events taking place in Europe and to closely cooperate with its European counterparts, as only a global effort can defeat this global enemy.

NOTE

1. Jordanian-born Abu Musab al-Zarqawi was best known as the leader of the terrorist group al Qaeda in Iraq (see p. 68 note 1).

3

"EUROPE HAS BECOME A CENTRAL 'FIELD OF JIHAD'"

Daniel Benjamin

On April 5, 2006, Daniel Benjamin testified before the Senate Foreign Relations Committee's Subcommittee on European Affairs regarding Islamist extremism in Europe. His prepared statement, reproduced below, reviews incidents of Islamist terror in Europe and analyzes both the growing alienation of European Muslims and the growing anti-immigration sentiment among Europeans.

* * *

Distinguished Members of the Senate Foreign Relations Committee: I want to thank you for the opportunity to appear before you today to discuss the critical issue of Islamist extremism in Europe. The growth of radicalism in virtually every part of the world today is a matter of concern. But there may be no regions in which American interests will be more profoundly affected by this phenomenon than in Europe. In my view, Europe has become a central "field of jihad," and so I commend the committee for taking an interest in this issue. I am particularly pleased to have the chance to speak with you just one day after the publication of "Currents and Crosscurrents of Radical Islamism: A Report of the Center for Strategic and International Studies Transatlantic Dialogue on Terrorism." European jihadism has been a core issue for the Transatlantic Dialogue, which is now in its third year, and I am glad to be able to share some insights from our conferences and to provide you with copies of the report.

It is an unwelcome irony that Europe, which emerged from the cold war more united, peaceful and prosperous than at any other time in history, may be threatened by jihadist violence as much as any other part of the world outside Iraq. Europe, as home to the world's largest Muslim diaspora, is at the heart of the battle over Muslim identity. Europe's experience with jihadist terror is already a long one: It served as the logistics and planning base for the September 11 attacks, which were prepared principally in

Hamburg, and as a haven for many Islamists who fled repression over several decades. In the 1990s the continent was roiled by fighting between Muslims and Christians in the Balkans that was primarily an ethnic conflict, but one that was exploited skillfully by jihadists for operational and propaganda purposes.

The March 2004 Madrid bombings, the assassination of Dutch artist Theo van Gogh in November 2004 and the July 2005 London attacks affected Europe profoundly, puncturing the feeling that many shared after September 11 that the United States was the primary target and that Europeans had little to fear. But the awakening came not because of a change in jihadist targeting but because the terrorists had failed repeatedly in their earlier attempts. In 2001 they had tried to bomb the Strasbourg Cathedral and the U.S. air force base in Kleine Brogel, Belgium; a cell in London was broken up in 2003 for conspiring to produce the toxic agent ricin, while another in Germany was planning a series of attacks against Jewish targets. European intelligence services estimate that radical Islamists have planned as many as thirty "spectaculars" since September 11. As one British official put it before the attacks of July 2005, "We've been very, very lucky." In light of a Home Office estimate of 10,000–15,000 British Muslims who "actively support" al Qaeda or related groups, strong evidence that Abu Musaab al-Zarqawi's network is growing in Europe and a raft of other indicators, the verdict remains a fair one even after July 7 of last year.

Much of Europe's problem owes to the fact that the individual Muslim's identity is sharply tested there. Most of the continent's Muslims arrived in the 1950s and 1960s as workers to fill postwar Europe's labor shortage, and they stayed on in countries that, for the most part, neither expected nor wanted to integrate them into their societies. It soon became apparent, however, that there was no easy way to send these workers back or to stanch the flow of family members seeking reunification with loved ones—let alone to stop them from having children. As a result, Europe has sleepwalked into an awkward multiculturalism. Its Muslim residents, many of them now citizens, live for the most part in ghetto-like segregation, receive second-rate schooling, suffer much higher unemployment than the general population, and those who do work are more likely than their Christian counterparts to have low-wage, deadend jobs. Indeed, it is this marginality that helps to explain the appeal of radicalization. The Madrid cell was composed of a host of men on the margins—drug dealers, part-time workers, drifting students—and this has been a pattern among jihadists for some time. The Hamburg cell that carried out the September 11 attacks was financially better off and its members tended to come from higher income families, but they too were drifting through Europe as their hatred deepened. L'Houssaine Kherchtou, a Moroccan al Qaeda member in the 1990s, described in a U.S. court how he had floated around the continent, working haphazardly and often illegally before finding his way to Milan and recruitment for jihad.

This class of potential terrorists may continue to exist for as long as Europe absorbs cheap labor from across the Mediterranean in North Africa. A parallel development has arisen out of the continent's ongoing political and economic unification, which has undercut the power of traditional national identity, especially among young people. The citizens of the various member states of the European Union still consider themselves to be French, or Polish, or British, but with the emergence of a single currency and EU passports, a world in which individuals choose from among multiple identities has come to be taken for granted. European Muslims have the same sense of choice when it comes to identity, and many are picking religion as their determining trait. For example, according to a 2002 survey of Muslims in Great Britain, 41 percent of the respondents under thirty-five years of age described themselves as solely "Muslim," rather than "British and Muslim," which was one of the other choices on the questionnaire. (One out of three respondents over the age of thirty-five felt the same.) Much the same trend has been documented in France, as well, where preferential identification with Islam among Muslims increased by 25 percent between 1994 and 2001. Given the inclination that Christian Europeans feel for a broader, transnational identity, it is not surprising that many Muslims also want to feel that they are part of something bigger. Identification with the new umma, or global community of Muslims, and its predominantly Salafi orientation has become an attractive alternative. The Internet, which delivers both news and an unambiguous interpretation of events from such distant places as the Palestinian territories, Chechnya and Kashmir, has had a profound impact in increasing the distribution of radical ideas. As a result, we have seen the emergence of the transnational identity in which there is a powerful sense of grievance in which the global and local are merged.

As the just-issued report of the CSIS Transatlantic Dialogue on Terrorism observes: Among individuals who actually do commit violence or seek to do so, there appears to be a greater sense of the inseparability of global and local grievances. Many Dialogue participants have echoed the generalization of former German Chancellory counterterrorism official Guido Steinberg's assessment that "Local motivations are key in what we call the global terrorist threat, but these local factors have diminished in recent years and are being replaced by international inspirations, by the international jihad." As one European participant put it, "recruitment takes place at a local level, but the motivations that guide the group can be both local, such as unemployment, discrimination, etc., and global, such as Iraq, Afghanistan and Guantanamo." An oft-cited example of how local and global grievances merge, the case of Mohammed Bouyeri, the young Dutch Muslim who murdered Theo van Gogh is frequently cited. In the manifesto-cum-poem that Bouyeri pinned to the chest of his victim, outrage was expressed at the United States, for the invasion of Iraq, and Israel, for the plight of the Palestinians, and, interestingly, comparable animus was directed against the Dutch state for considering a proposal to screen Muslim applicants for public sector jobs for radical leanings.

Iraq, as you have heard, receives prominent mention in this discussion. Let me simply note that, without a doubt, European Muslims had ample discontents before the U.S. toppled the regime of Saddam Hussein. Nonetheless, the invasion has had the effect of turbo-charging that unhappiness. The Madrid bombers were obsessed with Iraq and watched with delight a videotape of Iraqis gloating over the bodies of seven Spanish intelligence agents killed outside Baghdad in November 2003. The London bombers and Bouyeri are all known to have been outraged by America's military action.

The spread of Salafism—and within Salafism, the jihadist ideology, which has a potent minority voice—in Europe has been further facilitated by a lack of homegrown clerics. The number of mosques has grown dramatically in the past decade along with the sharp increase in Muslim population, but Europe does not have the thousands of clerics needed to meet this need. There are no privately endowed institutions for religious training, as are commonplace in the United States, and there are no state-funded seminaries, as are provided for officially recognized faiths. European governments are now wrestling with the complex issue of providing religious training and licensing preachers, but it will be years before such a system is in place and begins to graduate the imams needed to meet the spiritual needs of Europe's Muslims. In the meantime, European Muslim communities must rely on clerics from the Middle East and South Asia for religious guidance and leadership in prayer. Saudi Arabia, Egypt, North Africa, and Pakistan have been producing a surplus of imams, but many of them are imbued with a Salafist orientation and hostility toward secular European values. The result is that Salafist clerics wield an outsized influence on the debate over the evolving shape of Islamic belief and practice in Europe.

Prospects for the containment of radicalism must be seen in the near term as limited. Although the news media have paid much attention in recent years to the emergence of European anti-Semitism, a burgeoning anti-Muslim sentiment may yet become the bigger and more troubling phenomenon; it is already helping to drive the deepening alienation of European Muslims. In France, researchers found that 20 percent of those they spoke with conceded a dislike of North Africans, the largest Muslim group in the nation, and 62 percent told pollsters that Islamic values were incompatible with the French Republic. A larger percentage said that they considered Islam to be an intolerant religion, and almost two in three respondents stated that there are too many immigrants in France—immigrants, of course, being code for Muslims. The situation in Germany is similar. One in five Germans agrees with the statement, "Germany is a Christian country and Muslims have no business here." More than two out of three respondents believe that Islam does not fit in with Western culture and almost as many say Germany has too many foreigners. Over 80 percent of those polled in 2004 associate Islam with the word "terrorism." In Britain, one in ten people think that peaceful coexistence of non-Muslims and Muslims in Britain is impossible. One in three disagreed with the statement, "In general, Muslims play a valuable role in British society," and two-thirds thought that Britain's Muslims do "little" or "nothing" to promote tolerance. Not surprisingly, Britain's Muslims are not particularly happy with how they are treated by the wider society. One-third of them say that either they or someone they personally know has been subjected to abuse or hostility because of their religion; over half say that the position of Muslims has worsened since the Iraq war began in March 2003. Two in three stated that antiterrorism laws are applied unfairly against Muslims, nearly half would oppose an oath of allegiance to Britain, and 70 percent think that Muslims are politically underrepresented. When some of the British government's top civil servants met after the Madrid bombings to discuss how to defeat al Qaeda domestically, the picture that confronted them was deeply unsettling. Muslims had three times the unemployment rate of the entire population—only 48 percent of the Muslim population was working, well below the level for the population as a whole (68 percent)—and Britain's ten most underprivileged districts were home to three times as many Muslims as non-Muslims. Although terrorists rarely come from the poorest sectors of society, their sense of grievance is often nourished by the impoverishment of their fellow Muslims. In all, the Home Office estimated, "There may be between 10,000 and 15,000 British Muslims who 'actively support' al Qaeda or related groups."

This is more than a matter of a bad atmosphere: Europe's right-wing political parties have profited significantly from popular antipathy to Islam and have made real inroads by stressing anti-immigration politics. In the 2002 presidential election in France, Jean-Marie Le Pen of the National Front won a place in the runoff against incumbent Jacques Chirac. Belgium's Flemish Bloc, Denmark's People's Party, Italy's Northern League, and Switzerland's People's Party have all registered gains, though none has actually gained power. In Britain the Conservative Party leader Michael Howard centered much of his 2005 election campaign against Prime Minister Tony Blair on an anti-immigration theme. The ascendancy of nativist sentiment has pushed political discourse to the right. The center has moved and popular support for the liberal policies that have long characterized the relationship between state and society within Europe has diminished. Among the first fruits of the rightward shift has been the ban on headscarves in French schools and the Dutch decision to expel 26,000 asylum seekers from the Netherlands. The next steps will likely be in the realm of tightened law enforcement and immigration controls. European Muslims will naturally interpret these measures as being directed against them and may well become even more defensive and less interested in assimilation. Thus accelerates a dynamic of alienation, with the Christian Europeans becoming increasingly hostile to the self-segregating Muslims.

The sense of antipathy Muslims encounter in Europe is not just a matter of quiet slights on the street. Anti-immigrant sentiment is on the rise, and the inroads made by rightwing parties that espouse it have fueled many Muslims' sense of embattlement. The remarks of some European leaders have also displayed a remarkable hostility. In 2001, Italian Prime Minister Silvio Berlusconi set off an international furor when he declared the superiority of European civilization to that of Islam, adding that the West, "is bound to [Westernize] and conquer new people. It has done it with the Communist world and part of the Islamic world, but unfortunately, a part of the Islamic world is 1,400 years behind." More recently, the Queen of Denmark announced flatly that "We are being challenged by Islam these years.... We have to show our opposition to Islam."

These tensions will worsen in the coming years as Europe's demographic crisis and its antipathy to outsiders sharpen—as Christian Europe continues to shrink and Muslim Europe grows. Approximately one million Muslims arrive in Western Europe every year, about half seeking family reunification and half in search of asylum. As many as another half a million are believed to be entering the EU illegally annually as well. More important is the fact that the fertility rate among these immigrants is triple that of other Europeans. Consequently, the Muslim population is younger than the non-Muslim population, and Europe's Muslim population is likely to double from about 15 million in 2005 to 30 million by 2025. At the same time, current demographic projections show that Europe's non-Muslim population is stagnant or shrinking. Europe could well be 20 percent Muslim by 2050. Bernard Lewis, the renowned historian of Islam, may turn out to be right in his prediction that by the end of the twenty-first century the European continent would be "part of the Arabic west, the Maghreb."

Friction in Europe between Muslims and non-Muslims is likely to increase as these demographic changes take hold and as anti-immigration policies become more commonplace. Larger youth populations tend to be associated with higher levels of criminal activity, which will further rankle the non-Muslim population. Some of the greatest irritants will be over matters of religious practice: wearing headscarves, obtaining halal meat—ritual slaughter is controversial in several European countries and is banned in Switzerland because it is seen an inhumane—and the provision of workplace facilities for prayer five times a day. The socioeconomic problems that make the lives of many Muslims in Europe miserable—ghettoization, unemployment, lower wages, unequal access to education, discrimination in the workplace—are unlikely to disappear and the resulting discontent is likely to be expressed in religious terms. Against this background of anomie, jihad looks good to young European Muslims. It is empowering, promising the chance to do something dramatic, to assert oneself and punish one's tormenters.

It is impossible to say how far the radicalization will go. Olivier Roy, the French scholar who has done the most to describe the globalization of Islam, argues that the jihadist phenomenon will be contained by Muslim communities that recognize it as a danger to their well being. If that means that jihadists are not likely to dominate the communities, the prediction is probably correct—the numbers of those committed to violence is low. But we should not commit the fallacy of numbers. Small increases in the number of terrorists can make a big difference in the dimensions of the threat in an era when the technologies of destruction are increasingly available.

The eruption of jihadist violence in Europe must become a major concern for Washington for reasons that transcend concern for the safety of friends across the Atlantic. For one thing, the United States and Europe share a security perimeter. Not only are there more Americans and American businesses in Europe than virtually anywhere else, but most Europeans have easy access to the United States through the visa waiver program. (It is a disturbing oddity that the U.S. immigration system is now optimized to allow in people from the area of the world where Islamist radicalism may be growing fastest.) Moreover, the numbers of radicals in Europe and the civil liberties protections means that the continent will remain the most likely launching pad for attacks against America.

If terrorist attacks multiply, the consequences for intercommunal relations in Europe could be severe. After the Madrid bombings, there was little backlash against Spain's Muslim community. But after the van Gogh murder, the story in the Netherlands, historically one of Europe's most tolerant societies, was different. Within a week, there were at least twenty reported cases of arson involving Muslim schools and mosques. After the London bombings, half a dozen more arson attacks were reported in Britain, though there was no serious damage.

A Europe distracted by intercommunal tensions and violence will make a poor partner for America in many areas, not least dealing with the global threat of radical Islam. As we all know, pressing broad reform agenda in the Muslim world will, over the long term, be a vital part of a strategy for rolling back the jihadist threat. Yet if European countries become absorbed by strife within their borders, their willingness to work with the United States on a more global approach could well decline. Already, there are clear signs that Europe will not follow through on its commitment to allow Turkey to negotiate accession to the European Union, and this is a source of real worry because strengthening Turkey's place in the West is one of the steps that has widely been considered a key part of the effort to strengthen moderates in the Muslim world. Moreover, if Europe becomes preoccupied with its own internal security issues, and in the very worst case, if the continent is incapable of controlling the terrorists within its borders, the security challenge for America could be of profound proportions.

4

LONDONISTAN

Melanie Phillips

The bombings of the London transit system in July 2005, followed by the aborted plot to blow up several transatlantic flights, showed that London had become a center for Islamic extremists, many of whom were born, reared, and educated in Britain. Exploiting British liberty and tolerance and the naiveté of British officials, radical Islamists had recruited and trained jihadists eager to engage in terrorism in Britain and other countries. That these Muslim terrorists,, who were prepared to kill and maim their fellow citizens in large numbers, were radicalized, not in the religious schools of Pakistan but "within the British society that had nurtured them," was a wake up call for British and European security agencies. Two years later, Britain faced two other terrorist attacks, one in London and the other in Glasgow, that did not succeed. The eight Muslim suspects arrested were medical professionals, seven of them foreign-born physicians residing in Britain, another sign that terrorists are often educated and far from poor. In her controversial book, *Londonistan* (2006), excerpted below, Melanie Phillips, a columnist for London's *Daily Mail*, analyzes the rise and growth of a jihadist network in Britain.

* * *

Two months after the London bombings in 2005, the British public was further jolted by a videotape that was suddenly all over the TV screens. It featured Mohammed Sidique Khan, the apparent leader of the first bomb plot, dressed in an anorak and Arab keffiyeh [headdress] and calmly talking the language of homicidal hatred against his own country, Britain, in a broad Yorkshire accent. He warned his fellow countrymen to expect more death and destruction unless the British government ceased to take part in the oppression of Muslims. "Our words are dead until we give them life with our blood," he said. "Therefore, we are going to talk to you in a language you understand.... We are at war and I am a soldier. Your democratically elected governments continuously perpetuate atrocities against my people and your support of them makes you directly responsible, just as I am directly responsible for protecting and avenging my Muslim brothers and sisters. Until we feel security, you will be our target. Until you stop the bombing, gassing, imprisonment and torture of my people, we will not stop this fight."

The "you" was Britain, and the "my people" and "we" were Muslims. Thus he drew a lethal line between the two. This Leeds boy had no allegiance to, nor identification with, the Britain where he was born and brought up. His allegiance was instead to the worldwide community of Muslims, the ummah.

Since the London bombings, both British Muslims and the wider community have systematically downplayed the religious significance of those atrocities and the religious motivation of those who carried them out. The ritualistic nature of the suicide attacks and their continuity with similar attacks around the world, whose one overwhelmingly consistent feature was their inspiration by religious fanaticism, were brushed aside. The radical hostility and disengagement displayed by Mohammed Sidique Khan towards the country of his birth were similarly not ascribed to the ideology of Islamism, at the core of which lies an irrational hatred of the West and a desire to subjugate it to the tenets of Islam. Instead, the British heard the phrase "atrocities against my people" and decided that Britain had been bombed because of its role in the invasion of Iraq. Despite the fact that the bombers had not been poor or marginalized but had been well educated, held down jobs and been to all eyes integrated members of the wider community, the British intelligentsia also decided that the roots of this impulse to mass murder lay in the segregation of Muslims within British cities. And the reason for such segregation was economics, discrimination, racism— anything but religion.

This played well with British Muslims, whose main reaction to the bombings was to disclaim responsibility for what had happened, to maintain that it was utterly "un-Islamic" and the bombers had been not proper Muslims, that the overwhelming majority of British Muslims were wholly opposed to violence and of moderate opinions, and that the main victims of the London bombings were in fact the Muslim community, who were being oppressed and victimized by "Islamophobic" reactions.

In the wake of such atrocities, it is certainly important not to demonize an entire community for the misdeeds of a few. With emotions so heightened, there is a risk of victimizing innocent people who have been besmirched by the activities of a small number doing violence in the name of the religion they all share. Last but not least, across the world it is Muslims who have been victims of Islamist terror in greater number than anyone else.

However, it is unfortunately not so easy to agree that British Muslims are overwhelmingly moderate in their views, and that those holding extremist views are so small in number as to be statistically insignificant. The crucial question is what exactly "moderate" is understood to be.

If "moderation" includes reasonableness, truthfulness and fairness, the reaction by British Muslims to the London bombings was not moderate at all. Yes, they condemned the atrocities. But in the next breath they denied that these had had anything to do with Islam. Thus they not only washed their hands of any communal responsibility but—in denying what was a patently obvious truth that these attacks were carried out by adherents of Islam in the name of Islam—also indicated that they would do nothing to address the roots of the problem so as to prevent such a thing from happening again.

In the immediate aftermath Mohammed Naseem, chairman of the Birmingham Central Mosque, said there was no proof that the London suicide bombers were Muslims. He called Tony Blair a "liar" and an "unreliable witness" and questioned whether CCTV footage of the suspected bombers actually showed the perpetrators. He said that Muslims "all over the world have never heard of an organisation called al Qaeda."

From such nonsense, it was but a short step to saying that those who did point out that the roots of such terrorism lay in Islamist ideology, and therefore expected the Muslim community to do something about it, were guilty of prejudice. Accordingly Sir Iqbal Sacranie, secretary general of the Muslim Council of Britain, was quick to say that "the real victim of these bombings is the Muslim community of the UK." And if the Muslim community was the real victim, then it followed that the British, far from being the targets of terrorism, were actually to blame for causing it by supporting the war in Iraq. This moral inversion was then turned into a threat that unless the British changed their foreign policy they could expect more of the same.

Thus Dr. Azzam Tammimi of the Muslim Association of Britain said:... "and God knows what will happen afterwards, our lives are in real danger and it would seem, so long as we are in Iraq and so long as we are contributing to injustices around the world, we will continue to be in real danger. Tony Blair has to come out of his state of denial and listen to what the experts have been saying, that our involvement in Iraq is stupid." The marketing manager for the *Muslim Weekly* newspaper, Shahid Butt, said: "At the end of the day, these things [violent incidents] are going to happen if current British foreign policy continues. There's a lot of rage, there's a lot of anger in the Muslim community. We have got to get out of Iraq, it is the crux of the matter. I believe if Tony Blair and George Bush left Iraq and stopped propping up dictatorial regimes in the Muslim world, the threat rate to Britain would come down to nearly zero."

Other Muslim groups went even further and supported terrorism in countries other than Britain, including by implication the violence against British and American forces in Iraq by relabeling it "resistance." A joint statement signed by groups including the Association of Muslim Lawyers, the Federation of Student Islamic Societies, the Islamic Human Rights Commission, the Muslim Association of Britain and *Q-News* magazine said: "The Muslim community in Britain has unequivocally denounced acts of terrorism. However, the right of people anywhere in the world to resist invasion and occupation is legitimate." The statement, which also opposed the banning of [the radical] Hizb ut-Tahrir and any proposal to close "extremist" mosques, went on: "If the government hopes to pander to Zionist pressure by condemning and excluding from this country people who are critical of Israeli apartheid, it is in fact supporting apartheid."

The charge that Israel is an "apartheid" society is of course one of the Big Lies propagated by the Muslim world. And relabeling terrorism as "resistance," if it takes place in connection with one of the iconic conflicts of Islamist demonology, is a sleight of hand to conceal support for the murder of innocents. It was therefore no surprise that the same statement dismissed the word "extremism" as having "no tangible legal meaning or definition" and being "unhelpful and emotive." For such views were indeed extremist. Yet most of these were supposedly mainstream organizations....

Concern about the extremist character of British Muslims does not rest solely on their responses to the London bombings. Survey evidence suggests that, while the vast majority do not support violence, a frighteningly large number do; and, beyond them, a much larger proportion dislike British values and would like to replace them by the tenets of Islam.

A survey carried out by the Home Office in 2004 provided deeply alarming evidence. It found that no fewer than 26 percent of British Muslims felt no loyalty to Britain, 13 percent defended terrorism and up to 1 percent were "actively engaged" in terrorist activity at home or abroad, or supported such activity. This last number, deemed "extremely small" by the Home Office, added up to at least sixteen thousand terrorists or terrorist supporters among British Muslims. Meanwhile the former Metropolitan Police commissioner Lord Stevens revealed that up to three thousand British-born or British-based people had passed through Osama bin Laden's training camps. Security agencies believed that the number who were actually prepared to commit terrorist attacks might run into hundreds. Polling evidence revealed similar numbers who supported attacks on the United States. In 2001, a BBC poll had found that 15 percent of British Muslims supported the 9/11 attacks on America. In 2004, a Guardian poll recorded that 13 percent of British Muslims thought that further terrorist attacks on the USA would be justified.

In addition, polling evidence revealed a dismaying amount of anti-British feeling among Britain's Muslim citizens. Following the London bombings, a poll found that the overwhelming majority rejected violence, with nine in ten believing it had no place in a political struggle. Nevertheless, one in ten supported the attacks on July 7, and 5 percent said that more attacks in the UK would be justified, with 4 percent supporting the use of violence for political ends.

The evidence of Muslim alienation from Britain was no less disturbing. Between 8 and 26 percent have said they feel either not very or not at all patriotic. Another poll revealed that while 47 percent said they felt "very loyal" to Britain, nearly one in five—more than one hundred thousand British Muslims—said they felt little or no loyalty at all. And while 56 percent said Muslims should accept Western society, 32 percent believed that "Western society is decadent and immoral and that Muslims should seek to bring it to an end."

These numbers were simply horrifying. While the vast majority were opposed to terrorism, the numbers who supported it were wholly intolerable and almost certainly unique; no other community in Britain contains such an enormous reservoir of potential violence against the state. Moreover, to have almost a third of the community hostile to Western society and wanting to bring that society to an end clearly makes a mockery of the claim that British Muslims are overwhelmingly moderate. That is a huge pool in which terrorism can swim.

Why are so many British Muslims so angry and alienated? After the Muslim riots of 2001 in northern English towns, a clutch of official reports concluded that the essence of the problem lay in the fact that Muslims tended to be segregated from the rest of the community, in terms of both where they lived and how they behaved. But this failed to address the further question of why they were segregated. To some extent, it was because poor, vulnerable communities with very different traditions do tend to stick together for mutual support in a strange culture. But there were two obvious flaws in this argument.

The first was that other minorities, like the Hindus, had no problem integrating at all. The second was that British Muslims drawn into terrorism were not necessarily poor or marginalized. As British officials had noted, they tended to fall into two groups: "a) well educated, with degrees or technical/professional qualifications, typically targeted by extremist recruiters and organizations circulating on campuses; b) under-achievers with few or no qualifications, and often a non-terrorist criminal background—sometimes drawn to mosques where they may be targeted by extremist preachers and in other cases radicalized or converted whilst in prison."

So it would appear that there is something particular to Islamic culture at this present time that makes it vulnerable to this kind of extremism. Indeed, since a number of terrorists are Muslim converts who have not come from these segregated communities, the reason goes beyond ethnicity or economics. And although many in Britain lean over backwards to deny this, the case that the cause lies in the religious culture itself is overwhelming.

One must acknowledge that the Muslim community in Britain is extremely diverse, consisting of many subcommunities with different geographical and cultural antecedents and views as well as different positions on the religious spectrum. Many British Muslims just want to get on with life and have no leanings towards religious extremism, let alone violence.

But the fact that so many do not succumb to religious extremism does not mean that it doesn't have a profound influence on others. And all the evidence suggests that a doctrinal radicalization that took root in Britain more than twenty-five years ago has fed upon a widespread sense of cultural dislocation, resulting in a disastrous effect upon many Muslim youths.

In recent decades, the Islamic world has succumbed in large measure to an extreme version of the religion that emerged out of the postcolonial ferment and the rise of Arab nationalism in the late nineteenth and early twentieth centuries. This version, which gave rise to the Muslim Brotherhood in Egypt in 1928, was promulgated by hugely influential Islamic thinkers such as Sayed Qutb and in India by Sayed Abu'l Ala Maududi, and later fused with the puritanical Wahhabi doctrine, that was the orthodoxy in Saudi Arabia.

THE ALIENATION OF
BRITISH MUSLIMS

Sayed Qutb (see part 1, chapter 3) laid down that Muslims must answer to God alone and that human government was illegitimate. It was therefore a proper target for jihad, which would be waged by true believers, "destroying the kingdom of man to establish the kingdom of heaven on earth." This approach is the basis of Islamism, whose defining characteristic is the belief that the world should be conquered for Islam. It is a doctrine that forms a continuum of clerical fascism which has at its extremity al Qaeda—but with many other punctuation points along its route....

The Islamic Foundation in Leicester espouses the ideas of the Jamaat al-Islami, whose guiding star was Sayed Maududi. He said: "The truth is that Islam is a revolutionary ideology which seeks to alter the social order of the entire world and rebuild it in conformity with its own tenets and ideals." In 1982, the Leicester foundation said in its declaration that the Islamic movement "is an organised struggle to change the existing society into an Islamic society based on the Koran and the Sunna and make Islam, which is a code for entire life, supreme and dominant, especially in the socio-political spheres." In 2005, the foundation's chairman and rector, Kurshid Ahmad, said that a revolutionary idea that lets people "try to change the world on the basis of values of faith in Allah, justice, service to humanity, peace and solidarity" was nothing to be frightened of.

For more than twenty years, therefore, the Islamic Foundation, a prestigious and influential institution in the Muslim community, has been effectively teaching sedition to British Muslims. In line with prevailing Islamic religious and political authority, it has preached the message that they have a religious duty to change Britain into an Islamic society. While not everyone who passed through its portals will have been thus influenced, a considerable number will have been, along with graduates of many other similarly radicalized Islamic institutions—profoundly altering the way British Muslims see themselves in relation to the wider community.

Dr. Taj Hargey, chairman of the Muslim Education Centre in Oxford, which promotes what he calls "progressive inclusive Islam," has said there is a virtual apartheid in parts of Britain, self-imposed by those Muslims who regard non-Muslims as *kuffar,* or inferior—although they would never say so in public. "We see it from the time you're a child, you're given this idea that those people they are *kuffar,* they're unbelievers. They are not equal to you, they are different to you. You are superior to them because you have the truth, they don't have the truth. You will go to heaven, they will go to hell. So we have this from a very young age."

This deeply alienating message has been amplified by the widespread perception of Western decadence. British Muslims are overwhelmingly horrified and disgusted by the loose and dissolute behavior of a Britain that has torn up the notion of respectability. They observe the alcoholism, drug abuse and pornography, the breakdown of family life and the encouragement of promiscuity, and find themselves therefore in opposition to their host society's guiding values. What they are recoiling from, of course, is the *breakdown* of Western values. After a visit to the United States in 1948, Sayed Qutb wrote: "Humanity today is living in a large brothel!" Similarly British Muslims have concluded that the society that expects them to identify with it is a moral cesspit. Is it any wonder, therefore that they reject it? . . .

The mosques have been widely blamed for preaching this radicalism, particularly through imams brought over from India and Pakistan who are supporters of Saudi Arabian Wahhabism or other similar ideologies. True as this may be, however, they are by no means the only or even the most important conduit for hatred and incitement. Even worse damage is being done over the internet, and within Britain in addition by a silent army of highly influential community interlocutors including youth workers, peripatetic teachers, prison counselors and a host of voluntary organizations moving below the official radar.

Moreover, British universities have been exceptionally important breeding grounds for Islamist radicalism—and almost wholly overlooked. The list of terrorists who have been through the British university system is striking. Ahmed Omar Saeed Sheikh, who masterminded the kidnap and murder of the U.S. journalist Daniel Pearl in Pakistan, attended a British public school before dropping out of the London School of Economics. Among the London bombers, Mohammed Sidique Khan and Shehzad Tanweer had studied at Leeds Metropolitan University. Zacarias Moussaoui, one of the Hamburg cell responsible for 9/11, had completed a master's degree at South Bank University, London. Afzal Munir, who was killed fighting in Afghanistan, had studied at Luton University. And there are many more.

5

"The French Path to Jihad"

John Rosenthal

Several French nationals or residents have fought with the Taliban in Afghanistan and the insurgency in Iraq. Zacarias Moussaoui, the most famous French jihadist, is now serving a life sentence in an American prison for his connection to 9/11. In the following selection, John Rosenthal, who writes on European politics, analyzes a published collection of interviews of suspected members of al Qaeda and fellow travelers in French prisons by social scientist Fared Khosrokhavar. Almost all these inmates were either born in France or were long-term residents of France who came originally from the Mahghreb, the North African area that had once been under French control. French was either their native language or they spoke it fluently. One theory challenged by Khosrokhavar is that jihadists are poor and uneducated. As the research shows, "jihadists are largely recruited from relatively more privileged social strata in their countries of origin. As a rule, the inmates interviewed are highly educated, well-traveled, and multilingual."

The interviewees generally did not come from devout families but turned to Islam as a means of self-identification and self-respect, which they felt that French society denied them. As one of the inmates stated: "In France, a part of my personality was under attack, pushing me toward schizophrenia. It was under attack from infancy. I had the choice between schizophrenia as a Frenchman and the recovery of my identity in struggle against the society that denies me my dignity and the most ancestral part of my identity." Another inmate said that before turning to Islam, he had "admired the French and Westerners for their technical knowledge [savoir-faire] and their power. Now, Islam has given me self-respect, and I know that it is the West that incarnates vice and adultery, moral depravation and imperialism." Now no longer despising himself, he asserts that "all my rage is turned toward the West with its viciousness and lies."

The inmates expressed a hatred of France that was personal and deeply felt, as they testified to suffering from racism and expressed their firm belief that no matter how well-educated they were and whatever their efforts to live a typical French life, they would "always be outside the system" and treated as "criminal associations."

But ultimately France was not the target of their jihadist activities. Rosenthal describes how the inmates transfer their hatred from the "lived" experience of France to an imagined enemy, the United States/Israel, two countries fused into one entity in their minds. Lacking the personal experience of America that they have of France, the inmates obtain most of their ideas and imagery from the media. They are constantly exposed to images on TV that show the Palestinians struggling against Israeli oppressors, and they are convinced that an all-powerful and malevolent United States is ultimately responsible for this oppression and all other evil in the world. Rosenthal points out that these strong anti-American and anti-Israeli convictions mirror those of the European left that also shape much public discourse in Europe.

* * *

[A] just-published collection of interviews with suspected members of al Qaeda in French prisons, *When al Qaeda Talks: Testimonials from behind Bars,* provides us with an unprecedentedly large body of evidence on the backgrounds, worldview, and motivations of those who make the choice for violent jihad in the name of Islam.

The interviews were conducted between 2001 and 2003 by Farhad Khosrokhavar of France's preeminent social science faculty, the École des Hautes Études en Sciences Sociales. . . . [The interviewees] make no secret of their adherence to a radical or "rigorist" practice of Islam, nor of their acceptance of violent jihad as a legitimate—and, under certain circumstances, even obligatory—aspect of it. In more unguarded moments, some admit their own participation in jihad: either implicitly and without entering into details or explicitly in relation to actions—for instance, fighting with foreign mujahideen forces in the Bosnian civil war—that will not complicate their legal situation in France. Others reflect openly upon joining the jihad—in order, most often, to fight against the U.S. and Israel—upon their release. Still others seem indeed to have merely had casual contacts with jihadist circles, a fact that under France's remarkably broadly written statute on "criminal associations" was sufficient to earn them prison time. Even the members of the latter group, however, do not hide their admiration for the jihadists whose friendship or acquaintance has landed them in jail.

In addition to the ten interviews with the suspected al Qaeda members, the Khosrokhavar volume also includes four interviews with other inmates, for the most part convicted on lesser charges, who might best be described as fellow travelers. (One of these, a convert to Islam, has also been charged with membership in a "criminal association" preparing a terrorist act, so it is not clear why he is treated separately from the ten al Qaeda.) The subjects of the Khosrokhavar interviews defy the stock image that many Western observers will have of Islamists as highly exotic Arabic-speakers from the Middle East. On the contrary, they are, in effect, "Western" or at least "nearly Western." They all speak fluent French, and French for the most part—not

Arabic—is their mother tongue. The learning of Arabic—in order to be able to read the Qur'an in the original—is indeed frequently mentioned in the interviews as a crucial stage in the process of the inmates' Islamic radicalization. Several of the inmates—perhaps as many as half—were born in France, including the convert. The rest come from the Maghreb, the formerly French-controlled territories of the southern shore of the Mediterranean, with the largest contingent from Algeria. All but one, however, have lived for extensive periods in France. (The one exception is "Mohammad," the veteran of the Bosnian war, who astonishingly claims never to have set foot in France prior to his extradition.) Most are French citizens; some have earned advanced degrees from French universities; and even if they happen to have grown up in the Maghreb, French culture, as their testimonials make abundantly clear, has been a constant point of reference in their lives.

While Khosrokhavar's sample of Islamists may not be "typical," in light of this strong French connection, the fact is that Islamism as a self-consciously transnational ideology—in this respect, as in so many others, resembling twentieth-century Marxism-Leninism—draws its adherents from widely different parts of the globe: both from the *Dar al-Islam*, the traditional Islamic lands, and from the *Dar al-Dawa*, the lands of Islamic proselytism. In contemporary Islamist discourse—in the fatwas of Yusuf Al-Qaradawi, head of the European Council for Fatwa and Research, for example, or in the writings of Qaradawi's admirer Tariq Ramadan (see part 6, chapter 5)—Europe precisely represents a privileged terrain for Dawa: for proselytism. It is thus distinguished from, say, Russia or Israel or, for that matter, the United States, all of which, as judged by the practice of the jihadists, clearly fall within the *Dar al-Harb*: the lands "of war" targeted for military defeat. . . .

THE PRIMORDIAL ENEMY

The Khosrokhavar interviews burst numerous clichés about the jihadists and the sources of their militancy. Lest anyone still cling to the illusion that the root cause of Islamic terror is poverty and economic inequality, for instance, the interviews massively reinforce the findings of the already substantial body of research on Arab Islamists showing that jihadists are largely recruited from relatively more privileged social strata in their countries of origin. As a rule, the inmates interviewed are highly educated, well-traveled, and multilingual. . . . The inmates' more or less openly avowed enthusiasm for jihad is clearly not the product of a spontaneous reaction to desperate circumstances, but rather the outcome of an often highly intellectualized process of reflection. . . .

. . . [A] remarkable fact that emerges in the course of the Khosrokhavar interviews: that many—perhaps the majority—even of those inmates who obviously merit being described as Islamists come precisely from nonpracticing or, so to say, barely practicing families. "He's a slacker Muslim (*musulman faineant*)," complains one "Moussa" about his father. The rigorism of their Islamic faith is clearly not inherited, but rather acquired. The same, indeed, is true of Zacarias Moussaoui[1], whose mother, according to Moussaoui's brother Abd Samad Moussaoui, resolutely refused to teach her children about Islam and took to celebrating Christmas when Zacarias and Abd Samad were teenagers.

It is in this connection that the learning of Arabic takes on its full significance in the biographies of many of the inmates. Several of the inmates place great emphasis on the importance of reading the Quran in the original and, as one "Ahsen" puts it, "without any intermediary." Even inmates whose connection to Islam is more superficial and who do not know Arabic recognize this as a worthy goal. "For me reading the Quran was a real revelation, an inner awakening," says Ahsen, who admits to having spent several years in Afghanistan with the Taliban. "I came to realize that one had to fight against the *mulhidun* (heretics) and the *rafhidun* (deviants), against the people of other religions who oppose Islam." In light of the violence associated with Islamism, it has become common to hear from Western observers that Islam as such needs to pass through its "reformation." But the emphasis placed by these inmates on their personal and unmediated relation to the text of the Quran suggests, on the contrary, that contemporary Islamism may well be the Islamic equivalent of the Reformation. It is worth recalling in this connection that the historical Reformation of Christianity also gave rise both to extreme rigorist currents (Calvinism) and to violent Millenarian sects.

But perhaps the most important—and, in light of conventional wisdom, surprising—revelation of the Khosrokhavar interviews concerns the identity of the nation that is virtually without exception the principal object of the Islamists' obviously fervent hatred: a nation that they are convinced despises and humiliates Muslims and has committed unpardonable crimes against them—namely, France. Hatred of France is the unifying thread running through the testimonials of the inmates and, as we shall see, clearly provides the primordial affect that has fueled the process of their radicalization (or that could fuel such a process in the case of the younger French-born inmates who have yet to take the plunge into organized political violence).

As would be expected, the U.S. also comes in for severe criticism from the inmates. So too, of course, does Israel, which is often treated—according to the well-known motif shared by Islamists and a large part of the European left—as of a piece with the U.S. The alleged "crimes" of Israel against Palestinian Arabs are, needless to say, a constant refrain, and the complicity of the U.S. in these "crimes" is taken for granted. It is clear that in the current state of the global jihad, the U.S. is thus regarded as the privileged target. France is evidently a lesser priority. . . .

Nonetheless, in comparison to the passionate and thickly detailed indictment that Khosrokhavar's Islamist interlocutors draw up against France, their hostility toward the U.S. has an abstract, theoretical air to it. It is, in short, a matter of doctrine. None of the interviewees exhibit any firsthand knowledge of the United States, nor could any of them plausibly claim to have witnessed American mistreatment of Muslims, much less to have been victims of such themselves. "Mohammad," for example, the veteran mujahideen who fought in the Bosnian war, allows: "As much as I detest the Americans, I have to admit it: the presence of the Americans in Bosnia saved the Bosniacs." This realization does not, however, prevent him from describing America as a "mad dog" in need of a good kick, nor from observing that on 9/11 Americans "reaped what they sowed."

By contrast, the hatred of France that the interviewees express is clearly a heartfelt product of experience, an experience that has both a historical and a personal dimension. As concerns the historical dimension, the testimonials of virtually all the suspected al Qaeda members leave no doubt that the single episode that most substantially contributed to their radicalization was the military coup in Algeria in January 1992—a coup that is widely believed to have been carried out with French complicity and support. The coup prevented an Islamist party, the Islamic Salvation Front (FIS), from coming to power despite its clear victory in the first round of voting in elections the previous December. It was followed by the prohibition of the FIS and the mass arrest of FIS members. . . .

FRENCH MASKS, MUSLIM FACES

Ousman also speaks, and with sometimes remarkable eloquence, to the second, personal, dimension of the experience that, on the account of Khosrokhavar's Islamist interlocutors, led them not only to reject French society, but, in the phrase of Zacarias Moussaoui, to become France's "sworn enemies," namely, what they almost to a man perceive (or, at any rate, denounce) as French racism. The feelings the inmates express toward France in this connection are not necessarily without nuance and complexity. Indeed, Ousman's account of what he presents as his failed attempt at assimilation into French society resembles a tale of unrequited love—a love that, precisely by virtue of its lack of reciprocation, is transformed into hate. Here again it is worth quoting from his interview at length:

> Earlier France was my model—even if I also resented this. But my ideal was to be French, to act like the French: to have my wife, my kids, my car, my apartment, my house in the country, to become an average Frenchman and live in peace. . . . [E]ven before I had French citizenship or I had work, in my mind, I wanted to conform to the image of the average Frenchman, to be like them, to make myself in their image. But at the same time I had the feeling that this was more or less impossible: they didn't want me, even if I had citizenship and all the rest. They looked down on me, they treated me like I was nothing, they despised me. This contempt was killing me. Were we really so despicable? . . . I went back and forth between what I was and what I wanted to be: a little Frenchman. Whereas I was an Algerian. I was tortured by it. Some days, I couldn't fall asleep, I had the impression that my life had no meaning, that my part in life had been unjustly denied me.
>
> Islam was my salvation. I understood what I was: a Muslim. Someone with dignity, whom the French despised because they didn't fear me enough. Thanks to Islam, the West respects us in a certain way. One is scared of us.

We're treated as fanatics, as holy madmen, as violent people who do not
hesitate to die or to kill. But one doesn't despise us anymore. That is the
achievement of Islamism. Now, we are respected. Hated, but respected.

Ousman describes the process of his coming to Islam—in effect, on the
"bounce-back" from what he perceives as his rejection by French society—as
an "awakening," as his "reconquest of myself."

Even if the accounts of the other inmates do not attain the degree of
psychological vividness of Ousman's, it is remarkable how often the same
motif—of a "false" attempt to be or "become" French versus the "authentic"
Muslim "self"—is repeated in their testimonials. The younger French-born
inmates from immigrant families are, as a rule, particularly categorical about
the "impossibility" of their "becoming French"—even though, from a legal
standpoint, they are and always have been—and about the discrimination from
which they claim to have suffered. Thus, the "young banlieusard"[2] reports:

I have French citizenship. Even if it is written "French nationality" on your
identity card, in the eyes of the French you are not French. And, by the way, I
don't feel French any more than I feel Moroccan. I'm a Muslim: a true Muslim
who doesn't want to let himself be stepped on anymore.

Nonetheless, there is reason to doubt that his charges of French racism
amount to much more than alibi-making. At the same time, he admits that
his brothers and sisters are continuing with their studies and that they feel
"at home" in France. "They're frenchified [sic]," he complains. "They've lost
their roots, lost their honor, lost their sense of Islam."

It is important to note that in the most psychologically informative
accounts, the primary feeling is of "not being French." The "discovery" that
the "authentic"—or, at any rate, "not French"—self is in fact Muslim is a
secondary interpretation of this sense of "otherness." Thus, even an inmate
like Jacques [raised by his French Caribbean mother], who is not Muslim and
who has had very little personal connection to Islam, can claim that, by virtue of his "otherness" and his eagerness to defy the alleged racism of "the
French," he is, in effect, Muslim

To become someone who is feared, if not respected, one has to be openly
Muslim. Islam liberates. In this sense, I feel very Muslim. I even do Ramadan
with my "beur" [North African] brothers. I'm ready to embrace the religion of
Allah. I'm already Muslim in body and soul....

THE TRANSFERENCE OF HATE

In a long scholarly essay appended to the interviews, Khosrokhavar also
identifies the primordial importance of their grievances and/or complexes
vis-à-vis France in the biographical itineraries that have led the inmates to
radical Islam and its "anti-Western" jihad. He notes in this connection what
he calls a process of "generalization" of their hatred of France to "the West"

as such. The morose broodings of an Ousman provide just one illustration. But the interviews bear witness not only to such a process of generalization of the inmates' hate, but also—and, from the point of view of the real conduct of jihad, more crucially—to a process of transference of their hate from, so to say, its "lived" object, namely, France and French society, to an "imagined" object or, more precisely, two imagined objects that in the perspective of the inmates are fused into one, namely, Israel and the U.S. "The West," after all, is an abstraction. Inasmuch as it is a question of taking action—i.e., violent action in the framework of jihad—the designated target that stands in for the West in general and is substituted for France in particular is invariably the imagined Israelo-American monolith. The tight association of Israel and the U.S. in the discourse of the Islamists interviewed by Khosrokhavar is not, for the most part, given an openly anti-Jewish inflection. One highly revealing exception, however, is the "native French" convert. America, he says, "is hand in glove with the Jews," and he denounces the "domination" of Muslims by "the *yhudis* [Jews] and American Zionists."

One of the most fascinating and significant features of the Khosrokhavar interviews is that the mechanism of this transference of hate is clearly observable. Time and again, an inmate, having provided an inventory of the sources of his frustration in France, suddenly announces his intention to purge the full charge of his hatred in fighting against Israel and the United States. In virtually every instance, the switch that permits this transference to take place is explicitly designated. It is neither the preaching of radical Imams nor the indoctrination of Islamic organizations. Indeed, in a sense, it is not an ideological instrument at all, since the certainty with which it invests the inmates' convictions about American and Israeli infamy—a quasi-certainty tantamount to what they know from their own experience—is created through nonverbal means.

Consider, for instance, the diatribe of "Moussa," an Algerian-born Islamist who has lived for roughly a decade in France and is suspected of having ties with both the GIA [a radical Islamist group] and al Qaeda. "Islam is what saves us from the West," he says,

> from America, from all those who commit injustices against Muslims and oppress them: like Israel oppresses the Palestinian people. One sees on the television how the Israeli Army, with the help of America, mistreats the youth of the Intifada. When I see that, I want to go fight against them, against the Americans, against all those who repress Islam.

"Karim," a French national and another al Qaeda suspect, says that "France is pushing people toward extremism.... If you suspect the worst of us, we'll end up doing what we are accused of." Where exactly does such extremism lead? Karim explains further:

> You see: in prison the Jihadists are very respected by the other Muslim inmates. The others think that the Jihadists have dared to do what they, the other inmates, think is right but have not had the courage to do. They have taken action and

given a good lesson to the Americans who are repressing our brothers in Palestine or in Afghanistan. *Just watch the TV and the humiliation to which the Israeli army subjects the Palestinian chebab* [youth] [Rosenthal's emphasis].

When asked "Who are the enemies of Islam?" "Jacques," the Parisian-born fellow traveler, responds:

> You don't see? There are the Jews who are trying to push the Palestinians into the sea.... There is America, which is the closest ally of Israel. It's as if Israel were the 53rd state! They're hand in glove. When one sees on the TV how the Israeli tanks fire on youths armed with slingshots or Molotov cocktails and no one moves a finger. One asks oneself whether there is any justice in the world?

The implication of Jacques' remarks is clear: something should be done. And pressed by Khosrokhavar on the matter, he explains: "There are days when I am ready to enlist in the struggle against the Americans and the Israelis"—before adding: "and then I calm down and I think of my life and my future."

The source of the inmates' convictions about the injustices of which they accuse France is experience. What, then, is the source of their convictions about the injustice they believe Palestinian Arabs suffer at the hands of Israel and its presumptive American accomplice? "The TV." ...

It is, in effect, by way of the false immediacy of images of the Middle East conflict on the nightly news that the hatred the Islamists feel for France gets transferred to Israel. In the images of the Palestinian *chebab* doing battle with their homespun weaponry against the massively superior force of the Israeli Army, the French candidates for jihad see their own sense of victimhood reflected back to them in heroic guise. The Palestinian gunmen with their less wholesome Kalashnikovs and MI6s remain outside the frame. So too, needless to say—since, in any case, it is not accessible in images—does all the background and context that could render Israeli military actions in the West Bank or Gaza comprehensible and/or dissipate the aura of absolute victimhood in which Palestinian Arabs are almost invariably bathed in the French media....

The effects of such would-be representative and symbolically charged images of the Middle East conflict upon French and, more generally, European public opinion are well enough known. But the Khosrokhavar interviews clearly reveal the incitement they represent—incitement, namely, to jihad—for those in Europe or, for that matter, around the world who are psychologically predisposed to identify most intimately with Palestinian grievances. "When I see that," Moussa says, "I want to fight against them." ...

...The images of supposed Israeli mistreatment of Palestinians are taken by [the] inmates as bearing a constant meaning that is fully independent of the specific context of the events being depicted. Revealingly, Ousman associates these images with, as he puts it, "all injustice": "the sexual exploitation of children, the Americans who exploit Asia with their dollars, a girl who is prevented from wearing the veil." "All of that," he concludes, "drives me wild with rage." Palestinian suffering is thus elevated to a sort of summum of all unjust suffering, by which it follows that to redeem Palestinian suffering would be to redeem the injustice of the world. The religious structure of such thinking is obvious. The images are indeed "iconic" in more than just a metaphorical sense. But it is equally obvious that there is nothing specifically Islamic about such religious thinking and that it is also in evidence in the apotheosis of the Palestinian cause by a large part of the European and global left.

FIGHTING THE MALEVOLENT FORCE

Whereas such images in the media clearly provide the vehicle for the French Islamists' transference of their hate, they do not in themselves explain how America comes to be associated in their worldview with the "evil" or injustice that the images represent. Needless to say, this association is likewise taken for granted by the virtual entirety of the European left and is largely assumed in European public discourse more generally. In light of actual American support for Israel—support that has been set in relief over the past several years by the positioning of the EU as the principal external sponsor of the Palestinian Authority and diplomatic champion of Palestinian interests—this association might appear to be rational; and for those inclined to make it, undoubtedly it does.

If one considers the inmates' testimonials in their entirety, however, it is clear that the sources of the association are anything but rational. For in the discourse of the Islamist inmates—just as in the ambient discourse of contemporary European anti-Americanism—the U.S. is quite simply held to be responsible for every possible evil, real or imagined. Or, more precisely, in the discourse of the French Islamists, the U.S. is held to be responsible for every possible "evil" of which they do not themselves have direct personal experience. As we have seen, it is rather France that they hold accountable for perceived injustices that they have lived. With respect to matters, however, of which they have no experience and limited knowledge, the ambient anti-Americanism rushes to fill the void. Several of the inmates who do not share Mohammad's experience in the Bosnian war even manage somehow to blame America for the persecution of Bosnian Muslims!

It is indeed remarkable how little of a concrete character the Islamist inmates can cite to explain their hostility to the United States. Ousman's bizarre remark about "the Americans who exploit Asia with their dollars" is symptomatic in this regard. Significantly, virtually the only somewhat more concrete charge against the U.S. that the French Islamists can muster concerns the effects on Iraq's civilian population of the Iraqi trade embargo voted by the UN Security Council in 1990....

The French Islamists' conception of the U.S. as a kind of omnipresent and malevolent force, obscurely but all the more certainly implicated in the most various "evils" of a fundamentally unjust world, is clearly theological in nature. Testifying in his own defense in April [2006] and quickly finding himself at a loss to provide examples of the alleged American wrongdoing that he had come to the U.S. to combat, Zacarias Moussaoui managed to reduce this theology to its purest essence.... "Every child in Palestine is being killed because of you. What happened in Bosnia is because of you. You run the show." ...

The French Islamist inmates are evidently well aware that their ideas about the malevolence of American power, like their ideas about the exemplarity of Israeli "oppression," place them well within the French intellectual mainstream....

In any case, the "Islamism" of the inmates, like that of their comrade-in-arms Zacarias Moussaoui, is clearly a product not of the "Muslim world" alone, but rather of a certain encounter between Islamic traditions and modern European culture and society. When one considers that many of the leading intellectual figures in the history of the Islamist movement lived for extensive periods in Europe and did advanced studies in European universities, there is reason to believe that this mixed heritage is also characteristic of Islamist ideology more generally. The Iranian Ali Shariati, for instance, studied in Paris; the Sudanese Hassan Al-Turabi holds degrees from both the University of London and the Sorbonne; the Egyptian Said Ramadan—father of Tariq and son-in-law of Hassan Al-Banna, the founder of the Muslim Brotherhood—wrote a thesis on Islamic Law at the University of Cologne before settling in Geneva. Of course, the better-known European *cursus* of Muhammad Atta, Ramzi Binalshibh, and the other members of the "Hamburg Cell" who planned the 9/11 attacks shows that some of the key operatives of Islamic terror have followed a similar itinerary.

As the testimonials collected in the Khosrokhavar volume make clear, the encounter with Europe has often been a traumatic experience for Arabs and Muslims more generally. In a sense, the United States has not had much to do with the episodes that have made it such: neither with the history of European colonialism in northern Africa and the Middle East nor with the tensions and discontents that have accompanied Muslim immigration to Europe in the aftermath of decolonization. Indeed, in some contexts—for instance, the Suez Canal crisis—America even served as a brake upon the neocolonial ambitions that certain European powers continued to nourish vis-à-vis Arab countries in the aftermath of World War II.

But it is perhaps precisely America's exteriority to the relationship of Europe and the "Muslim world" that accounts for the ease with which a metaphysical anti-Americanism of distinctly European provenance could be grafted onto the discourse of contemporary Islamism. If, as Zacarias Moussaoui puts it, America "runs the show," then everything of which one disapproves in the "show" is, in the final analysis, America's fault. This simple postulate converts the United States into the universal scapegoat. The Khosrokhavar interviews amply illustrate how the specter of U.S. power permits resentments that have their sources in France and French policy to be "safely" channeled toward an external "enemy." Another example of the capacity of the anti-American postulate to dissipate—or indeed, in this, case, fully to volatilize—the sources of tension in Europe's relationship both to traditionally Muslim countries and to its own Muslim population comes from none other than Osama Bin Laden. Thus, in his "Letter to America," Bin Laden, in a remarkable feat of legerdemain, accuses the United States—not France—of being responsible for the 1992 Algerian coup and the repression that followed:

> When the Islamic party in Algeria wanted to practice democracy and they won the election, you unleashed your agents in the Algerian army onto them, and to attack them with tanks and guns, to imprison them and torture them—a new lesson from the "American book of democracy!!!"

The contrast with the testimonials of Bin Laden's own Algerian followers, as recorded by Khosrokhavar, is striking.

The integration of a metaphysical anti-Americanism with the rigorist canon of the Islamists represents a particular danger because it creates the prospect of a sort of "reconciliation" of Europe and Islamic extremism: in shared hostility to America. Such a prospect may be only an illusion. Nonetheless, the eagerness of some political currents in Europe to seek "dialogue" with precisely the world's most reactionary Islamic forces—from Hamas to Hezbollah to Mahmoud Ahmadinejad—bears unmistakable witness to the power of attraction it exerts. This being the case, it is clear that the solution to America's much-trumpeted "image problem in the Muslim world" is not be found in the "Muslim world" alone.

NOTE

1. Zacarias Mousaoui, the so-called "20th hijacker," was convicted by a U.S. court for his role in the 9/11 attack and sentenced in May 2006 to life in prison.
2. Literally, a resident of the suburbs. However, the term is applied here specifically to residents of suburbs with large Muslim populations and high rates of poverty and crime.

6

NOW THEY CALL ME INFIDEL: WHY I RENOUNCED JIHAD FOR AMERICA, ISRAEL, AND THE WAR ON TERROR

Nonie Darwish

Unlike European countries, the United States does not have large numbers of poor, unemployed, unassimilated, and frustrated Muslims living in low-income enclaves that are breeding centers of jihadism. Although there are exceptions, it is fairly common in American mosques for imams to preach the virtues of assimilation. Well-integrated into American society, educated, facing little discrimination, and solidly middle class, American Muslims are much less attracted than their European co-religionists to militant organizations committed to jihad and terrorism. Since 9/11 the authorities have found little evidence of "sleeper" cells operating in the United States. The government has deported several Muslim extremists, but relatively few individuals have been indicted, much less convicted, on the charge of involvement in terrorist acts. For these reasons, say some analysts, the real danger, emanates from terrorists coming from abroad, particularly from Europe.

Other analysts maintain that documented evidence of Islamic extremism in the past indicates the need for ongoing vigilance, for it is likely that Islamists have insinuated themselves into American society. These analysts refer back to February 1993, when Islamic terrorists set off an explosive device in the World Trade Center causing significant structural damage and leaving six people dead and more than one thousand injured. Also in 1993, the FBI uncovered a plot to bomb simultaneously several landmarks in New York City, including the Holland and Lincoln tunnels. In July 1997, acting on a tip, police thwarted an impending attack by two Palestinians intended to blow up a subway in Brooklyn during the morning rush hours as the train was passing through the tunnel under the East River. In 2001, six Yemeni-Americans from Lackawanna, New York were arrested for attending al Qaeda training camps overseas. In the spring of 2007, authorities broke up a cell of mostly ethnic Albanian Muslims planning to attack soldiers at Fort Dix in New Jersey and thwarted a conspiracy to blow up aviation fuel tanks and pipelines at John F. Kennedy International Airport in New York by men with links to Islamic extremists in South America and the Caribbean. Several Muslim charities in America had operated as fund-raising fronts for al Qaeda and other jihadist groups, and radical imams preaching virulent hatred of the West had, no doubt, enticed some Muslims to embrace the jihadist ideology, even if they would not take up arms in its support. Some groups on college campuses demonstrate support for Middle East terror organizations, and Saudi Arabian texts, tapes, and videos, which continue to circulate in Muslim schools and mosques, propagate an extreme fundamentalist and jihadist Wahhabi doctrine.

In *Now They Call Me Infidel: Why I Renounced Jihad for America, Israel, and the War on Terror* (2006), Nonie Darwish discusses, among other topics, Islamic extremists in the United States. Daughter of the former Egyptian military commander of Gaza, who died in battle with Israeli forces, Darwish worked as an Egyptian journalist before emigrating to America. Growing enamored of the religious and political freedom and the personal liberties, particularly for women, that she experienced in America, she felt compelled to warn her adopted country of the danger of radical Islam.

> My life has been a journey from hatred to love, from a culture that stifled joy and creativity, to a life of freedom and endless possibilities. Because I love my adopted country, I have a duty to alert my fellow Americans to a real and present danger. Radical Islam has declared war on America and the West and the majority of Muslims either support or make excuses for terrorism.

In the following excerpt from her provocative book, Darwish analyzes radical Islam and vents her anger at American Muslims for either supporting it or not doing enough to oppose it.

*   *   *

... I believe that the majority of Muslims who left Muslim countries, even if they don't admit it, have come to live under Judeo-Christian freedoms in America in search of a better future just as I did, a world that encourages personal responsibility and self-discipline and discourages envy, shaming, pride, and anger. Such a society is easier to live in. Nevertheless, once in America, some of them fall under the influence of the radical networks and organizations that dominate the mosques. There are many Arab and Muslim organizations that encourage Arab Americans to vote as a block and not as individuals with different preferences. It is hard to get rid of the bad habits of the old country since these behaviors are often spontaneous and seem normal. Many American mosques show no respect to their host country. They have come with the agenda of changing the culture and not to be part of America. Many of the imams get their salaries directly from oil-wealthy

Muslim nations who have sent them to America on religious visas and built their mosques. They don't have to pass the plate in the mosque for donations from worshippers and their salaries are guaranteed. Thus, they continue teaching the only thing they ever knew and are trained to do, and that is hate speech and anti-Semitism. Instead of being a source of comfort and wisdom, these preachers become a source of rage, hate, and subversion right here in America, working the worshippers into a frenzy of anger and paranoia not only against Western values and Israel but also against moderate Muslims who represent the majority of Arab Americans.

Unfortunately, these Muslim radicals within the United States are not here to live in a pluralistic society that has respect for all. They have come to Islamize America. They have also come to manipulate the new Muslim immigrants to the United States, keep them within their camp, and spread doubt and rejection of America among their ranks. Many of them are easy prey since that was the way they have lived in the old country. These immigrants are then tragically prevented from fully experiencing the American way of life.

Furthermore, to recruit new Muslims in America, radical leaders often go to the most angry and vulnerable population; that is, inside American jails, to turn them against America. And when it comes to converting African Americans, they use the race card. However, they fail to mention that Arabs were among the first cultures to enslave sub-Saharan Africans and promote the slave trade around the world, not to mention that slavery is still practiced by Sudanese Muslims. Radical mosques also work to recruit Middle Eastern immigrants...to the larger jihadist worldview that has one goal: to overtake and overwhelm America and other Western societies, bring the evil infidels to their knees, and conquer the world for Islam.

Many devout Muslims hold at heart a dream of an Islamic Caliphate, a totalitarian political system encompassing the whole Muslim world—and eventually the entire world—which functions under one constitution (the Koran) and one law, Islamic sharia law. This is not some crazy notion espoused by some lunatic fringe Islamists. Conquering the world for Islam is the stated goal that emanates from powerful, ruling Islamic clerics throughout the Middle East, whether it is the Wahabis of Saudi Arabia, the mullahs of Iran's Islamic revolution, the Muslim Brotherhood of Egypt, the Taliban of Afghanistan, or the followers of Osama bin Laden. This is also the goal of many Islamic organizations operating under false pretenses in America and financed and supported by radical Muslim states. Is the Islamic invasion of the seventh century on the superpowers of that time being reincarnated again on the superpowers of today?...

[In Muslim schools] in America, the same indoctrination and hate speech against non-Muslims I experienced back in Gaza is now creating a new generation full of alienation and rage, a subculture that rejects the larger society. The indoctrination of these schools here and elsewhere in the West is producing angry young Muslims who cannot relate to the larger community. It is a ticking time bomb waiting to explode....

I avoided radical Muslims in America who appeared fake and two-faced to me. But their presence and power was increasing.…

Furthermore, I see Arab professors on U.S. campuses who are equally if not even more radical…than any imam in a radical mosque. They are merely more clever in conveying their message of hate and anti-Semitism than the crude preachers are.…

Muslim defenders…insist that Islam is a religion of peace and tolerance while ignoring the daily prayers in Middle Eastern mosques for the violent exploits of great heroes and martyrs. Religious leaders across the Middle East are blessing and approving of suicide bombers and those who kill the infidels. Even Muhammad Sayyed Tantawi, the sheikh of Al-Azhar University in Cairo, who is the highest-ranking cleric in Sunni Islam, has issued fatwas in favor of violent jihad against America and in support of suicide bombings.

The notion that Islam teaches peace and tolerance is ridiculous in light of the record of Islamic countries' treatment of their minorities or the sermons preached in neighborhood mosques. Even in the new, supposedly "democratic" Afghanistan, in the spring of 2006 a Muslim who converted to Christianity was sentenced to death, a punishment mandated by sharia law. His life was spared only after Western governments pressured Afghan authorities, and the man was secretly whisked away to Italy in the midst of death threats from top Muslim clerics. So-called moderate Muslim leaders unfortunately were silent and did nothing to protect or defend that poor Afghani convert. There were no Muslim riots to save his life. The only outrage came from the mob wanting to kill him themselves if the government set him free.…

The defenders cannot reconcile the huge gap between the idealism of Islam and the reality of the actions of many Muslims. If they truly believe Islam is a religion of peace, then why do they tolerate the teaching of hatred, violence, and jihad in Muslim schools? Why do they not teach peace in their schools, mosques, media, and political institutions? If they truly believed in the ideals of Islam and the verses they quote from the Koran, they would have to stand up to terrorists and stop defending their actions. If the majority of Muslims are defending the actions of Osama bin Laden—openly or secretly—then we cannot tell the world Islam is a religion of peace. Then it is a lie. If Islam is a religion of peace, then we must teach peace as a major part of Islamic teachings.

After the prominent role Saudi citizens played in the attacks of 9/11, the West criticized Saudi schools for teaching hate. In response, the Saudi government launched an internal review and revision of their textbooks. After new textbooks were published, the Saudi government took out a full-page ad in *The New Republic* to trumpet the program's success, and an embassy spokesman said, "We have removed materials that are inciteful or intolerant towards people of other faiths." However, a translation of the new textbooks reveals otherwise. An eighth-grade Islamic-studies text reads: "As cited in the Ibn Abbas[1]: the apes are Jews, the people of the Sabbath, while the swine are the Christians, the infidels of the communion of Jesus." This is only one of many such examples and serves as a telling example not only of the gap between idealism and reality, but also the huge gap between what the Arabs tell the West and what is in fact really happening within the Arab world....

After 9/11, my fellow Americans should never be in the dark again. They must understand the brutality and persistence of their enemy. As a loyal and grateful American, I feel I must help the American public understand what is at stake. America must understand that Islam is not just a religion. It is a political system; it is a legal system, both civil and criminal. Penalties under Islamic law can be death, limb amputation, or stoning. It is a system that gives power to the vice police to hold a stick in public and use it on women's ankles if they are uncovered. Everyone's rights and duties are spelled out very clearly in Islam, and, no, there is no equality under Islamic law between Muslims and non-Muslims or between men and women. This is what they want for the whole world.

Radical Islam has lofty plans to conquer the West and won't let go. That is something Americans don't understand and have trouble believing. They may be able to understand why the Islamic world hates them; they may get the dynamics behind why they blame America, Israel, and the West for all the ills in their society. They may even be able to understand how these extremists justify, violence. But what Americans still don't understand is that the goal of jihad is to conquer the world, literally, for Islam, and to usher in a Caliphate—that is, a supreme totalitarian Islamic government, a lifestyle by force, one nation, one party, one constitution (the Koran), and one law (sharia Islamic law). Anyone who reads and speaks Arabic and monitors Web sites and listens to speeches and sermons in mosques around the world knows how seriously many Muslims believe in their mission to dominate the world for Islam, the one true religion.

Make no mistake about it: They are sacrificing their men, women, and children for this goal of world domination. They are willing to bring about an Armageddon to conquer the world to Islam. We are already in World War III and many people in the West are still in denial. Unlike during the cold war with communism, the enemy is not a superpower, but a fanatical religious movement equipped with a very powerful weapon of mass destruction called suicide/homicide bombers. For generations, thousands if not millions of suicide bombers have been bred, trained, and nourished to give up their lives in service of jihad. That makes this an unprecedented world war....

When I started speaking out, of course I was accused of defaming Islam. Some even called me an infidel. It is not me—or those few moderate Muslims who are speaking out—who have given Islam a bad name, rather it is the terrorists, their sympathizers, and the silence of the Muslim majority that defames a great religion and a great people. We cannot continue denying the undeniable that there is a major problem within Muslim and Arab society that has produced terrorism. Now is the time to own up to the dysfunction in the Islamic world and seize the moment to bring about change. Good and loyal Muslims all over the world should demand an end to the violence and terror. They should work to reform their institutions, beginning with the education of young children. They should join the other great religions of the world to advocate peace and tolerance, love and harmony.

NOTE

1. Ibn Abbas is an important seventh-century religious scholar who was a cousin of Muhammad.

Part 6

Jews as Targets: The Islamization of European Anti-Semitic Myths

Although Jews suffered legalized humiliation as second-class citizens and, at times, massacres, for centuries they generally lived in greater security in Muslim lands than they did in Christian Europe. Unlike the Latin West, medieval Muslims did not teach that Jews were endowed with Satanic qualities. Nevertheless, there are passages in the Qur'an and later Islamic writings that denigrate Jews, and that provided a foundation for Muslims to embrace, since the early twentieth century, the worst elements of European anti-Semitism.

The advent of Zionism, the creation of Israel on what is perceived as inviolable Muslim land, the Jewish state's humiliating defeats of Arab armies and its ongoing conflict with the Palestinians have stirred the cauldron of Jew-hatred in the Arab-Muslim world. Islamists, in particular, view Israel as another example of Western colonialism and a glaring affront to Muslim dignity. They also regard the Jewish state as a threat to Islamic identity, for by so successfully assimilating into Western culture, Israelis constitute a dangerous model that Muslims might be tempted to imitate. Now reaching epidemic proportions, anti-Semitism has become a principal theme of jihadists and justification for terrorist acts committed against Israelis and Jews in other lands. As Cardinal Tucci, the director of Vatican Radio, stated in November 2003: "Now in the whole Muslim world, in the media, the radio, television, in schools, a whole system inciting to anti-Semitism exists. It is the worst anti-Semitism that can be imagined after Nazi anti-Semitism, if not its equal."[1]

The recycling of the ugliest elements of Nazi propaganda has led several theorists, notably Robert Wistrich, to stress the continuity between the thinking of radical Muslims and Nazi ideology. Like the Nazis, Islamists and jihadists—and many "moderate Muslims"—perceive the Jews as a criminal people that threatens all humanity, blame the Jews for their misfortunes, and hold out the image of a utopian future once Israel is eradicated and the Jews eliminated. As in Nazi Germany, the media in the Arab/Muslim world are often filled with repulsive caricatures of Jews—dark, stooped, sinister, hook-nosed, devil-like creatures—many of them taken from Nazi works. In Arab sermons, classrooms, school books, and on the

Internet, Jews are often referred to as "descendants of apes and pigs," "the scum of the human race," "the rats of the world," "bacteria," "vampires," "usurers," and "whoremongers." Like their Nazi forbears, Islamic anti-Semites, many of them popular imams or members of the educated elite, strip Jews of their humanity. Thus Fatma Abdallah Mahmound, an Egyptian columnist, wrote in *Al-Akhbar*, considered a moderate newspaper sponsored by the government, that the Jews

> are accursed in heaven and on earth. They are accursed from the day the human race was created and from the day their mothers bore them.... These accursed ones are a catastrophe for the human race. They are the virus of the generation, doomed to a life of humiliation and wretchedness on Judgment Day.... Finally, they are accursed, fundamentally, because they are the plague of the generation and the bacterium of all time. Their history always was and always will be stained with treachery, falseness, and lying.[2]

No accusation against Jews is too absurd not to be included in the litany of Jewish evil. To prove their inherent wickedness, Jews are held responsible for the French Revolution, the Russian Revolution, both world wars, and the atomic bombing of Hiroshima and Nagasaki. The Egyptian media accuses Zionist agents of using HIV-infected prostitutes to spread AIDS among Egyptian youth, disseminating candy that sterilizes Egyptian children, and supplying Egyptian university students with chemically laced chewing gum that arouses lust. Bin Laden maintains that Jews "in accordance with their religion, believe that human beings are their slaves and that those who refuse [to recognize this] should be put to death."[3] The Arab media have even revived the medieval canard that Jews are required to murder non-Jewish children in order to obtain their blood for making unleavened bread for Passover. In the tradition of Josef Goebbels, Hezbollah's popular satellite TV channel, Al-Manar, which reaches millions of homes throughout the Middle East, depicts a gory scene of Jews seizing a terrified Christian child, slitting his throat, and collecting the spurting blood in a metal basin.

Pervasive in the Muslim world is the myth—a staple of Nazi ideology—that a secret cabal of Jews plots to dominate the world. Like the Nazis, Muslims widely circulate the *Protocols of the Learned Elders of Zion*, that notorious forgery written by order of the Russian tsar's secret police and first published in 1902, which purported to reveal a plot by Jewish elders to take over the world. The book is a bestseller in the Arab world and dramas based on the *Protocols* have been featured in prime time on both Egyptian and Syrian television. In October 2003, in the library at Alexandria, the *Protocols*, described as "a Jewish sacred text." was placed next to the Torah. In accordance with the bizarre fantasy contained in this fraudulent work, many Muslims remain convinced that the disasters occurring on 9/11 were engineered by the Mossad, Israel's intelligence service, in an effort to inflame the Christian West against Muslims. Sheikh Muhammad al-Gemeaha, Imam of the Islamic Cultural Center and Mosque of New York City, who returned to

Egypt several days after 9/11, was interviewed by an Arab website on October 4, 2001. He said that because of 9/11

> Muslims do not feel safe even going to the hospitals because some Jewish doctors in one of the hospitals poisoned sick Muslim children, who then died.... [O]nly the Jews are capable of planning such an incident [9/11].... [T]he police arrested a group of Jews rejoicing in the streets at the time of the incident.... The Jews who control the media acted to hush it up so that American people would not know.[4]

A month after 9/11, an article in *The Jihad Times,* a Pakistani paper, claimed that obeying the *Protocols,* the "300-member apex Zionist body [of Elders]" launched the attack and issued a "secret directive" to four thousand Jews not to report to work on September 11 so that "not a single Israeli or American Jew working in the World Trade Center was reported killed or missing." (In actual fact, some 300 Jews perished in the World Trade Center on that fateful day.) Similar interpretations were voiced in Muslim publications in other lands.

Government-controlled newspapers and television networks in Saudi Arabia, Egypt, and other Arab lands employ the language, themes, and authority of the *Protocols,* never apprising their audience that the book is a proven forgery. Indeed they insist that it is an authentic exposition of the Jews' insidious spirit, occult powers, and sinister aim to subvert Islam and dominate the planet. In a series of articles entitled "The Serpent Around Our Necks," published between July and October 2005 in the Saudi daily *Al-Madina,* columnist Najah Al-Zahhar maintained that the Protocols reveals the plans of the "Zionist serpent"; that "the match between the *Protocols* and the real events is the most convincing proof of their authenticity"; that Jews believe "the best way to take over the world is by violence and terrorism"; and that "Zionism seeks to destroy all religious beliefs so that only Judaism will remain."[5] In an interview with Al-Jazeera TV on October 31, 2006, an Iraqi researcher living in Europe invoked the *Protocols* to explain why the Jews have been awarded so many Nobel prizes and the Arabs so few: "Democracy does not explain how it was awarded to 167 Jews from among those 15 million scattered around the world while abandoning...380 million Arabs. This prize stems from the core of the Elders of Zion,"[6] that is, Jewish control extends not only over the world's media and financial institutions but also encompasses the Nobel Prize.

Like anti-Semites in the West, jihadists and a surprisingly large number of Muslim intellectuals, journalists, statesmen, and religious leaders, publicly and vigorously deny the Holocaust, agreeing with Fatmah Mahmound that it is "a fabrication, a lie, and a fraud!...[a] carefully tailored [plot]...completely unconnected to the truth."[7] If only the Holocaust had really happened, he laments, the world would have been rid of a criminal people. When Arab/Muslim Jew-haters are not denying the Holocaust they are celebrating Hitler's mass murder of Jews—"thanks to Hitler of blessed memory," writes another columnist for *Al-Akhbar*—but with one reservation: not enough Jews perished. On several occasions Mahmoud

Ahmadinejad, president of Iran, has called for the obliteration of Israel and dismissed the Holocaust as a Zionist myth. In 2006 he arranged for two vile events: a contest of cartoons lampooning the Holocaust and a conference to "debate" whether the Nazi annihilation of European Jewry really happened. The conference was attended principally by anti-Semites and neo-Nazis from many lands; speaker after speaker maintained that there were no gas chambers, no crematoria, and no mass executions, that Jews invented these lies in order to extort money from Germany and to deceive the world into creating Israel. Sadly, but tellingly, Muslim leaders throughout the Middle East, political, spiritual, and intellectual, raised no voice in protest. (Some Iranian academics and Iranians in exile did denounce the spectacle as did some American Muslim groups.)

Both Arab spiritual leaders and academics have taught that killing Jews is a religious obligation, that their annihilation would benefit humanity and fulfill God's will. The following statement broadcast on the official television channel of the Palestine Authority by Dr. Ahmed Abu Halabiyah, rector of advanced studies at the Islamic University in Gaza, is more representative than unique; similar sentiments are frequently voiced in the Arab media and even school textbooks:

> The Jews are the Jews....They do not have any moderates or advocates of peace. They are all liars. They must he butchered and must be killed.... The Jews are like a spring—as long as you step on it with your foot it doesn't move. But if you lift your foot from the spring, it hurts you and punishes you.... It is forbidden to have mercy in your hearts for the Jews in any place and in any land, make war on them anywhere that you find yourself. Any place that you meet them, kill them.[8]

And a Syrian text for tenth graders instructs the reader: "The logic of justice obligates the application of the single verdict [on the Jews] from which there is no escape: namely, that their criminal intentions be turned against them and that they be exterminated."[9]

For Islamists, anti-Semitism has become an ideological imperative. Either because of conviction, fear, or state-controlled media, virtually no condemnations of anti-Semitism have emerged within Arab/Muslim lands. (Some Muslims living in the West have spoken forcefully against the Judeophobia rampant in the Middle East [see part 6, pp. 235–241]) The pervasive anti-Semitism in the Islamic world—and its revival in Europe—portends a serious danger for Western civilization. In the last two centuries, anti-Semitism has been a central feature of ideologies hostile to the Enlightenment tradition of reason, political freedom, and tolerance. Deeply ingrained in European Christian culture, starting in the late nineteenth century it was employed by the Right in order to mobilize masses of people from different classes in the struggle against liberal democracy and socialism. Expropriated by the radical Right, Jew-hatred became a core element of an extreme racial-nationalist ideology that culminated in Nazism, which threatened to destroy Western civilization as we know it. It now serves as a rallying cry for Islamic jihadists and fundamentalists hostile to the core values of the Western tradition. For them, Israel is an outpost of the hated West, its elimination an important step in the removal of anti-Islamic Western ways and ideas from the Muslim world. As such, anti-Semitism and the irrational myths associated with it that undermine rational thinking and incite barbaric violence, transcend a purely Jewish concern. There are already signs that Americans and other westerners—the infidels—are becoming the object of that same pristine hatred that is now directed at Jews. Having experienced the horrors of Nazism, westerners are impelled to reflect on the immense implications for humanist and democratic values of a resurgence of Nazi-like demonology of the Jew that openly calls for and justifies genocide.

NOTES

1. Quoted in Bat Ye'or, *Eurabia: The Euro-Arab Axis* (Madison, NJ: Farleigh Dickinson University Press, 2005, 2006), pp. 250–251.
2. Quoted in Gabriel Schoenfeld, *The Return of Anti-Semitism* (San Francisco, CA: Encounter Books, 2004), pp. 17–18.
3. Quoted in Raymond Ibrahim, ed. and trans., *The Al Qaeda Reader* (New York: Broadway Books, 2007), p. 277.
4. Middle East Media Research Institute (MEMRI) No. 288, October 17, 2001 <http://www.memri.org>.
5. MEMRI, Special Dispatch Series, No. 1311, October 6, 2006 <http://www.memri.org>.
6. MEMRI, Special Dispatch Series, No. 1359, November 16, 2006 <http://www.memri.org>.
7. Ibid.
8. Quoted in Itamar Marcus and Barbara Crook, "Kill a Jew—Go to Heaven: The Perception of the Jew in Palestinian Society," *Jewish Political Studies Review*, Vol. 17, Nos. 3–4 (Fall 2005), p. 127.
9. Fiamma Nirenstein, "Observations: How Suicide Bombers Are Made," *Commentary*, 112 (September 2001), pp. 52–55.

1

"ISLAMIC ANTI-SEMITISM
IN HISTORICAL PERSPECTIVE"

Anti-Defamation League

Seeking to alert people to the rising tide of Islamic anti-Semitism, the Anti-Defamation League, an organization founded in 1913 to combat prejudice against Jews, issued a special report, "Islamic Anti-Semitism in Historical Perspective," in 2002. This report, excerpted below, traces the roots of anti-Jewish sentiment in classic Muslim theology and analyzes the spread in recent decades to the Muslim world of long-standing European anti-Semitic myths, lies, and imagery.

* * *

INTRODUCTION

This report takes as a given the existence of widespread anti-Semitism throughout the Middle East. This anti-Semitism is endorsed or tolerated by governments, disseminated by the media, taught in schools and universities, preached in mosques. No segment of society is free of its taint. Not everyone makes anti-Semitism a part of his or her profession like the columnist in Egypt's largest newspaper who writes encomiums to Hitler every now and then. Individuals in the Middle East, like people everywhere, have other, more practical concerns in their daily lives. Some may reject anti-Semitism entirely. But to the extent that we are able to speak of an attitude or ideology permeating a society, informing the beliefs of the masses, the debates of the intelligentsia and the decisions of the leaders, the Middle East is permeated with anti-Semitism.

At the outset we must state that this anti-Semitism should not be confused with opposition, however impassioned, to Israeli policies and actions. Opposition and censure, the results of healthy debate and differing points of view, can hardly be condemned. But neither should we allow the terms of political opposition to be used to mask or legitimize hatred, bigotry, and paranoia. When "Zionist" becomes a curse-word and "Zionists" can be blamed, as if by reflex, for September 11, when Israelis are caricatured as *Ostjuden* [Eastern European Jews] and blood libel imagery applied to Israel's prime minister, we have clearly moved beyond opposition to concrete policies and actions and entered the realm of chimerical anti-Semitism [that is, an anti-Semitism based on pure myths and lies]. In the contemporary Middle East, malevolence and betrayal are cast as parts of an essential "Jewish nature," endemic either to the Jewish "race" or to Judaism as a religion. Jews, whether Israeli or in the Diaspora, are behind the misfortunes that have befallen the Arab people; they are known to many as the "eternal enemies" of Islam and Allah.

"Traditional" Muslim Anti-Judaism

The demonization of Jews was not a traditional component of Islam, and even today it must not be assumed to characterize Islam throughout the world. Islam as a religion has viewed Jews—and Christians for that matter—as the bearers of respective versions of Allah's truth, distorted by human agency, however, and superseded by Islam, the perfect expression of the one true religion.... Jews and Christians were permitted to live in Muslim lands as tolerated, second-class minorities, subject, however, to the humiliations of their *dhimmi* status.

Jews in particular had to live with the legacy of Muhammad's historical interactions with their co-religionists from Medina; the ire he felt at their opposition to his expanding influence, recorded in the Qur'an, was followed by his triumph over them and their subjugation to his word. This presaged and set the tone for Islam's subsequent perspective on the Jews: the descendants of those who distorted God's truth and opposed His prophet, Jews would rightly be humbled before Muslims and live in second-class status.

Of course this theological perspective on the Jews varied from time to time and place to place. Not all Arab governments were equally anxious to impose strict interpretations of the dhimmi paradigm on their Jewish subjects, and many Arab societies, especially during the High Middle Ages [twelfth and thirteenth centuries], were suffused with a rare premodern cosmopolitan tolerance for Jews and other minorities. But even in these societies, alongside those Arabs who dealt with Jewish neighbors and associates with friendship and esteem there were those who stressed that the proper Islamic approach called for Jewish debasement.

The New Demonization

Yet such debasement is far different from the abject vilification of Jews so prevalent today. A new theology of anti-Semitism and demonization of Jews has arisen, in which stereotypes derived from Muhammad's experience with the Jews of seventh century Arabia were now made relevant to today's politics. These were made central in explaining the decline of Islamic power and in motivating Muslims to resist historic trends.

This theology was expressed most famously in the proceedings of the 1968 Al-Azhar Conference in Cairo and in the writings of the Egyptian Sayyid Qutb (d. 1966), which removed the ancient alleged Jewish distortion of Allah's initial revelation to them and the Jewish opposition to Muhammad from their legendary and historical contexts. Instead these two events were portrayed as describing an essential evil in Jewish nature.

Muhammad Azzah Darwaza wrote at the Al-Azhar conference that:

[The Qur'an reveals that the Jews of ancient times] coated what was right with what was wrong. The Jews were also stubborn in telling lies and contradicting the truth. They told lies about Allah and let people suspect their religion. They were notorious for covetousness, avarice and bad manners. They were not ashamed of embracing polytheism or performing the rites of paganism. They sometimes praised the idols and were in collusion with idolaters against monotheists. They displaced the words of Allah and disfigured the laws of Heaven and God's advice. They were hard-hearted and sinful, they committed unlawful and forbidden crimes.

   It is extremely astonishing to see that the Jews of today are exactly a typical picture of those mentioned in the Holy Qur'an and they have the same bad manners and qualities of their forefathers although their environment, surroundings and positions are different from those of their ancestors. These bad manners and qualities of the Jews ascertain the Qur'anic statements about their deeply rooted instinct which they inherited from their fathers. All people feel this innate nature of the Jews everywhere and at all times....

Other negative Islamic traditions about Jews throughout the ages were veneered in darker hues and incorporated into a new narrative of Jewish malevolence towards Allah and to Muslims generally. Even what had previously been positive Islamic traditions about Jews—as in the story of Samaw'al, a Jew who was held by Arabs as the paradigm of fidelity for his willingness to allow his son to be killed rather than surrender items entrusted to his safekeeping—were revised with an anti-Semitic animus: Samaw'al's action demonstrated merely that he loved money more than his son's life.

Ultimately, Jews came to be described as the "eternal" enemies of Allah and of Islam, a satanic, diabolical force, locked in a lethal struggle with Islam. Sayyid Qutb (see part 1, chapter 3) wrote that "the struggle between Islam and the Jews continues in force and will thus continue, because the Jews will be satisfied only with the destruction of this religion [of Islam]." In the same vein, the rector of Al-Azhar University in Egypt, Shaykh Abd-al-Halim Mahmud, identified the Jews as Islam's worst enemies:

As for those who struggle against the faithful [Muslims], they struggle against the elimination of oppression and enmity. They struggle in the way of Satan. Allah commands the Muslims to fight the friends of Satan wherever they may be found. And among Satan's friends—indeed, his best friends in our age—are the Jews.

One participant at the Al-Azhar conference, described Jews as "hostile to all human values in this world," and another, the Mufti of Tarsus in Syria, claimed that Jews "have always been a curse that spread among the nations and sought to extinguish all manifestations of civilization."

Similarly the Imam of the main mosque in Amman blamed the Jews for all the evil in the world:

> Jews are treacherous, ungrateful killers of their prophet. Wherever they went they generated disaster. They stand behind all conspiracies and corruption in the world. God protect us from their evil!

Spreading the Message of Hate

This new theological paradigm of Jews was adopted and promulgated by a variety of Islamist groups. The Muslim Brotherhood, the main Islamist pan-Arab grass-roots movement for most of the twentieth century, popularized the notion that Jews were the first and most dangerous of the "four horsemen of apocalypse." In a children's supplement to the Brotherhood's *al-Da'wa'* publication in October of 1980, an article entitled merely "The Jews" exhorted:

> Brother Muslim Lion Cub, Have you ever wondered why God cursed the Jews in his Book? God grew weary of their lies. They associated others with God, they were infidels. Such are the Jews, my brother, Muslim lion cub, your enemies and the enemies of God. Such is their particular natural disposition, the corrupt doctrine that is there. [T]hey have never ceased to conspire against their main enemy, the Muslims. In one of their books they say: "We Jews are the masters of the world, its corrupters, those who foment sedition, its hangmen!" Muslim lion cub, annihilate their existence, those who seek to subjugate all humanity so as to force them to serve their satanic designs.

Younger Islamist groups have also adopted this theological anti-Semitism, at least in their internal publications. Sayyid Muhammad Husayn Fadlallah, the spiritual mentor of the Hezbollah terrorist group, states that "The struggle against the Jewish state, in which the Muslims are engaged, is a continuation of the old struggle of the Muslims against the Jews' conspiracy against Islam."

A famous teaching of the Hadith which stated that the resurrection of the dead will only occur when "Muslims will war with the Jews and kill them," and that even "rocks and trees" will betray Jews to the Muslim warriors, came to be cited in the Hamas charter and became a blueprint for a political program that puts hatred of Jews at its center and makes adherence to this hatred essential to proving loyalty to Islam.

This theology is echoed and reinforced every Friday in the sermons of radical a'immah and 'ulema that are televised throughout the Middle East.... [An] explicit example was broadcast on Saudi Arabia's TV1 television station on April 19, 2002, which featured Sheikh Abd Al-Rahman Al-Sudais preaching from the Al-Harram mosque in Mecca:

> Read history and you will know that yesterday's Jews were bad predecessors and today's Jews are worse successors. They are killers of prophets and the scum of the earth. God hurled his curses and indignation on them and made them monkeys and pigs and worshippers of tyrants. These are the Jews, a continuous lineage of meanness, cunning, obstinacy, tyranny, evil, and corruption. They sow corruption on earth.
>
> O Muslims, the Islamic nation today is at the peak of conflict with the enemies of yesterday, today, and tomorrow, with the grandsons of Bani-Quraydah, Al-Nadiri, and Qaynuqa [Jewish tribes in the early days of Islam]. May God's curses follow them until the Day of Judgment. The conflict is exploding and magnifying, the exploitation and greed are increasing, and the indulgence in humbling Arabs and Muslims and their holy places has become very serious by the world rodents that have revoked pacts and agreements. Treachery, sabotage, and cunning dominate their minds and injustice and tyranny flow in their veins. They cannot but remain arrogant, reckless, corrupt, and harmful. Thus, they deserve the curse of God, His angels, and all people.

WESTERN-STYLE ANTI-SEMITISM

Still, traditional Islamic images, however radicalized and distorted, do not nearly account for the variety of negative representations of Jews and Judaism, in the twentieth century Middle East and today. The use by Islamists of the ancient Muhammadean conflict with Jews as a model for their contemporary disaffection with modern Jews still does not turn naturally into the sort of Satanic rhetoric commonly in use since the 1960s. To explain the demonization of contemporary Jews we must look not to the roots of Islam but to the West: the ancient blood libel, and charges of ritual murder and well-poisoning, as well as the belief that Jews are engaged in a fantastic world conspiracy.

Blood Libel and Ritual Murder

These charges are not indigenous to the Middle East. They originated in various parts of Europe in the medieval and early modern periods, and were imported to the Middle East by European traders, missionaries, and occasionally even government officials, in the Imperialist nineteenth century. The first major blood libel, for example, occurred in the famous Damascus Affair of 1840, in which Jews were blamed for the disappearance of a Capuchin friar and his Muslim servant. The accusation of ritual murder in the Damascus Affair, like the majority of some twenty charges of ritual murder in the Middle East before the twentieth century, was made by Christians. Indeed, since its genesis in the Middle Ages, the blood libel had been invested with christological significance and, like the charge of Host Desecration, was inspired by an alleged Jewish desire to "continue" their millennia-old attack on Jesus Christ and his followers.

But in the twentieth century, the blood libel and the charge of ritual murder had been recast by Muslims as merely another part of the Jewish religion, directed against not only Christians but Muslims and any non-Jew as well. "The God of the Jews is not content with animal sacrifices," wrote the Egyptian 'Abdallah al-Tall in his 1964 book entitled *The Danger of World Jewry to Islam and Christianity.* "He must be appeased with human sacrifices. Hence the Jewish custom of slaughtering children and extracting their blood to mix it with their matzot on Passover." By 1967 Israeli academic Y. Harkabi had identified eight Arabic books asserting that Jews perform ritual murder and/or drink the blood of non-Jews as part of their religion. Although Harkaby himself noted at the time that such accusations form only a small part of the anti-Jewish rhetoric in the Middle East, they continued to appear in Arab media through the 1970s to today. Arabic mass-circulation newspapers in Qatar, Egypt, Saudi Arabia, Kuwait, Bahrain, and Jordan have reprinted similar claims about Jews and Israelis.

In August 1972 King Faisal of Saudi Arabia reported in the Egyptian magazine *al-Musawar* that while he was in Paris "the police discovered five murdered children. Their blood had been drained, and it turned out that some Jews had murdered them in order to take their blood and mix it with the bread that they eat on that day." Another instance of high-profile Arab personalities asserting the blood libel occurred in 1984, when Syrian Defense Minister Mustafa Tlass published a book *The Matzah of Zion* in which he returned to the Damascus Affair of 1840, claiming that the Jews had indeed murdered the Capuchin friar. In 2001 an Egyptian producer, Munir Radhi, announced that he was adapting Tlass' book into a movie. "It will be," he said, "the Arab answer to Schindler's List."

Conspiracy Theories and the Protocols

As the medieval world entered the early modern world era, the conspiratorial aspect of the ritual murder charge took on a life of its own. This tendency culminated in The *Protocols of the Elders of Zion*, a document purporting to be the notes of a secret meeting of Jewish leaders plotting to subvert Christianity, destroy modern civilization and enslave humankind. Though a contemporary Western reader of the *Protocols* will likely view them as an absurd caricature, they attained worldwide circulation after World War I and were taken seriously by many in those tumultuous times.

The *Protocols* were discredited in the West by the late 1920s, when the original text on which the *Protocols* were modeled—a tract from the 1860s attacking Napoleon III—was discovered. Since then their influence has been limited to the extremist fringes in the West. But in the late 1920s the popularity of the book in the Arab world was only beginning, and their authenticity, according to historian Bernard Lewis, was not seriously questioned until the late 1970s. As of 1967, Y. Harkaby had identified nine different complete Arabic translations of the *Protocols*, many of them published and republished by government presses in Egypt in the 1960s and early 1970s. By all indications they are perennial bestsellers in the Middle East.

The seriousness with which they appear to be taken in the Middle East may be partly explained by the number of prominent Muslims who have endorsed them. Nasser endorsed the *Protocols* in 1958, as did President Sadat, President Arif of Iraq, King Faisal of Saudi Arabia, Colonel Qaddafi of Libya, and others. The *Protocols* form part of the worldview of extremist groups, as attested to by their mention by name in Article 32 of the Covenant of the terrorist group Hamas in describing the aspirations of Israel:

> The Zionist plan is limitless. After Palestine, the Zionists aspire to expand from the Nile to the Euphrates. When they will have digested the region they overtook, they will aspire to further expansion, and so on. Their plan is embodied in the "Protocols of the Elders of Zion" and their present conduct is the best proof of what we are saying.

On the other extreme, excerpts from the *Protocols* have even appeared in the Jordanian school curriculum.

Even today *the Protocols* continue to be cited by public figures and in the media in the Arab world. In December 1997 Mustafa Tlas, the Syrian defense minister, cited the *Protocols* as an explanation for the warm relations between Israel and Turkey. On June 23, 2001, the Egyptian government daily *Al-Ahram* wrote:

> What exactly do the Jews want? Read what the Ninth Protocol of "The Protocols of the Elders of Zion" says: "We have limitless ambitions, inexhaustible greed, merciless vengeance, and hatred beyond imagination. We are a secret army whose plans are impossible understand by using honest methods. Cunning is our approach, mystery is our way. [The way] of the freemasons, in which we believe, cannot be understood by those among the gentiles who are stupid pigs. The ultimate goal of the freemasons is to destroy the world and to build it anew according to the Zionist policy so that the Jews can control the world and destroy the [world's] religions."

Barely two weeks after September 11, 2001, a columnist in the Egyptian newspaper *Al-Wafd* wrote that the "Zionists" must have known in advance that the September 11 terrorist attacks were impending, but refused to share that information with the United States "in order to sow disputes and troubles" throughout the world. "Proof is found," he added, "in the *Protocols of the Wise Men of Zion*."

Even where the *Protocols* are not mentioned by name, the theme they express—that Jews are engaged in secret machinations to "take over the world," or alternatively, that Jews already control the world—would, by the frequency of its expression by leaders, intelligentsia and media forums, appear to pervade the Arab worldview. A few examples will suffice:

Al-Ahram, November 14, 1998
"The Jews have been behind all the wars and their goal was corruption and destruction. This is their means of getting rich quick after wars."

Al-Hayat Al-Jadeeda, July 2, 1998

"Everywhere, the Jews have been the subjects of hatred and disdain because they control most of the economic resources upon which the livelihoods of many people are dependent. There is no alternative but to say that the success of the Jews is not coincidental but rather the result of long years of planning and a great investment of effort in order to obtain their wretched control over the world's media."

Al-Hayat Al-Jadeeda, November 6, 1997

"We must act on the international level in the framework of a detailed information plan which will expose the Zionist-Colonist plot and its goals, which destroy not only our people but the entire world."

Damascus Radio, September 2, 1998

"[Jewish] history is full of devising conspiracies, even against the countries in which they live, whose citizenship they bear and whose benefits they enjoy. Anyone interested in documents from World War I can learn about the role German Jews played in organizing conspiracies to undermine Germany, harm its economy and weaken its capabilities, which deteriorated to the extent that it led to its defeat. Whoever studies these documents can also understand why the hatred of Jews consequently increased so severely."

Nazism and Holocaust Denial

What Is Holocaust Denial?
Why Is It Anti-Semitic?

One specific conspiracy theory which receives much play in the contemporary Arab press deserves special mention: Holocaust denial. Here, facts that are universally acknowledged throughout the rest of the world are questioned in the Arab world, and hinge on conspiracies of frightening scope.

Holocaust denial—the claim that approximately six million Jews were not methodically killed, many by poison gas, by the Nazis during World War II—now regularly occurs throughout the Middle East, in speeches and pronouncements by public figures, in articles and columns by journalists, and in the resolutions of professional organizations. While some voices oppose this denial or deliberate distortion of the historical record, the main tenet of Holocaust denial—that Jews invented the Holocaust story in an attempt to advance their own interests—appears to be an increasingly accepted belief for large numbers of people in Arab and Muslim states. Even as many Western countries have enacted legislation identifying Holocaust denial as a form of hate crime, the Middle East is one of the few regions in the world today where governments do not condemn, and sometimes even sponsor, such anti-Semitic propaganda.

Though some try to portray the deniers as "revisionists" conducting legitimate inquiry into the historical record, scratching the surface of their theories will demonstrate the anti-Semitic conspiracy theory they are really espousing. To make their claims credible, Holocaust deniers are forced to reject enormous volumes of historical evidence from World War II. In so doing they resort to fantastic conspiracy theories about Jews. Records from the period, including thousands of pages of evidence used immediately after the war in the Nuremberg trials, are dismissed as forged by a secret committee; survivors are rejected as greedy charlatans; American GI's who saw the death apparatus in the camps are told that they were duped by the American military itself, which was corrupted by Jewish concerns and also complicit in the conspiracy. As for a motive (for why would Jews claim that millions of their brethren were killed in World War II?): deniers claim that the Jews wanted to defraud the West of billions of dollars in reparations and other payments; to "purchase" world support for the creation of the state of Israel; to demoralize "Aryans" and the West so that the Jews could more easily take over the world.

Holocaust Denial Takes
Root in the Middle East

In the Middle East, in some cases, Holocaust denial is actively sponsored by national governments—by Iran, for example, which has become a sanctuary for Western Holocaust deniers fleeing legal entanglements in their home countries, and whose leader, Ayatollah Ali Khamenei, suggested in 2001 that the statistics of Jewish deaths during the Holocaust had been exaggerated. The numerous expressions of Holocaust denial that have appeared in *Teshreen*, Syria's main daily newspaper, which is owned and operated by the ruling Baath party, suggests that the Syrian government also condones the propaganda. The same holds true for the Palestinian Authority, whose newspaper, *Al-Hayat Al-Jadeeda*, and television station have frequently denied basic facts of the Holocaust in their reporting....

...Among the newspapers that have consistently featured Holocaust denial are the Jordanian daily, *Al Arab Al-Yom*, the Syrian daily, *Teshreen*, the English-language Iranian *Teheran Times,* and the Palestinian Authority's *Al-Hayat Al-Jadeeda*. Several noted religious leaders in the region have also rejected the facts of the Holocaust, including Sheikh Mohammad Mehdi Shamseddin of Lebanon, Sheik Ikrima Sabri of Jerusalem and Iranian religious leader Ayatollah Ali Khamenei.

On July 4, 1998, for example, the establishment Jordanian newspaper *Al-Arab Al-Yom* told its readers that "most research prepared by objective researchers" has "proven in a manner beyond the shadow of a doubt" that the Holocaust is "a great lie and a myth that the Zionist mind spread in order to lead the world astray." Earlier that year (April 27, 1998), the same newspaper had published an article claiming that "there is no proof" that the Holocaust occurred, except for "the conflicting testimonies of a few Jewish 'survivors.'" On July 14, 1998, the Egyptian newspaper, *Al-Akhbar,* stated that regarding the crematoria remaining at Buchenwald and Auschwitz, "even if these crematoria operated day and night, it would take dozens of years to burn six million people and not merely three years." A Lebanese politician, Dr. Issam Naaman wrote in a London-Arab newspaper on April 22, 1998, that "Israel prospers and exists by right of the Holocaust lie and the Israeli government's policy of intentional exaggeration." . . .

The best-known flare-up of Holocaust denial in the Middle East occurred in response to the trial of Roger Garaudy in France in 1998. Garaudy was charged with violating a 1990 French law that makes it illegal to deny historical events that have been designated as "crimes against humanity," and with inciting racial hatred. These charges stemmed from his 1995 book, *The Founding Myths of Modern Israel,* in which he stated that there was no Nazi program of genocide during World War II, and that Jews essentially fabricated the Holocaust for their financial and political gain. Garaudy was convicted on these charges in 1998.

Before, during, and after the trial, he was hailed as a hero throughout the countries of the Middle East—the trial was covered by media from Saudi Arabia, Qatar, Egypt, Iran, Syria, Lebanon, Jordan, and the Palestinian Authority. Formerly Roman Catholic and Communist, Garaudy had converted to Islam in 1982, and married a Jerusalem-born Palestinian woman, but this alone did not explain the outpouring of support he received; the "revisionist" message of his book—whose Arabic translation was a best-seller in many of the region's countries—clearly resonated across the region. The former president of Iran, Ali Akbar Hashemi Rafsanjani, announced in a sermon on Radio Tehran that his personal scholarship on the subject had convinced him that "Hitler had only killed 20,000 Jews and not six million," and added that "Garaudy's crime derives from the doubt he cast on Zionist propaganda." The main establishment newspaper in Egypt, *Al-Ahram,* defended Garaudy in a March 14, 1998, article that argued that there is "no trace of the gas chambers" that are supposed to have existed in Germany, and that six million Jews could not have been killed in the Holocaust because "the Jews of Germany numbered less than two million" at the time. Numerous professional and social organizations throughout the region issued statements supporting Garaudy as well, including the Palestinian Journalists' Syndicate, the Palestinian Writers Association, the Jordanian Arab Organization for Human Rights, the Qatar Women's Youth Organization, the Federation of Egyptian Writers, and the Union of Arab Artists.

Support for Garaudy did not end merely with words. Seven members of the Beirut Bar Association volunteered to defend the writer in France, and Egypt's Arab Lawyers' Union also dispatched a five-man legal team to Paris in Garaudy's support. The United Arab Emirates daily, *Al-Haleej,* was inundated with contributions and messages of support for Garaudy after it published an appeal on his behalf. The most surprising contribution came from the wife of United Arab Emirates leader Sheikh Zayed ibn Sultan al-Nahayan, who gave the equivalent of $50,000, in cash, to cover the maximum fine that Garaudy would be required to pay if found guilty.

The Great Contradiction: Holocaust Denial and "Jews as Nazis"

Of course the Arab perception of the Holocaust has never been monolithic, and has often been influenced by the vicissitudes of the Arab-Israeli conflict. The perception that the West created Israel out of guilt over the attempted genocide of the Jews during World War II is widespread in the Middle East; coupled with their hostility towards Israel, this leads many Arabs to complain that they are "paying" for the sins of the West. This opinion was especially widespread among Palestinian opinion-makers—until the breakdown of the 2000 Palestinian-Israeli peace process, when many came to view the recognition of any historical Jewish suffering as a political liability, and the Palestinian Authority-controlled media outlets increased their dissemination of Holocaust denial.

Another, more troubling approach to the Holocaust also exists in the Middle East. Hatred of Israel has led some Arabs to embrace Nazism itself, and to applaud its attempted genocide of the Jews. "[Give] thanks to Hitler," wrote columnist Ahmad Ragab recently in the Egyptian newspaper, *Al-Akhbar.* "He took revenge on the Israelis in advance, on behalf of the Palestinians. Our one complaint against him was that his revenge was not complete enough." Nazi-style anti-Semitism has in fact had a long history in the Middle East, beginning as early as 1937, when Nazi leaders conducted propaganda campaigns in the region.

The Mufti of Jerusalem during World War II, Hajj Amin al-Husayni, attempted to establish an alliance between Nazi Germany, Fascist Italy and Arab nationalists, for the ultimate purpose of conducting a Holy War of Islam against "international Jewry." Several Nazi-influenced political parties arose in the Middle East in the 1930s and 1940s, some of which went on to play important roles in shaping the leadership of Arab nations in the post–World War II period. Egypt, Syria, and Iran are widely believed to have harbored Nazi war criminals, though they do not admit doing so. *Mein Kampf* has been published and republished in Arabic since 1963.

HISTORICAL PERSPECTIVE, AND LOOKING TO THE FUTURE....

...The constant trumpeting of the anti-Semitic Islamist paradigm since the late 1960s, and the apparent absence of an opposing, moderate voice of Islam emanating with any real force from the Middle East, suggests that this new, theologically based demonization of Jews is being accepted by masses of

Muslims throughout the region. Weaving together a theological, metahistorical opposition to Jews with the worst of Western anti-Jewish conspiracy theories, today's anti-Semitism in the Middle East cannot be easily resolved. Religions are self-propagating, and theologies possess remarkable staying power across generations. A theologically based anti-Semitism gripped Christian Europe for hundreds of years; it took further centuries of reformation and revolution and an all-encompassing reordering of society for its domination to be broken. Even today its aftereffects linger. It would be prudent to not underestimate its potency.

2

"KILL A JEW—GO TO HEAVEN: THE PERCEPTION OF THE JEW IN PALESTINIAN SOCIETY"

Itamar Marcus and
Barbara Crook

The image of the Jew as propagated in Palestinian society is a microcosm of how much of the Arab/Muslim world views Jews. In the following essay, published in fall 2005, Itamar Marcus, founder and director of the Palestinian Media Watch, and Barbara Crook, the organization's North American representative, illustrate how the depiction of Jews by Palestinian religious and secular elites as inherently evil and an existential threat to humanity legitimizes their annihilation. The triumph of the radical Islamist organization Hamas (see part 6, chapter 4) in the 2006 Palestinian elections, and its seizure of complete control of Gaza in June 2007 exacerbated an already virulent anti-Semitism among the Palestinians.

* * *

INTRODUCTION

It was always my wish to turn my body into deadly shrapnel against the Zionists, and to knock on heaven's doors with the skulls of Zionists.
Reem Riyashi, 13 January 2004

The day after twenty-one-year-old Palestinian terrorist Reem Riyashi read these words for her farewell video, she murdered four Israelis in a suicide terror attack. She, or those who wrote the statement for her, believed that her act would guarantee her entry into heaven.

It will be demonstrated here that Palestinian religious, academic, and political elites are teaching an ideology of virulent hatred of Jews. The killing of Jews solely because they are Jews is presented as a religious obligation, necessary not only for Muslims and Arabs but as self-defense for all humankind.

Palestinian Authority (PA) elites have systematically built a three-stage case against Jewish existence, much as a prosecutor might build a case in court to demand a death sentence. As their expert witness they bring Allah Himself, Who is said to have sent a message through the Prophet Muhammad that killing Jews is a necessary step to achieve world redemption through Resurrection.

Stage 1 is characterized by collective labeling of Jews as the inherently evil enemies of Allah. Jewish traits are portrayed not as negative behavior that can be improved, but as the unchangeable Jewish nature. Stage 2 teaches that because of these immutable attributes, Jews represent an existential danger to all humanity. Stage 3 presents the necessary solution predetermined by Allah: the annihilation of Jews as legitimate self-defense and a service to humankind.

This inculcation began well before the outbreak of violence in September 2000, and continues in 2005 under the new Palestinian leadership.

These findings are based on eight years of analysis of teachings and statements by PA elites through television, radio, and newspapers and are representative of a much greater body of similar material conveyed in the PA-operated or strictly controlled media. This constitutes the Palestinian leadership's message to its populace. Numerous arrests and disciplinary beatings of Palestinian journalists by the PA's security forces have been documented. It is too early to judge whether the Mahmoud Abbas regime will permit press freedom. So far, on no issue has there been an exchange of a broad range of opinions that is indicative of change.

STAGE 1: COLLECTIVE LABELING
OF JEWS AS EVIL

The PA teaches that Jews are malevolent and immoral by nature. To support these claims it presents, through its controlled media, a steady stream of religious figures, academic authorities, political leaders, and others to corroborate the existence of fundamental Jewish evil.

Dr. Muhammad Mustafa Najem, a lecturer in Koranic interpretation at Gaza's Al-Azhar University, taught in a PA-televised sermon that Allah described the Jews as "characterized by conceit, pride, arrogance, savagery, disloyalty and treachery...[and] deceit and cunning." Just a month later he declared, also on PA TV: "The Jews are Jews, and we are forbidden to forget their character traits even for a moment, even for a blink of an eye."

Such indoctrination coming from the spiritual elite is particularly problematic in religious cultures such as the PA. Palestinians' allegiance to religious doctrine is so great that in a recent poll, when asked if the PA should "adopt laws endorsed by the Palestinian Legislative Council [PLC] or the Islamic shari'a," 68.6 percent of Palestinians inclined toward shari'a while only 15.9 percent preferred laws endorsed by the PLC.

The teachings of religious leaders in PA society are seen as the word of God—not opinions to be challenged, but dogma to be accepted.

The anti-Jewish indoctrination, however, is not limited to religious elites. Dr. Khader Abas, a lecturer in psychology at Gaza's Al-Aksa University, taught the origins of Jewish evil from a different perspective: "From the moment the [Jewish] child is born, he nurses hatred against others, nurses seclusion, nurses superiority...." It should be stressed in assessing statements by PA academics that the freedom that Western universities take for granted is nonexistent in PA institutions. There are numerous documented instances of the PA arresting or forcing the dismissal of Palestinian academics.

Palestinian children are taught disdain of Jews through children's entertainment programs. One such show, ostensibly teaching youngsters to stay out of "dangerous places," included this warning: "Watch but! You can't trust the Jews, because they can strike us suddenly at any moment."

Jews are also depicted as having inherent negative traits in popular entertainment. An example is crossword puzzles in daily newspapers, as in a clue that read: "Jewish character trait spelled backward." The solution: "Treachery."

Indeed, the religious leaders who speak on PA TV confer on Jews the ultimate iniquity: they are said to be the cursed enemy of Allah. Jews, it is claimed, rebelled against God by distorting the Torah He had given them. A historical educational program, already broadcast twice on PA TV in 2005, reiterated this common religious indictment: "The Jews in Medina had forsaken the commandments of Moses and returned to worshiping gold.... The Jewish scholars would make business of the Torah: they hid [selected] pages of it, attached pages, falsified pages, and went on to become rich."

As enemies of Allah, Jews are therefore the enemy of every Muslim. In the words of Najem, "Praise unto Allah, Who cursed our enemies; curse upon curse up to Judgment Day."

Reinforcing such notions is the portrayal of Jews as animals. In three instances, the Koran tells of Muhammad turning people into monkeys and/ or pigs. Another passage compares the Jews to donkeys. PA religious leaders, such as Imam Dr. Muhammad Ibrahim Maadi in his weekly lessons and official Friday sermons that are shown on PA TV, routinely apply these references to Jews. In one TV sermon Maadi proclaimed: "We are waging this cruel war with the brothers of the monkeys and pigs, the Jews and the sons of Zion."

Palestinian children have incorporated this language into their image of Jews. A girl on PA TV introduced herself as follows: "My name is Ala from Rafah. [I am] ten years old. Let the pigs and monkeys know and their leaders Sharon and Bush...."

Complementing the verbal dehumanization of Jews are visual images. Odious caricatures of Jews in Palestinian media appeared long before the eruption of violence in September 2000. For instance, in 1999, a cartoon in the official daily *Al-Hayat Al-Jadida* depicted a Jew as a subhuman dwarf with the caption: "The disease of the century."

Palestinian commentators commonly malign Jewish traditions. The following appeared in an opinion piece in *Al-Hayat Al-Jadida*:

> The Jews until today keep the rituals of Passover.... This holiday has various meanings.... Murdering foreigners is a godly virtue that should be emulated.... There is nothing in history more horrible than the theft, the greatest crime in history, that the Jews carried out the night of their Exodus [from Egypt].... In other words, robbing others is not only permitted, it is considered holy. Especially since this thievery was done under the direct command of God, [that is,] the God of the Jews.

The PA not only distorts Jewish tradition but also presents fictitious libels as authentic Jewish documents. Prominent among these is *The Protocols of the Elders of Zion*, which the PA routinely treats as the Jewish plan for world domination.

Dr. Riad Al-Astal, a lecturer in history at Al-Azhar University in Gaza, brought up the Protocols when discussing the rise of political Zionism in Europe. "What is known as the Zionist Renaissance," he asserted, "grew and the seeds of what is called The Protocols of the Elders of Zion appeared at the end of the eighteenth century [really nineteenth century]. They are the protocols that were presented in Basel [First Zionist Congress]."

Religious leaders stamp their indictments of Jewish nature with the irrefutable authority of the Prophet himself: "[Muhammad] warned us about the Jews, and about the Jews' evil and the Jews' deceit.... He clarified the character of the Jew ... so we would beware of them at every moment and at all times."

STAGE 2: JEWS AS EXISTENTIAL DANGER TO HUMANITY

Jews are said to be planning and executing massive crimes that endanger all humanity. They are claimed to be responsible for all civil strife, financial crises, conflicts, and wars.

Senior Palestinian academics regularly portray Jews as a threat to stable society, and Zionism as a European attempt to solve its Jewish problem. The aforementioned Dr. Riad Al-Astal asserted: "Britain's first aim was to be rid of the Jews, who were known to provoke disputes and disturbances and financial crises in Germany, France, and other European states."

This notion of Zionism as a European defense plan to be rid of its Jews has been taught as history in the PA for years. In 1998, an opinion piece in *Al-Hayat Al-Jadida* compared Hitler to Britain's pro-Zionist foreign secretary, Arthur Balfour:

> The difference between Hitler and Balfour was simple: the former did not have colonies to which to send the Jews, so he destroyed them, whereas Balfour turned Palestine into one of his colonies and sent Jews there. Balfour is Hitler

with colonies, while Hitler is Balfour without colonies. They both wanted to get rid of the Jews.... Zionism was crucial to the defense of the West's interests in the region, [by] ridding Europe of the burden of its Jews....

Palestinian children have embraced this teaching. In the words of a teenage girl named Majda: "...the Jewish presence in the land of Palestine was nothing but the liberation of all the countries of the world from the source of evil—that evil, which is widespread among the Sons of Zion..."

The Jews, however, have concealed their menacing nature from most of the world thanks to their "repulsive control over the world media." Once again, the *Protocols* are said to be the source of this policy:

> The *Protocols of the Elders of Zion* did not ignore the importance of using propaganda to promote the Zionist goals. In the second protocol is written: "Through the newspapers we will have the means to propel and to influence." In the twelfth protocol: "Our governments will hold the reins of most of the newspapers, and through this plan we will possess the primary power to turn to public opinion."

A PA religious leader taught that Jews were responsible for the tsunami that struck Asia in December 2004, as well as for all catastrophes on earth: "[the Jews] spit their poisons at the international and regional level; and more so at the domestic level. Those who are the reason for every disaster of the world...these are the Jews, Allah's curse be upon them."

The PA augments the picture by teaching that Judaism is a racist, murder-promoting religion. In an educational broadcast, Jirar Al-Kidwa, head of the PA Public Library, taught: "The commandments of their Hebrew Bible or their Talmud say that we are goyim—that is, non-Jews. They view all non-Jews as barbarians or as their servants, void of any human rights, and [one] may destroy them and kill them."

Al-Aziz Shahin, then PA minister of provisions, propounded the same message: "In their religious schools, where they learn that they are the chosen people of God and we are the others, we are considered the stage between the Jew and the monkey. This is a basis of the Jewish religion, and from this comes the killing of the Arab people in Palestine."

Palestinian children have internalized these messages and affirm that Judaism is life-threatening for them as Arabs. For instance, a child in a children's TV program said: "They [Israeli soldiers] fight the Arabs—not only Palestinians—by killing Palestinians, expelling Palestinians, and expelling Arabs. All this is permitted according to their dictionary, their constitution, and their religion...."

The PA also uses cultural expression and entertainment media to promote these messages. A full-length movie, *Garden of Death,* depicting Jews as evil murderers was broadcast numerous times over several years. Typical of this movie's script are lines in which a rabbi avers: "Palestinians have no place on this land. Never! If we ever keep one of them alive, it would be as if we had done nothing. May God exterminate all Palestinians!"

Accusations that Israel is committing a holocaust are common in the PA. Even children's education includes this message. In a play for children aired on PA TV, an actor cried: "They are the ones who did the Holocaust. . . . They opened the ovens for us to bake human beings. . . . When an oven stops burning they light a hundred [more] ovens."

Academic and religious leaders use metaphors to emphasize the danger posed by Jews. Dr. Issam Sissalem, senior lecturer in history at the Islamic University in Gaza, said of Israelis: "They are like a parasitic worm that eats a snail and lives in its shell. We will not let anyone live in our shell!" In a TV sermon, senior PA cleric Ibrahim Mudayris defined Jews as a "cancer." He is the PA's most popular choice as TV imam. In the last year, he presented 60 percent of the official Friday PA TV sermons.

Children have internalized this imagery and are likewise shown on television referring to Jews as germs and cancer, as in this statement by a child on PA TV: "That evil which is found in the Jews has become a germ among us; it is a cancer that buried us and is still burying and we are the ones who suffer from this cancer."

Setting the stage for the demand that Jews be killed, PA religious leaders explain that left unchecked, the Jews could bring about the destruction of the world. As Mudayris put it: "The Jews—a mere seven million [actually about 13 million]—trouble the entire earth. The cause of our nation's problems and the world's problems is the Jews."

He also asserted:

> The Jews will not rest until they ignite the whole world with the fire of their conflicts. . . . Our war against Zionism is not a war against the Israeli government alone, but a much greater war. It is a war against World Zionism that has begun controlling decision centers, controlling the Security Council, controlling the U.S. government, controlling Arab countries, controlling many countries around the world. Allah warned us of the Jews and their conflicts. The Jews are behind any conflict that can cause world destruction.

Stage 3: Eliminating the Threat

The first two stages define the PA's "objective" reality: Stage 1 characterizes the Jews as evil, and Stage 2 posits this evil as a threat to humanity. The verdict is inescapable: the world has no choice but to defend itself by fighting, subjugating, and killing Jews.

Indeed, according to the PA, all outbreaks of anti-Semitism can be explained as the world's response to this threat. Because Jews are said to have been so detrimental to the societies where they have lived, a common message taught in Palestinian society is that their persecution throughout history was justified by nations' need to protect themselves and take revenge on them.

The above-mentioned lecturer in psychology, Khader Abas, expounded this point on PA TV:

> The Israelis brought on themselves, I emphasize, brought on themselves in every society they lived, disasters and massacres. First, they concentrated money in their hands, denying it to others. Second, they spied against the nations where they lived. And the third important and basic aspect: they were condescending.... Thus the people of the societies they were in took revenge against them, or tried to punish them.

A month after Yasser Arafat died, Hassan Al-Khater, founder of the *Al-Quds Encyclopedia*, justified on PA TV the Pact of Omar—which in 637 CE prohibited Jews from living in Jerusalem—as a necessary defensive action:

> They did not ask for this condition, because they were racists or anti-Semites....The Muslims are familiar with the conspiracies of the Jews. For approximately four hundred or five hundred years, the Jews were forbidden from living in Jerusalem, before the arrival of Islam, and that due to the experience of those nations and of those cultures with this people.... If we presented this before a judge [today]...he would renew this condition.... The solution is that no Jew should live there.... The prosperity of that city [Jerusalem] and of this land necessitates that no Jew should ever live there.

The avowal that fighting Jews is legitimate self-defense continues under Abbas. As Mudayris stated in May 2005:

> Read the history....You'll find that Jews are behind every conflict on earth. The suffering of nations? The Jews are behind it! Ask Britain! What did it do to the Jews at the beginning of the sixth century [actually, end of the thirteenth century]? Chased them down, made them suffer, and prevented them from entering for more than three hundred years....Ask France what it did to the Jews! They made them suffer, chased them down, and burned their Talmud, for the conflicts that they [Jews] tried to ignite in France....Ask Portugal what it did to the Jews! Ask Czarist Russia—which hosted the Jews, and they plotted to murder the Czar! And they were massacred again and again. Don't ask Germany what it did to the Jews, since the Jews are the ones who provoked the Nazis so the world would go to war against it.

Once anti-Semitism by Arabs and other nations is legitimized as self-defense, fighting Jews becomes the fulfillment of a duty, as Maadi underlined in a televised Friday sermon: All weapons must be aimed at the Jews, Allah's enemies, the cursed nation in the Koran, whom Allah describes as monkeys and pigs.... [The] Koran says clearly that the worst enemies of the Muslim nation are the Jews, may Allah fight them....

The call to fight Jews solely because of their ethnicity is widespread in the PA. Ismail Radwan, professor at the Islamic University in Gaza, justifies the ongoing battle: "It is no coincidence that the Noble Koran mentions the story of Muhammad's heavenly ascent while talking of the Israelites—as though Allah was preparing the Islamic nation that Jews will be in this land and as if He was addressing the Muslims: 'O Muslims, prepare yourselves for the struggle with world Jewry.'"

Self-defense is cited together with religious sources as the justification for genocide. Dr. Ahmad Abu Halabiyah, rector of advanced studies at the Islamic University, explained on PA TV:

> The Jews are the Jews....They do not have any moderates or any advocates of peace. They are all liars. They must be butchered and must be killed....The Jews are like a spring—as long as you step on it with your foot it doesn't move. But if you lift your foot from the spring, it hurts you and punishes you...It is forbidden to have mercy in your hearts for the Jews in any place and in any land. Make war on them anywhere that you find yourself. Any place that you meet them, kill them.

Beyond self-defense, the PA teaches that the death of Jews at the hands of Muslims is a precondition of world redemption. The PA promotes this belief by repeatedly propounding in their print and television media the following hadith, that is, a tradition attributed to Muhammad: "The Hour [Resurrection] will not take place until the Muslims fight the Jews, and kill them. And the Jews will hide behind the rock and tree, and the rock and tree will say: 'O Muslim, O servant of Allah, there is a Jew behind me, come and kill him!'"

Frequently in recent years, Palestinian religious leaders and academics have taught publicly that this genocidal hadith, articulated more than a thousand years ago, is a religious obligation today. This is often blended with the self-defense argument, as in this statement by Mudayris from another TV sermon:

> Why is there this malice? Because there are none who love the Jews on the face of the earth: not man; not rock; and not tree—everything hates them. They destroy everything; they destroy the trees and destroy the houses. Everything wants vengeance on the Jews, on these pigs on the face of the earth, and the day of our victory, Allah willing, will come.

On numerous occasions, suicide bombings have been presented as fulfillment of this obligation, as in a sermon by Maadi:

> All the weapons must be aimed at the Jews, Allah's enemies....They will not be deterred unless we blow ourselves up, willingly and as our duty, in their midst....We will blow them up in Hadera. We will blow them up in Tel Aviv and in Netanya so that Allah will make us masters over this riff-raff. We will fight against them and rule over them until the Jew will hide behind the tree and rock and the tree and rock will say: "Muslim! Servant of Allah, there is a Jew behind me, kill him."

The call for genocide has continued since Arafat's death. On 10 January 2005, the above-mentioned Hassan Al-Khater cited the same hadith requiring the killing of all Jews everywhere. This came just two weeks after he devoted an entire TV lecture to analyzing this hadith and concluded that its demand for genocide was specifically directed at the Palestinians: "Allah meant our land and our people and meant our trees and our stones."

In May 2005, Mudayris taught on PA TV that the final stage of history would be the subjugation of Christian countries under Islam. However, the Jews could not be subdued and therefore the solution awaiting them was death—literally, the extermination of every Jew.

> We [Muslims] have ruled the world [in the past] and a day will come, by Allah, when we shall rule the world [again]. The day will come and we shall rule America, Britain, we shall rule the entire world, except the Jews. The Jews will not live under our rule agreeably and permanently, since they have been treacherous in nature throughout history. A day will come when all shall have relief from the Jews, even the tree and the stone, which have suffered from them. Listen to your Beloved [Muhammad], who tells you about the most dire end awaiting the Jews.

Muhammad Abd Al-Hadi La'afi, responsible for religious teaching and instruction in the Office of the PA Wakf, likewise wrote of the impending extermination of the Jews: "The battle with the Jews will surely come....The Prophet spoke about it in more than one hadith and the Resurrection will not come without the victory of the believers over the descendants of the monkeys and pigs and with their annihilation."

CONCLUSION: PARALLELS TO NAZI IDEOLOGY

There are striking parallels between PA and Nazi ideology. In *Mein Kampf,* Hitler used the same two justifications for his hatred of Jews: self-defense against the threat they posed to humanity, and fighting for God. He wrote: "[the Jews] would have as their final result the collapse of human culture, thereby leading to the desolation of the world...the funeral wreath of humanity...believe today that I am acting according to the will of the almighty Creator: when I defend myself against the Jew, I am fighting for the work of the Lord."

The PA has built an extensive case against Jewish existence based on libels and stereotyping. Jews are said to be inherently evil and an existential danger. Their annihilation, then, is legitimate self-defense, a service to humanity, and an enactment of God's will.

Although the PA is not reticent about its plans, the world remains apathetic except for an occasional criticism of what is called "incitement." This, too, seems to be a repetition of the world's indifference to Hitler's open calls for genocide. As Justice Robert H. Jackson, chief U.S. counsel to the Nuremberg Trials, wrote: "We must not forget that when the Nazi plans were boldly proclaimed, they were so extravagant that the world refused to take them seriously."

3

"Jews Use Teenagers' Blood for Purim Pastries"

Dr. Umayma Ahmad Al-Jalahma

"Of all the accusations which fanaticism and ignorance have used as a weapon against Judaism, there is none which can be compared in terms of improbability and absurdity to that of ritual murder," wrote a Jewish scholar more than a hundred years ago. During the Middle Ages, Jews were accused of murdering Christian children in order to use their blood for making matzo, the unleavened bread, for the Passover holiday. To Christians it seemed totally consistent with Jewish behavior that the people who had spilled Christ's blood would seek to reenact the crucifixion by torturing and draining the blood of an innocent child and that they would use that blood for some magical rite. The charge of ritual murder, which led to the torture and burning alive of thousands of Jews, demonstrated the power and appeal of myths that disparaged and demonized the Jewish people. It showed the willingness, even eagerness, of many Christians to believe any absurdity about Jews and to expect the worst of them.

The libel of ritual murder persisted in Europe into modern times; in the late nineteenth and early twentieth century Jews accused of this act were put on trial in several European lands and on July 4, 1946, just fourteen months after the end of World War II and the almost total extermination of Poland's Jews, a frenzied Polish mob, stirred by the ritual murder allegation shot, axed, and clubbed to death forty-two Jewish survivors of the Holocaust, including children.

Today in the Western world the charge is now seen as blatantly absurd, a medieval superstition that had no basis in fact. But it has found a new home in the Muslim world, the subject of numerous books, articles, television programs, and cartoons. The following article, "Jews Use Teenagers' Blood for Purim Pastries," written by columnist Dr. Umayma Ahmad Al-Jalahma of King Faisal University, was published on March 10, 2002 in the Saudi government daily *Al-Riyadh*. It purports to show how Jews use the blood of a Gentile youth in order to make pastries for the holiday of Purim.

*　*　*

Special Ingredient for Jewish Holidays Is Human Blood from Non-Jewish Youth

I chose to [speak] about the Jewish holiday of Purim, because it is connected to the month of March. This holiday has some dangerous customs that will, no doubt, horrify you, and I apologize if any reader is harmed because of this.

During this holiday, the Jew must prepare very special pastries, the filling of which is not only costly and rare—it cannot be found at all on the local and international markets.

Unfortunately, this filling cannot be left out, or substituted with any alternative serving the same purpose. For this holiday, the Jewish people must obtain human blood so that their clerics can prepare the holiday pastries: In other words, the practice cannot be carried out as required if human blood is not spilled!!

Before I go into the details, I would like to clarify that the Jews' spilling human blood to prepare pastry for their holidays is a well-established fact, historically and legally, all throughout history. This was one of the main reasons for the persecution and exile that were their lot in Europe and Asia at various times.

This holiday [Purim] begins with a fast, on March 13, like the Jewess Esther who vowed to fast. The holiday continues on March 14; during the holiday, the Jews wear carnival-style masks and costumes and overindulge in drinking alcohol, prostitution, and adultery.

This holiday has become known among Muslim historians as the "Holiday of Masks."

How the Jews Drain the Blood from Their Young Victims

Who was Esther, and why the Jews sanctify her and act as she did, I will clarify in my article next Tuesday[1] Allah willing. Today, I would like to tell you how human blood is spilled so it can be used for their holiday pastries. The blood is spilled in a special way. How is it done?

For this holiday, the victim must be a mature adolescent who is, of course, a non-Jew—that is, a Christian or a Muslim. His blood is taken and dried into granules. The cleric blends these granules into the pastry dough; they can also be saved for the next holiday. In contrast, for the Passover slaughtering, about which I intend to write one of these days, the blood of Christian and Muslim children under the age of 10 must be used, and the cleric can mix the blood [into the dough] before or after dehydration.

The Actions of the Jewish Vampires Cause Them Pleasure

Let us now examine how the victims' blood is spilled. For this, a needle-studded barrel is used; this is a kind of barrel, about the size of the human body, with extremely sharp needles set in it on all sides. [These needles] pierce the victim's body, from the moment he is placed in the barrel.

These needles do the job, and the victim's blood drips from him very slowly. Thus, the victim suffers dreadful torment—torment that affords the Jewish vampires great delight as they carefully monitor every detail of the blood-shedding with pleasure and love that are difficult to comprehend.

After this barbaric display, the Jews take the spilled blood, in the bottle set in the bottom [of the needle-studded barrel], and the Jewish cleric makes his co-religionists completely happy on their holiday when he serves them the pastries in which human blood is mixed.

There is another way to spill the blood: The victim can be slaughtered as a sheep is slaughtered, and his blood collected in a container. Or, the victim's veins can be slit in several places, letting his blood drain from his body.

This blood is very carefully collected—as I have already noted by the "rabbi," the Jewish cleric, the chef who specializes in preparing these kinds of pastries.

The human race refuses even to look at the Jewish pastries, let alone prepare them or consume them!

Note

1. In the article's sequel (March 12), the columnist tells the story of the *Book of Esther* and concludes, "Since then, the Old Testament, the Jewish holy book, requires the Jews to glorify this holiday and show their joy. This joy can only be complete with the consumption of pastries mixed with human blood." This note comes with the translation.

4

"Their Plan Is the 'Protocols of the Elders of Zion'"

Covenant of the Islamic Resistance Movement (Hamas)

Organized by radical Palestinian Islamists, the Islamic Resistance Movement, or Hamas, openly calls for the destruction of the Jewish state. It started as an armed terrorist movement that recruited suicide bombers and instructed them to set off their devices in crowded restaurants, buses, and shopping centers. These attacks gained Hamas popularity and in 2006 it was voted into power by a surprising majority of Palestinians, and in June 2007 it seized total control of the Gaza region of the Palestinian territories, driving out by force Fatah, its competitor for power.

Whereas al Qaeda sees itself engaged in a global religious struggle and runs terrorist operations in many parts of the world, Hamas' agenda is totally nationalistic—destroying Israel and erecting an Islamic state on its ruins—and its suicide bombings and rocket launchings are confined to Israel. Despite economic pressure from the West, Hamas refuses to honor past agreements the Palestinian leadership had made with Israel, renounce terrorism, or recognize Israel's right to exist. Its unrelenting hatred of Israel is revealed in the following statement by Khaled Mash'al, political bureau head of Hamas: "Before Israel dies it must be humiliated and degraded....We will make them lose their eyesight, we will make them lose their brains."[1] Hamas remains true to its covenant, issued on April 18, 1988, which employs themes from the *Protocols of the Learned Elders of Zion* and other notorious anti-Semitic sources. Excerpts from the covenant follow.

*   *   *

Our enemies [the Jews] have planned from time immemorial in order to reach the position they've obtained now. They strive to collect enormous material riches to be used in the realization of their dreams. With money, they've gained control of the international media beginning with news agencies, newspapers and publishing houses, broadcasting stations...with their money they have detonated revolutions in different parts of the world to obtain their interests and reap their fruits. They were behind the French Revolution and the Communist Revolution and were responsible for most of the revolutions we've heard about elsewhere. With their money, they've created secret organizations which spread throughout the world in order to destroy societies, and to achieve the Zionist interest such as the Free Masons, the Rotary, and the Lions Club. All these are destructive espionage organizations. With their money, they've been able to take control over the imperialist countries and spread corruption there. The same goes for international and local wars. They were behind World War I in order to destroy the Islamic Caliphate [Ottoman Empire] and make material profit. Then they obtained the Balfour Declaration [of November 1917, by which the British government committed itself to facilitate the restoration of a Jewish homeland in Palestine] and established the League of Nations in order to rule the world through this organization.

They were also behind World War II where they made enormous profits from speculation in war material; paved the way for the creation of their state and inspired the establishment of the United Nations and Security Council to replace the League of Nations in order to rule the world through them. There is no war anywhere in which their fingers do not play. . . . The Imperialist powers in the capitalist West and the Communist East support the enemy with everything they can. And they switch roles. . . . In the day that Islam will appear, the powers of heresy will unite to confront it because the nation of heresy is one. . . . [Clause 22.]

World Zionism and the imperialist powers are trying through wise movement and careful planning to get Arab countries one-by-one out of the circle of struggle with Zionism so that finally they will face only one Palestinian people. . . . [T]oday it will be Palestine, but tomorrow it will be some other country since the Zionist plan has no limits. After Palestine, they aspire the destruction of the area they reach, they will still aspire to further expansion. Their plan is the "Protocols of the Elders of Zion" and their present [conduct] testifies to the truth of what we say. [Clause 32.]

NOTE

1. Matthias Kuentzel, "Hitler's Legacy: Islamic Antisemitism in the Middle East," a paper presented at the international seminar series Antisemitism in Comparative Perspective under the auspices of the Institution for Social and Policy Studies at Yale University, New Haven, CT, November 30, 2006 http://www.yale.edu/isps/seminars/antisemitism/index.

5

"Muslims Against Anti-Semitism: Ways to Promote Common Values"

Tariq Ramadan

Condemnation of the myths and lies directed against Jews by the Arab/ Muslim media is virtually nonexistent in the Middle East. In Europe and the United States, some Islamic organizations and intellectuals have protested the anti-Semitism propagated by their coreligionists in the Middle East. One such intellectual is Tariq Ramadan, a controversial Swiss-born Islamic philosopher who is a Senior Research Fellow at St. Antony's College, Oxford, and is also associated with other educational institutions and foundations. He has written and lectured extensively on Islamic philosophy, European Muslims, and the relationship between Islam and the West. Ramadan has often been praised as a moderate who has sought to adapt Islam to the modern world and Western society. On the other hand, he has also been accused of tailoring his views to appeal to the sympathies of different audiences, of supporting terrorism and its apologists, and of harboring anti-Semitic sentiments. In 2004, Ramadan, who had been appointed to a special chair at Notre Dame University in Indiana, was denied a visa by the American government because of his alleged terrorist sympathies and, specifically, contributions he had made to two Palestinian charities that were accused of providing support to Hamas.

In the following selection, published late in 2004, Ramadan speaks with the voice of a moderate, as he argues against anti-Semitism, pleading for mutual respect between Jews and Muslims and a recognition of shared values. He asks his fellow Muslims in the West to focus on the positive references to Jews in the Qur'an and to view "certain equivocal texts" in context, to stop blaming the Jews for the racism and discrimination they encounter, and to be sensitive to the pain and suffering caused to the Jewish people by the Holocaust. He tells both peoples to "stop feeding sentiments of victimization," and asks the Jewish intellectuals, both secular and religious, to recognize that criticism of the policies of the state of Israel should not be interpreted as a lack of respect for Judaism.

*   *   *

The situation in our societies is becoming more and more difficult insofar as the increasing public expression of anti-Semitism and racism. We all know— Governments, official institutions, as well as citizens—that if we remain passive, the situation will worsen and drive us towards a new troubled era of racist and ethical stigmatizations.

There are many ways and strategies to try to face the problems of anti-Semitism and racism in our societies, but one can say that at the global level there are two main choices: either to let the Jews alone struggle against anti-Semitism while advocating that every ethnic or religious community should protect itself (even though it is against the others), or to call on all people of goodwill, from every community, to commit themselves within a global movement, acting against all kinds of racism in the name of common universal values. The latter perspective is, in my view, the only efficient way, even though it is a very demanding task at both intellectual and practical levels.

In order to find and build this shared ground of common values and proactive commitment, every one of us, from his or her respective Jewish, Christian, Muslim, agnostic or atheist background, must put into motion a twofold process: first, one has to try to extract and promote from one's religious or cultural tradition the values that are universal and common in order to be able to reach out and act and work with people of other belongings and faiths; second, one has to distinguish between the greatness of the message she/he believes in and the less noble use of it that is made by fellow-practising Jews, Christians, Muslims, etc. Self-criticism is an imperative prerequisite.

As we address the issue of anti-Semitism, it is urgent and necessary from a Muslim viewpoint to commit ourselves to promote from within our communities two concomitant intellectual stances: objective self-criticism and promotion of common values. As the relationships between the Muslim world and Jews are influenced and disturbed by the perpetual reference to the Israeli-Palestinian conflict, it is also crucial to differentiate the two problems and focus on this specific question: how to struggle with anti-Semitism from a Muslim viewpoint?

We should start by saying that the responsibility of Muslims and Jews in the West is tremendous: living together, both citizens of the same countries, they should raise their voices in the name of justice and mutual respect. In France, for example, one finds a unique situation, namely, the largest Jewish and Muslim communities in Europe living together. In America, we find the same situation, with two important religious communities sharing the same citizenship. That in itself should be an ideal opportunity for people to learn to live in harmony. However, the reality is that problems are on the rise. While tensions have been incidental in the past, the situation has been exacerbated during the second Intifada and more recently during the upsurge of violence in the Middle East. The trend appears to be that the Muslim immigrants, as well as native European and American Muslims, are becoming extremely sensitive to the events occurring in Palestine and are demonstrating their frustration quite overtly.

Malicious words, cries of "down with the Jews" [are] shouted during protest demonstrations and, in a few cities in France, reports of synagogues being vandalized. One also hears ambiguous statements about Jews, their "occult-like" power, their "insidious" role within the media and their "nefarious" plans. After September 11, the false rumor that 4,000 Jews did not show up for work the morning of the terrorist attacks against the World Trade Center was relayed throughout predominantly Muslim areas.

It is very rare to hear Muslim voices that set themselves apart from this kind of discourse and attitude. Often, one will try to explain away these phenomena as being a result of extreme frustration and humiliation. That may be true, but one must be honest and analyze the situation deeply. This is the real meaning of self-criticism. Much like the situation across the Muslim world, there exists in the West today a discourse which is anti-Semitic, seeking legitimacy in certain Islamic texts and support in the present situation in Palestine. This is the attitude of not only the marginalized youth but also of intellectuals and Imams, who see the manipulative hand of the "Jewish lobby" at each turn or every political setback.

The situation is far too serious for one to be satisfied by simple explanations based on current frustrations. In the name of their faith and conscience, Muslims must take a clear position so that a pernicious atmosphere does not take hold in the Western countries. Nothing in Islam can legitimize xenophobia or the rejection of a human being due to his/her religious creed or ethnicity. One must say unequivocally, with force, that anti-Semitism is unacceptable and indefensible. The message of Islam requires respect of Jewish faith and spirituality as noble expressions of "The People of the Book." During the initial phase of the Prophet's settlement in Medina, prior to the conflicts of alliances, the Prophet Muhammad sternly admonished: "He who is unjust with a contractor (Christians and Jews of Medina), I shall bear witness against him on the Day of Judgment." Later, during a period of extreme conflict [between Jews and Muslims], eight Qur'anic verses were revealed to absolve a Jew who had falsely been accused of a crime by a Muslim. Mohammed constantly taught respect for all human beings, with all their differences. One day, he stood up out of respect when he saw a funeral procession nearby. When told it was that of a Jew, he replied, "Is it not a human soul?"

One cannot simultaneously neglect these teachings and continue to feed a tainted portrayal concerning Jews. It is the responsibility of Islamic organizations and Imams to send an unambiguous message about the profound link between Islam and Judaism; the recognition of Moses and the Torah as part of Islamic teachings; the necessary contextualization of certain equivocal texts within the Qu'ran; and on mutual respect and the rejection of all forms of explicit or implicit anti-Semitism. This also means to acknowledge the horrors of the Holocaust by studying its ramifications and respecting the pain and suffering which have shaped the Jewish conscience in the twentieth century.

In order for all Muslim citizens to understand this teaching, there must be a corresponding set of actions. One has to fight feelings of victimization, which colonize the spirit of many Muslim citizens in the West, especially those who are the most marginalized. The frustration within these communities leads to blaming the other, the State, the police and "the Jew who does not like us and who manipulates us...." It is here that Muslim intellectuals and the public authority should share the responsibility. The first step is to disseminate an Islamic awareness that is coherent and non-literal. It should emphasize personal responsibility and respect of others. As for public authorities, it is important that they encourage concrete actions that break the cycle of economic ghettos and encourage reform of social and urban politics at a local level. Whether we like it or not, unemployment and discrimination are one of the major roots of racism.

At another level, there is urgency for Jewish and Muslim representatives to start communicating and establish an honest dialogue in order to avoid knee-jerk, reflexive community responses that may undermine the principle of living together in harmony. Self-criticism must become a mutual exercise. If it is necessary to condemn the anti-Semitic language of some Muslims, it is also the responsibility of Jewish intellectuals, religious or secular, not to confuse the different spheres. The respect that we have towards Judaism should not be subject to suspicion once we denounce the unjust policies of the State of Israel. In fostering this type of amalgams, we will end by creating chasms between communities, and that is certainly to empty the ethical content of our common Western citizenship based on the values of justice and equality.

Muslims and Jews alike should stop feeding sentiments of victimization, and reconsider the discourse that one is creating towards the other. In the name of a common ethics of citizenship, our dignity will be based upon our ability to know how to criticize, transcending one's creed, a State or an organization, without considering that it is "clearly" a manifestation of anti-Semitism or Islamophobia. It is exactly this type of intellectual requirement that one must teach and which will help all Jews and Muslims to offer to their faith and to their respective belonging the magnitude of a self-conscience based on universal principals, and not a closed-minded ghetto identity.

In Europe and in America, the conditions are right to bring these challenges to light, and this will have a tremendous impact at the international level, and especially in the majority of Islamic countries. What remains is the mutual commitment to a constructive self-analysis and to refuse the destructive temptation of selective condemnations.

6

"Holocaust Denial Undermines Islam"

Shaykh Hamza Yusuf

In recent years Nazi apologists and anti-Semites have deliberately and cruelly manufactured a new myth—that of Holocaust denial. These people argue that during World War II the Germans had no policy of extermination; that Jews invented the Holocaust to gain world sympathy for Zionism and to wrest enormous indemnity payments from innocent Germans. Holocaust denial, which flies in the face of all documentary evidence, including the testimony of eyewitness survivors, perpetrators, and bystanders, demonstrates anew the willingness of anti-Semites to embrace and propagate the most grotesque beliefs about Jews. This myth now circulates widely in the Arab/Muslim media, including mainstream publications.

In the following piece, published in *Tikkun*, a liberal Jewish journal, Hamza Yusuf condemns the Iran-sponsored conference of Holocaust deniers as a tragic event which undermines respect for Islam. Hamza Yusuf was raised in California in a Greek Orthodox family. After surviving a life-threatening car accident at age seventeen, he began reading the Qur'an and eventually converted to Islam. Yusuf spent ten years studying Islam in the Middle East and West Africa. After 9/11 he appeared with President Bush as a symbol of Islamic moderation, and he continues to denounce terrorism as contrary to the true spirit of Islam.

* * *

Epistemology is a branch of philosophy that studies the nature and basis of knowledge. How do we know things? It also studies the veracity of "truth." How do we know the difference between belief, knowledge, opinion, fact, reality and fantasy?...We live in a world where facts are meaningful and opinions can be assessed, at least to the degree that we deem them sound or unsound....For instance, there is consensus among historians that the Normans invaded England in 1066; too many accounts of this momentous event exist and have been recounted in each generation through multiple sources. In the case of any solitary original source, healthy skepticism is warranted.... Much of what we know about the world and what we accept as truth comes from multiply transmitted accounts. Let's say I claim that Australia doesn't exist and is merely a figment of our imagination, that its origins lie in a whimsical cartographer in the Middle Ages who decided that such a large ocean needed a land mass. And, when confronted with people who claim to be from Australia and can prove it, I dismiss them as part of a conspiracy of cartographers who wish to perpetuate the myth of their forbearer. I would be laughed at, or ignored, or deemed "certifiable." While this example seems absurd, many people actually believe things just as fatuous and far-fetched.

Holocaust denial is one such example. As one who has read some Holocaust denial literature, with the poorly reproduced pictures and claims of the orchestration of these scenes in collusion with the U.S. government, I can attest to the tragic gullibility of people who take such literature as historical truth.... [Holocaust denial] is presented with utter certainty by the "researchers." In the end, reality is manipulated to meet the needs of the mythologist.

Indeed, we are each entitled to our own opinions, but not to our own facts. And those who present alternative versions of "reality" tend to reject everything that does not suit their theory, and cherry-pick and interpret everything—facts, innuendos or "coincidences"—that does.

In the case of the Holocaust, the facts are clear and transmitted from multiple sources. Tens of thousands of Jewish and other individuals who survived the death camps and other horrors of Nazi Germany lived to tell of it. Nazis were brought to trial, evidence was presented in court, and they were convicted. Mass graves were found, and gas chambers were discovered, which were clearly not delicing rooms as some callously claimed. The ovens exist and cannot be reduced to an efficient way of preventing cholera outbreaks or disposing of victims of starvation. I have personally met many Holocaust survivors and their children. I have seen tattoos. I have also heard firsthand accounts of the horrific events. The numbers and details of such events may be legitimate areas of research and inquiry for scholars, but questioning whether the events took place at all undermines the epistemological basis of our collective knowledge. Muslims, of all people, should be conscious of this as their religion is predicated on the same epistemological premises as many major events in history, such as the Holocaust. To deny such things is to undermine Islam as an historical event. That a "conference" examining the historicity of the Holocaust should take place in a Muslim country hosted by a Muslim head of state is particularly tragic[1] and, in my estimation, undermines the historicity of the faith of the people of that state.

In our inherent contradictions as humans, and in order to validate our own pain, we deny the pain of others. But it is in acknowledging the pain of others that we achieve fully our humanity. A close friend of mine, a professor of religion in a Muslim country for many years, recently told me that his wife, an English teacher in that country, had wanted to use Anne Frank: *The Diary of a Young Girl* as a text for her Muslim pupils. But the school administrators repeatedly denied her request because they deemed it inappropriate reading for young Muslims. It is sad that the current political morass in the Middle East has led to this intolerable refusal to confront a people's collective suffering. Perhaps in acknowledging that immense past of Jewish suffering, in which the Holocaust is only the most heinous chapter, Muslims can better help the Jewish community to understand the current Muslim pain in Palestine, Iraq and other places. In finding out about others, we encourage others to find out about us. It would greatly help our Jewish brethren to know the historical facts of Jewish experience in the Muslim world, which are often heartening and humanizing and very different from their European experience. In our mutual edification, we grow together.

NOTE

1. The allusion is to the conference organized in 2006 by the president of Iran, Mahmoud Ahmadinejad, to "debate" whether the Holocaust really happened.

Glossary

Caliph, Caliphate   The title caliph designates a ruler who is recognized as the successor to the Prophet Muhammad and therefore has religious and political authority over all Muslims. The caliphate is a state ruled by the caliph that represents the unity of the Muslim world. The sultan of the Ottoman Empire was the last caliph. Following the dismemberment of the empire after World War I, the caliphate was officially terminated in 1924.

Dar al-Islam   Literally, the house of Islam, the term refers to lands that are or once were under Islamic rule.

Dar al-harb   Literally, the house of war, the term refers to lands ruled by non-Muslims.

Da'wa   Preaching or missionary activities.

Dhimmis   Members of non-Muslim religions granted the right to live in lands under Islamic rule.

Fatwa   A legal opinion or decree issued by a recognized religious scholar or authority.

Fiqh   Islamic jurisprudence, interpretations of *shari'a*.

Fitna   Communal discord or civil war.

Hadith(s)   Narratives of the teachings, sayings, and actions of the Prophet Muhammad.

Hajj   Pilgrimage to the holy city of Mecca required of all Muslims at least once in a lifetime.

Haram   Forbidden by Islam.

Hijira   The flight from Mecca to Medina by Muhammad in the year 622 that marks the year one in the Muslim calendar.

Ijtihad   The independent reinterpretation of Islamic texts by religious scholars who are not bound by existing interpretations and legal precedents.

Jahiliyyah, Jahili   Originally the term *jahiliyyah* referred to the ignorance and barbarism of the pre-Islamic tribes in the Arabian Peninsula. However, by extension, the term has come to include all non-Muslims, and some fundamentalists even consider Muslim's not living strictly according to the dictates of *shari'a* to be part of *jahili* society.

Jihad/Jihaad Warfare in the service of Islam or, alternatively, a spiritual struggle to achieve dominance over one's passions.

Jizyah A poll tax paid by non-Muslims *(dhimmis)* living in lands under Muslim rule.

Khutba The Friday sermon of an imam.

Mujahed/Mujahid (pl. Mujahideen/Mujahidin) Holy warrior(s).

Salafism A fundamentalist movement that seeks to purify Islam by returning to the religion as Salafis believe it was originally practiced by Prophet Muhammad and his early followers.

Shahadah The Muslim profession of faith.

Shahid (fem. Shahida) Martyr.

Shari'a The divine law of Islam.

Sirah Religiously inspired biographies of the Prophet Muhammad.

Sunnah Accounts of the religious actions of the Prophet Muhammad believed to have been transmitted and validated by his original companions. The term is sometimes used interchangeably with hadith.

Sura A chapter of the Qur'an.

Tawhid Belief in the absolute unity of God, the monotheism that is a central tenet of Islam.

Ulama (Ulema) Muslim religious leaders.

Umma(h) The worldwide community of Muslims.

Wahhabism An austere, puritanical Islamic movement, founded in the eighteenth century, that dominates religious practice in Saudi Arabia and whose propagation to other parts of the Muslim world is financed by Saudi Arabia and the Gulf states.

CREDITS

PART 1   JIHADISM: THEOLOGY AND IDEOLOGY

1. Shmuel Bar, "The Religious Sources of Islamic Terrorism," *Policy Review*, No. 125 (June/July 2004), pp. 27–37. Reprinted by permission of *Policy Review*.
2. Cited in Rudolph Peters, *Jihad in Classical and Modern Islam: A Reader* (Princeton, NJ: Markus Wiener, 1996), pp. 47–51.
3. From Sayyid Qutb, *Milestones* (New Delhi, India: Millat Book Centre, n.d.), pp. 71–72.
4. Ayatollah Ruhollah Khomeini, "Islam Is Not a Religion of Pacifists," in Amir Taheri, ed., *Holy Terror: Inside the World of Islamic Terrorism* (Bethesda, MD: Adler & Adler, 1985), pp. 241–243. Reprinted by permission of Adler & Adler Publishers, Inc.
5. From David Cook, *Understanding Jihad* (Berkeley and Los Angeles, CA: University of California Press, 2005), pp. 157–161. Copyright © 2005 by The Regents of the University of California. Reprinted by permission of the University of California Press.

PART 2   AL QAEDA: ACTIVATING JIHADISM

1. Osama bin Laden, "Declaration of Jihad against Jews and Crusaders," in Bruce Lawrence, ed., James Howarth, trans., *Messages to the World: The Statements of Osama bin Laden* (London and New York: Verso, 2005), pp. 58–62. Reprinted by permission of Verso.
2. From Ayman al Zawahiri, "Knights Under the Prophet's Banner," in Laura Mansfield, trans., *His Own Words: A Translation of the Writings of Dr. Ayman al Zawahiri* (USA: TLG Publications, 2006), pp. 203–215, 218–220, 222–225. Copyright 2006 by Laura Mansfield. Reprinted by permission of Laura Mansfield.
3. From Efraim Karsh, *Islamic Imperialism: A History* (New Haven, CT: Yale University Press, 2006), pp. 226–228, 230–232, 234. Copyright 2006 by Yale University Press. Reprinted by permission of Yale University Press.
4. From Mary R. Habeck, *Knowing the Enemy: Jihadist Ideology and the War on Terror* (New Haven, CT: Yale University Press, 2006), pp. 161–167, 170. Copyright 2006 by Yale University Press. Reprinted by permission of Yale University Press.
5. Mary R. Habeck, "Jihadist Strategies in the War on Terrorism," lecture delivered on August 12, 2004 (Heritage Lecture No. 855; Washington, DC: Heritage Foundation, November 8, 2004). Reprinted by permission of The Heritage Foundation.

6. Yassin Musharbash "What al-Qaida Really Wants," *Der Spiegel*, August 12, 2005 <http://www.spiegel.de/international/0,1518369448,00.html>. Reprinted by permission of *Der Spiegel*.

PART 3   THE WAR ON TERROR:
SEIZING THE INITIATIVE

1. Daniel Benjamin, Prepared Statement, U.S. Congress, Senate, Committee on Foreign Relations, *Hearing on Counter Terrorism: The Changing Face of Terror*, 109th Congress, Second Session, June 13, 2006 (Washington, DC: U.S. Government Printing Office, 2007), pp. 60–63.
2. From *The 9/11 Commission Report: Final Report of the National Commission on Terrorist Attacks upon the United States* (authorized edition; New York: W.W. Norton, 2004), pp. 365, 367, 374, 376–377, 379–382.
3. Bruce Hoffman, "Al Qaeda on the Run or on the March?" Written Testimony, U.S. Congress, House of Representatives, Armed Services Subcommittee on Terrorism Unconventional Threats and Capabilities, *Hearing on Challenges for the U.S. Special Operations Command (SOCAMM) by the Global Terrorist Threat*, 110th Congress, 1st Session, February 14, 2007 (Washington, DC: U.S. Government Printing Office, 2008), pp. 47–68.
4. Abdurrahman Wahid, "Right Islam vs. Wrong Islam: Muslims and Non-Muslims Must Unite to Defeat the Wahhabi Ideology," *Wall Street Journal*, December 30, 2005, p. A16. Reprinted by permission of the LibForAll Foundation.

PART 4   SUICIDE BOMBERS: MOTIVATION,
RECRUITMENT, INDOCTRINATION, AND
EFFECTIVENESS

1. From Walter Laqueur, *No End to War: Terrorism in the Twenty-First Century* (New York: Continuum, 2004), pp. 91–97. Reprinted by permission of Walter Laqueur.
2. From Robert A. Pape, *Dying to Win: The Strategic Logic of Suicide Terrorism* (New York: Random House, 2005), pp. 172–173, 179–181, 187–188, 197–198. Copyright © 2005 by Robert A. Pape. Used by permission of Random House, Inc.
3. Anat Berko and Edna Erez, " 'Ordinary People' and 'Death Work': Palestinian Suicide Bombers as Victimizers and Victims," *Violence and Victims*, Vol. 20, No. 6 (December 2005), pp. 608–617. Reproduced with the Permission of Springer Publishing Company, LLC, New York, NY 10036.

PART 5   THE THREAT TO THE WEST:
TERRORISTS IN OUR MIDST

1. Claude Moniquet, Prepared Statement, U.S. Congress, House of Representatives, Committee on International Relations, Subcommittee on Europe and Emerging Threats, *Hearing on Islamic Extremism in Europe*, 109th Congress, First Session, April 27, 2005, Serial No.1009-34 (Washington, DC: U.S. Government Printing Office, 2005), pp. 33–38.
2. Lorenzo Vidino, Prepared Statement, U.S. Congress, House of Representatives, Committee on International Relations, Subcommittee on Europe and Emerging Threats, *Hearing on Islamic Extremism in Europe*, 109th Congress, First Session,

April 27, 2005, Serial No.109-34 (Washington, DC: U.S. Government Printing Office, 2005), pp. 25–30.

3. Daniel Benjamin, Prepared Statement, U.S. Congress, Senate, Committee on Foreign Relations, Subcommittee on European Affairs, *Hearing on Islamist Extremism in Europe,* 109th Congress, Second Session, April 5, 2006 (Washington, DC: U.S. Government Printing Office, 2007), pp. 52–56.

4. From Melanie Phillips, *Londonistan* (New York: Encounter Books, 2006), pp. 77–80, 82–87, 90–91. Reprinted courtesy of the author c/o Writers Representatives L.L.C. All rights reserved.

5. From John Rosenthal, "The French Path to Jihad," *Policy Review,* No. 139 (October/November 2006), pp. 40–46, 48–50, 52–59. Reprinted by permission of *Policy Review.*

6. From Nonie Darwish, *Now They Call me Infidel: Why I Renounced Jihad for America, Israel, and the War on Terror* (New York: Sentinel, 2006), pp. 148–150, 152–153, 203–204, 212–214. Copyright © 2006 by Nonie Darwish. Used by permission of Sentinel, an imprint of Penguin Group (USA) Inc. For online information about other Penguin Group (USA) books and authors, see website at *http://www.penguin.com.*

PART 6   JEWS AS TARGETS: THE ISLAMIZATION OF EUROPEAN ANTI-SEMITIC MYTHS

1. Adapted and reprinted with permission from "Islamic Anti-Semitism in Historical Perspective" by the Anti-Defamation League. New York: Anti-Defamation League, © 2002. www.adl.org. All rights reserved.

2. Itamar Marcus and Barbara Crook, "Kill a Jew—Go to Heaven: The Perception of the Jew in Palestinian Society," *Jewish Political Studies Review,* Vol. 17, Nos. 3–4 (Fall 2005), pp. 119–129. Reprinted by permission of the Jerusalem Center for Public Affairs.

3. Dr. Umayma Ahmad Al-Jalahma, "Jews Use Teenagers' Blood for Purim Pastries" *Al Riyadh* (Saudi Arabia), March 10, 2002, trans. Middle East Media Research Institute (MEMRI), http://www.memri.org, MEMRI Special Dispatch Series, No. 354 (March 13, 2002). Reprinted by permission of MEMRI.

4. "Charter of the Islamic Resistance Movement," Hamas: Gaza, August 1988, in Simon Wiesenthal Center, *Selected Translations and Analyses* (Los Angeles, CA: Simon Wiesenthal Center, Fall 1988). Reprinted courtesy of Simon Wiesenthal Center Library and Archives.

5. Tariq Ramadan, "Muslims Against Anti-Semitism: Ways to Promote Common Values," *UN Chronicle,* No. 4 (December 2004–February 2005), pp. 35, 37. Reprinted by permission of the UN, the author of the original material.

6. Shaykh Hamza Yusuf, "Holocaust Denial Undermines Islam," *Tikkun* (July/August 2007), pp. 26–28. Reprinted from *Tikkun: A Bimonthly Interfaith Critique of Politics, Culture & Society,* and www.tikun.org.

INDEX